HOW TO STAY A
OF YOUR DOCTOR AND
INFLUENCE YOUR HEALTH

Simple, Practical and Effective Insider Tips to Utilise the Healthcare System to Your Advantage and Stay Healthy

By Dr Leke Asong MRCGP

Foreword by

Dr Michael Dickson LVO, OBE, FRCGP
Chair College of Medicine. Chair Institute for Social Prescription.

This book is intended as a reference volume
only and not as a medical manual.

The information provided here is designed to help you make informed decisions about your health. It is not intended as a substitute for any treatment that might have been prescribed by your doctor.

If you suspect that you have a medical problem, please consult with your doctor.

Please get in touch: www.guthealthmedic.co.uk

Book interior design by Velin@Perseus-Design.com

ISBN 978-1-9162714-0-1

DEDICATION

I would like to dedicate this book to the following people:

Mum and Dad

A big thank you to Mum and Dad (RIP) for instilling a Love of Books in me.

I remain eternally grateful and remember the multiple summaries of the classics you made me read.

My Family

A special thank you to my Wife and Daughters for their love, patience, and forgiveness for missed family activities while I worked endless hours on the computer.

Dr Tom Allen

Lastly, to Dr Tom Allen for believing in me and showing his relentless love over the years.

TABLE OF CONTENTS

PART 2: INTRODUCTION TO THE HUMAN BODY

PART 3: THE BASIC FUNDAMENTALS OF CLINICAL MEDICINE

PART 4: AN ALTERNATIVE APPROACH TO HEALTH AND DISEASE

ACKNOWLEDGMENTS

This book is an accumulation of my 20 years plus of study and experiences.

The idea for this book started as a medical board game, but slowly morphed into what you see today.

There is an African proverb that says if you want to go fast, go alone, and if you want to go far, go together.

I couldn't have done this work all on my own, and would like to acknowledge the following friends and colleagues:

I would like to thank the following friends and colleagues for their help and support:
Mrs Afua Basoah, Dr Agbor Ndip, Mr Akinlolu Akinwusi, Dr Ama Basoah, Mrs Amanda Williams, Mr Andy Rodgers, Mrs Angela Almond, Dr Ayan Panja, Dr Dave Morris, Miss Dione Mbong, Dr Gaynor Mountcastle, Mrs Harriet Bindloss, Dr James Greenwood, Mrs Jo Bridger, Mrs Katherine Pinder, Dr Leye Oginni, Mrs Linda Millard, Mrs Martha Foulger, Mrs Nicola Ryan, Dr Sam Modzabi, Mrs Olufunmilayo Ogunremi, Dr Richard Chalmers, Mr Roger Millard, Dr Roland Achenjang, Dr Michael Ash, and Mr Pete Williams.

I would also like to thank all the patients who presented with challenging health issues or asked me difficult questions.

You helped make me truly think and become a better doctor.

Last but not least, I would also like to thank you, the reader, for investing your time and money into reading this book.

I wish you everlasting health and prosperity.

FOREWORD

Dr Leke Asong has written the ultimate bedtime bible for anyone who wants to improve or maximise their health and well-being. It is a mountain of common sense packed with plenty of useful and important advice.

His book opens up every corner of medicine's mysteries to the layman, from how the health system works to ways of getting the best out of it and who better to explain how to get the best out of your doctor than a practising GP? He then explains all that you need to know about anatomy and physiology and how the body works. From there he proceeds to describe how we can better care for ourselves and stay well. He takes you behind the scenes to explore how things really work and what doctors really think, providing a springboard for the reader to take a far greater and more effective role in his or her own health and care.

His writing is lively, clear and intelligent, taking us on a mutual journey rather than preaching. It is spiced with interesting anecdotes, humanity and humour. It is not only a good read in itself, but with its well set out text it is also a book that you can dip into when you are looking for answers to specific questions.

The great medical iconoclast Ivan Illich wrote in Medical Nemesis, "The greatest single advance in medicine will not be some new drug or procedure but an increased ability of patients to care for themselves." Leke Asong's book marks a significant step forward on that journey towards patient emancipation.

Dr Michael Dixon LVO, OBE, FRCGP
Chair College of Medicine.
Chair Institute for Social Prescription.

INTRODUCTION

Uber yourself before you get Kodak'ed.

-Markus Sinclaire

What if I told you most of the ailments you present with to your doctor today would be managed entirely by yourself in the coming future?

Don't believe me? Please permit me to make my case.

Technology is shaping the world as we know it, and healthcare is no different.

There are gadgets on the market that can record your pulse rate, respiratory rate, and blood oxygen level, just to name a few.

Numerous smartphone applications (apps) are available for use by anyone with an interest in health, and telemedicine and remote monitoring allows doctors to obtain vast amounts of patient information without them leaving their home.

There is even talk of doctors being redundant in the near future with recent advancements in robotics and artificial intelligence (AI).

Alongside technological advancement is the rapidly evolving field of epigenetics and *personalised medicine.*

Epigenetics studies the environmental influence on gene expression.

In other words, modifiable factors like lifestyle and diet can indeed shut off expression of a gene you might have. As a consequence, I predict it would be the norm for disease treatment to be tailored to the individual, taking into account their genetic makeup and environmental influences on the very genes.

This would be a massive step forward compared to current practice where a manufactured drug is used by the general population without taking into account any *individuality* or environmental influence on the genes and the organism as a whole.

The advancement of personalised medicine and epigenetics in practice would mean an abundance of information that would be almost impossible to master by a single doctor. This is probably where health databases would come in to make sense of all the information—so-called *big data*.

So, as you can see, the paradigm could shift. Doctors would concentrate on deciphering all the sophisticated data while you took over what they diagnosed today.

However, we are not in the future yet, so what does all this mean for you now?

At the moment, the odds are against you. Healthcare systems all around the world are buckling under pressure. The National Health Service (NHS) is under severe strain as care is continuously rationed.

According to a Nuffield Trust report, the NHS spend has increased from 3.5% of the GDP to 10% in the last 50 years, and the total NHS spend on chronic conditions is estimated at about 70% [(1)].

We are all living longer, and patients presenting with multiple conditions account for up to 78% of all GP consultations. [(2)]

New drugs and technologies are also costing more, and a recruitment crisis means doctors are feeling the strain of overwork. They simply haven't got the time or energy to dedicate to everyone.

As the squeeze on healthcare provision increases, we are told to self-care.

At the same time, we are also bombarded with public health campaigns ordering us to rush to the doctor if we develop certain symptoms. When we try to research our symptoms, the internet opens us to a world of infinite possibilities, drawing us closer to the prospect of cancer with every click.

When we do finally get to see a doctor after weeks or months of anticipation, we have only ten minutes to explain what is wrong with us. In some cases, our issues are resolved. In others, they carry on, despite making the rounds of hospital consultants. In the end, we are left to our own devices once again.

Sound familiar? I see the above situation on an almost daily basis.

The average patient is in a difficult position, which arises from not knowing the basics while at the same time being constantly flooded with new information.

This leads to misinterpretation, the root cause of worry and anxiety in some cases.

I remember hearing a quote about a year ago from the famous actor Will Smith, about his relationship with his lovely wife Jada.

"It's unfair, and kind of unrealistic, and can be destructive to place the responsibility of happiness on anybody other than yourself."

Although Will was talking about relationships, it felt like the perfect analogy to health.

So, just to be clear, let me paraphrase for you. It's unfair, and kind of unrealistic, and can be destructive to place the responsibility of health on anybody other than you.

I see too many patients suffer on a daily basis, and it hurts me. My goal in writing this book is therefore to empower you to take care of your own health.

This is the best way to prepare yourself now and for the future, and I will show you exactly how.

This book is divided into four parts:

The first part takes you through the organisation of the health system and gives you tips on how to navigate every part of it.

The second part explores the human body, starting from the cells or building blocks of the human body right through to the body systems and how they work together in harmony.

The third part explores the signs and symptoms of common diseases and how doctors formulate a diagnosis, starting from history and leading to eventual treatment.

I teach you how to present your symptoms to your doctor in a more organised manner and make sense of any symptom you may have and any advice you may have been given.

Let's face it, the more you know, the higher the chance you have of making better decisions about your health together with your doctor.

I will share with you a mnemonic used by medical students and doctors for years, which you can use to dissect any symptom you have to reach a sensible probable diagnosis. You will also be able to search the internet in a smarter way to get the information you really want.

Finally, in the fourth part, I will share with you new models of looking at diseases while demystifying some difficult to treat symptoms you might have had. I will also divulge tips on how to stay healthy, lose weight and prevent disease.

This book is written from a general practice perspective and will be invaluable for anyone hoping to stay healthy, anyone who feels lost with regards to health, anyone frustrated with the current health system or anyone fascinated by the human body and how it works.

Remember there is no substitute to seeing a qualified medical practitioner, so please use this as an aid rather than a replacement for medical advice.

There is a lot of information packed into this book, and my hope is to stimulate your curiosity and broaden your horizons, with the ultimate aim of persuading and empowering you to take charge of your own health.

Being empowered doesn't weaken you, it makes you stronger. Being empowered gives you the independence not only to help yourself but your family members and friends too.

Let's go!

1) Department of Health. Improving the Health and Well-being of People with Long-Term Conditions

2) C Salisbury et al. (2011) Epidemiology and impact of multi-morbidity in primary care: A retrospective cohort Study. http://www.ncbi.nlm.nih.gov/pmc/articles/PMC3020068/

PART 1

ORGANISATION OF THE HEALTHCARE SYSTEM

CHAPTER 1

NAVIGATING THE HEALTHCARE SYSTEM SAFELY

I have come to believe that the world is an enigma, a harmless enigma that is made terrible by our own mad attempt to interpret it as though it had an underlying truth.

-Umberto Eco

Before we explore the body, it is helpful to understand how the healthcare system works.

The organisation of the healthcare system is designed in a way to maximise efficiency of healthcare resources while providing the best care available for patients.

In other words, careful decisions are made to allocate care to the right people at the right place, all from a limited pot of money.

Here are two examples that explain this concept:

So, if you develop an infected toe, it is best to book an appointment with your GP practice, rather than call an ambulance to take you to Accident and Emergency (A&E). Apart from the cost of dispatching an ambulance and crew for a relatively trivial complaint, their time is best spent taking care of genuine emergencies, a role they best serve.

Secondly, if, God forbid, you were to suffer from a rare disease and there was an expensive drug available to you, the National Health Service (NHS) might refuse to fund it based on the grounds that only a few people would benefit.

Due to an ageing population, with resulting increased healthcare needs of the population, the changes in healthcare service will remain a dynamic process in the foreseeable future.

With all of this coupled with a shortage of doctors in the country, it makes sense to avoid the healthcare services if possible. The best way to do this is by making sensible decisions about your health like eating a healthy diet, exercising regularly and getting adequate rest.

Of course, disease could strike at any time, and should this happen it is wise to be prepared by arming yourself with some knowledge.

Access to the healthcare system can be made at different points, firstly depending on what symptom you have and secondly on your personal inclination.

The healthcare system can be divided into primary, secondary and tertiary care.

Primary care is normally the first point of access for most patients and comprises general practitioners (GPs), practice nurses, dentists, pharmacists, opticians, family planning clinics, health visitors, midwives, district and community nurses. An often-forgotten service is the out-of-hours service that provides care outside normal surgery hours. This is usually from 18:30 to 08:00 weekdays, all day on weekends and bank holidays.

The out-of-hours service is designed in different ways depending on what part of the country you reside in and is usually manned by GPs and nurses. You can access the out-of-hours services by calling 111 or just turning up.

Secondary care comprises hospital-based services. These include hospital doctors, nurses, radiographers, physiotherapists and dieticians. Access to secondary care is usually via your GP.

Tertiary care comprises specialist hospitals or centres. Doctors and nurses here tend to be hyper specialised, dealing with certain pathologies. Tertiary centres usually have sophisticated equipment to carry out specialist tests. Referral to a tertiary centre is usually via secondary care although also possible via your GP.

In the next section, we will go into a bit more detail on the various services.

CHAPTER 2

SURVIVING THE MAZE

ACCIDENT AND EMERGENCY (A&E)/ EMERGENCY DEPARTMENT (ED)

Whatever hits the fan will not be evenly distributed.

-Unknown

This is the place to go to if you feel your symptom is an emergency, in which case you have the option of dialling 999 for an ambulance. Common emergencies include breathing difficulties, chest pain, suspected stroke and severe bleeding.

An ambulance normally arrives on the scene, attended by paramedics who assess or treat patients depending on the case.

Paramedics are trained clinicians and will typically examine you, take your blood oxygen levels (Denoted as SPO2), pulse (P), blood pressure (BP) blood sugar levels (BM) and perform an electrocardiogram (ECG) of the heart. In some cases, a defibrillator is used on unconscious patients on the scene.

Generally, true emergency cases make the trip to A&E, with most already receiving immediate treatment on the scene.

Most patients usually get high-flow oxygen through a face mask, with diabetics getting sugary drinks if they are found to have very low blood sugars (hypoglycaemia).

Patients with heart problems usually receive some type of cardiac drug.

Cases not deemed true emergencies by the paramedics are left at home for the GP to follow up, usually on the same day or later.

Due to pressures on the NHS, the wait for an ambulance can be quite long. It is not uncommon for ambulances to turn up late or not turn up at all. I have heard of stories where the GP drove patients themselves to the ER.

Please don't blame the ambulance crew, it isn't their fault—the system is under pressure.

If you realise the wait for the ambulance will be longer than the situation at hand, I suggest you ask someone to help you get to hospital as soon as possible if feasible.

A&E cases are traditionally divided into Minors and Majors, terms used to denote the severity of cases. A case brought in by ambulance would usually be sent to Majors, following a brief handover by the crew. If you were to arrive at the ER in a critical state by yourself or accompanied, it is imperative you immediately let the receptionist know. Failing this, you might end up waiting for hours on end without anyone taking notice.

Another route into the ER is via your GP who would have seen you in surgery and decided to refer you to hospital after having spoken to a junior doctor in the relevant specialty. A good GP will usually include your repeat medication list with an accompanying letter. If for some reason this is not included, politely ask if you can have your updated repeat medication list. This is usually of tremendous help for the junior doctor who will subsequently transcribe your medication onto a hospital medication chart to be used by the ward nurses should you be admitted.

You might think bringing all your medication along to hospital is the best way; however, occasionally they get lost in transition among some of your belongings.

Patients might also come to the ED via the police. This is sometimes related to patients with mental health issues who have been sectioned, people found on the street or cases associated with violence or crime.

I remember a man who absconded from the mental health ward, accusing the nurses of sitting around sipping coffee all day. He later called the ward threatening to kill himself.

He then wandered into the town centre and found a bridge, where he contemplated his suicide while gazing into the water. A few minutes later, he spotted a police car a few yards away. Walking up to the car, he knocked on the window and asked the pair of policemen if they were looking for him—they replied that they weren't! Minutes later, they took him to the ED.

When he narrated the story, he joked about the fact that no one cared about him—no one had been looking for him despite threatening suicide.

We both laughed at the whole episode, and I knew he was going to be just fine.

From the ED, you might be referred to another department, usually for additional assessments or admission. It is common for ED clinicians to utter the following popular phrase: "See your GP."

Once you hear this, politely ask what the specific reason for seeing your GP is.

This is important for three reasons as follows:

First, it might shed some clarity and enable you to do some research on the ailment when possible.

Secondly, the discharge letter might not have arrived by the time you see your GP.

Finally, what you have been told in the ER might not appear on the discharge letter. I have seen this happen occasionally.

In cases like this, your GP might just be as much in the dark as you.

A&E staff members are constantly on the go and should be commended on the hard work they put in, despite the occasional abuse and rowdiness that occurs especially over the weekends.

I once saw a patient complain of the intolerable level of noise on a Saturday night and he eventually left the department in his nightgown without being seen.

The ER can be a charged place to work, and staff usually use humour as a coping strategy.

I remember a shift during which an aggressive intoxicated man walked stark naked along the corridors of the ER, threatening staff. The police were called, and the two officers who arrived at the scene looked like they had just finished sixth form.

"What do you want us to do?" one of them said as the man obnoxiously paraded past them. It was at that point we realised we were on our own.

In a WWF (World Wrestling Federation) style tackle, a nurse, a tad on the big side, suddenly threw her weight over the man, with the rest of the staff following suit. A haloperidol syringe was plunged into the man's gluteus maximus (bottom) at about the same time, silencing him into a sleeping lamb a few minutes later.

The two officers, planted against a wall clutching their walkie talkies throughout the struggle, eventually walked off in silence.

"Thank God for the police", the porter gasped sarcastically during a moment of complete silence, sending the whole department into roaring laughter.

It was moments like this that always made work at A&E exciting.

CHAPTER 3

ACUTE MEDICAL UNIT (AMU)/ EMERGENCY MEDICAL UNIT (EMU) AND HOSPITAL WARDS

Rather, ten times die in the surf, heralding the way to a new world, than stand idly on the shore.

-Florence Nightingale

Cases in the emergency department (ED) deemed for further assessment are referred to the various specialties where they remain in a temporary holding ward called the acute medical unit (AMU) or emergency medical unit (EMU) depending on the hospital.

Some hospitals also have a temporary holding ward called acute treatment centre (ATC).

This is generally used to relieve ED beds, and reserved for patients who are thought to be fit for same-day discharge from the ED, pending good response to treatment and/or normal blood test results.

Most ATCs close at five (unless there is a shortage of beds when they are used as outlying wards).

At the AMU you will be assessed again by a junior doctor who will be waiting enthusiastically to draw vials of blood for analysis. Usually a consultant and team will see patients on AMU as well as on the wards, usually in the early hours of the morning, to formulate a treatment plan.

You will normally see junior doctors jotting items down, so-called jobs requested by the consultant.

A common job could be to check a patient's kidney function every 48 hours or arrange for an ultrasound scan of his/her abdomen.

During the ward round, the junior doctors will generally be quizzed. This is a good time for the keen doctors to demonstrate their knowledge but the worst time for those lacking in knowledge.

Sometimes on a round a consultant will stop all your medication while on AMU.

It is worth asking why this has been done as you never know, some information you provide might change his mind.

On the AMU ward round, keep your ears open and give a fresh history to the consultant if you can. Don't hesitate to correct a bit of information you think is incorrect. If your symptoms are changing or you remember some additional information, say so and don't assume the team are aware.

Once the AMU ward round is completed, you are then then taken to the wards for some peace and quiet.

At the end of the morning ward round, the consultant either goes off to clinic to sees routine cases booked from a few weeks or months before by a GP or to theatre depending on the specialty. There is usually a management meeting or two thrown in during the day as well.

Later in the night, another ward round is done with the consultant and team to see the rest of the patients who arrived AMU late. Similarly, a treatment plan is formulated and off you go to the wards.

After successful treatment on the wards it might be time to finally go home, but before you go, make sure you have a good read of your hospital discharge letter, which will invariably have some sort of medication change or a plan for your GP to follow. It is worth knowing that the discharge letter is not necessarily typed up by the doctor who admitted you and the quality does vary; therefore, spending a few minutes to read your copy and querying any changes while still on the ward before you leave is worth the extra time.

Common plans for your GP to arrange are Check U&Es (kidney function) in one week, or Check full blood count (FBC) in a month, right at the bottom of the page. I would suggest noting the date in a diary or smartphone to remind you, just in case a reminder from the GP practice does not show up in time or not at all.

Taking this proactive approach with all aspects of your health ensures you are always on top of things. In other words, you help your GP with your care rather than fully depending on them for every aspect of it.

CHAPTER 4

CONSULTANT CLINICS

Experts often possess more data than judgement.

-Colin Powell

As mentioned above, your GP might refer you routinely for a hospital clinic appointment instead of a same-day admission.

During your appointment with the consultant, always ask as many questions as you can. In my experience, many patients don't, only to come back to their GP asking the pertinent questions that would have been best answered by the consultant they just saw.

It might happen that on every occasion you are go to clinic you are seen by a different doctor. This can be a frustrating experience, but remember as part of medical training, doctors have to see patients to get the much-needed experience to practice safely.

The important thing, in my opinion, is to make sure that whoever sees you has a full grasp of your case. Different doctors manage things in different ways, so don't be surprised if a care plan is slightly modified from what it initially was.

Most importantly, a management plan has got to make sense, hence the need to have some idea of your condition in the first place.

Specialising in a particular field is a great accomplishment but can potentially make a doctor blinded to other aspects of health. So don't be surprised if your consultant hasn't got all the answers you were looking for, especially if they are slightly out of their field of expertise.

At the end of your clinic appointment, a consultant will typically dictate a letter typed by the secretaries, which will be sent to your GP. It is worth reminding the consultant politely to send you a copy for your records as well.

A good way of organising your health records is to collate and store them in a designated labelled section in your filing cabinet or A4 folder on a shelf.

If you are tech savvy, scan your letters and store as a PDF file or similar under a created folder on your home computer or laptop under the name "My Health."

If you haven't got a scanner, no problem—just download a scanning app on your smartphone and take pictures of any relevant letters. Most of these apps automatically convert files into PDF for you. I personally use CamScanner, but there are numerous options on the market.

Organising your medical records is a good habit to form, especially if you have many comorbidities and make frequent trips to hospital.

I once saw a patient who recounted his experiences during his clinic appointments.

"Each time I see the consultant, he says let me try you on this, let me try you on that. I am not a guinea pig. Half the time I have had what he wants to give me anyway—doesn't he have my notes?"

Bring a full updated list of your medications with you, and do not assume the consultant will know.

CHAPTER 5

NHS 111

People will soon forget what you said. They will never forget how you made them feel.

-Dr Maya Angelou

You might feel you only need advice, in which case you have an option to call the 111 number.

The 111 call handlers have different levels of experience and usually direct your call using the *NHS pathways software*, an algorithm-based diagnostic tool.

Disease algorithms are computer programs with set questions that aim to diagnose and give management options on conditions, depending on the answers fed into it.

Depending on the case at hand, your call might be directed to a healthcare professional who will then try to come up with a possible diagnosis and appropriate management option.

I once saw a lady with chest pain who had called 111 the previous day. After answering all the questions asked, the call handler mentioned, "The computer says call 999."

The lady replied, "I disagree, let's start again."

A rare instance of the computer saying, "Yes," in a way.

Medical algorithms have come a long way, and huge progress has been made with the advancement in artificial intelligence (AI)

Having said this, they are not perfect in all areas of medicine.

If you think the diagnosis you hear does not sound right, it is worth asking as many questions as you can to see if what you have been told makes sense. You might even be surprised to find your knowledge is better than the call handlers on occasion.

It must be said, however, that diagnosing over the phone is a tough job, and the call handlers do a commendable job to provide the best advice they can. I also think their job would be a lot easier had they been medically trained to some degree.

CHAPTER 6

WALK-IN CENTRES/URGENT CARE CENTRES & GP SURGERIES

Those who are unaware they are walking in darkness will never seek the light.

-Bruce Lee

Traditionally many patients with non-emergencies chose to book an appointment at their own surgery. However, there are other options available like attending a walk-in centre (WIC), urgent care centres (UCC), minor injuries unit (MIU) or the urgent treatment centre (UTC). There are slight differences in the level of services they offer with some offering X-ray services for example.

Generally speaking, they are reserved for minor illness and non-chronic conditions. They are not to be used for life-threatening cases.

Many of the above facilities have a mix of nurses, nurse practitioners and doctors available to see patients. Some centres are run exclusively by nurse practitioners with a supervising doctor on site.

You don't generally need an appointment to attend a walk-in centre, although some run a registered list of patients alongside.

At a walk-in centre, a clinician will either deal with your presenting complaint or refer you to hospital to be seen on the same day if need be.

It is worth noting that clinicians at a walk-in centre cannot make a routine hospital referral and can only advise you to, "See your own GP"—words you have probably heard many times.

Cases best suited for walk-in centres include rashes, insect bites and stings, burns, minor cuts and bruising, sprains, coughs and colds, ear infections and similar cases.

Walk-in centres are usually located in big cities and can get extremely busy, especially during bank holidays when GP practices are shut.

I remember arriving at a certain walk-in centre at 7:30 a.m., and witnessing a queue from the door up to the car park even before opening time at 8:00am. It was a tough shift due to the sheer volume of people who had attended, and I couldn't wait for 10:00 p.m. to go home.

At 9:40 p.m., I thought I had finished and made my way to the reception area.

As I looked onto the street, I saw the doors of a stationed mini-bus open.

Seconds later, streams of people got off the bus, making their way towards the entrance. I looked at the receptionist in dismay...

As it turned out, the local emergency department had a contract with the walk-in centre to see non-emergency cases. Once the numbers were significant, they were shuttled by bus to the walk-in centre!

I broke the news to the other GP who had already switched his computer off ready to leave and was on the phone to his loved ones. ☺

CHAPTER 7

HOW TO PICK AND REGISTER WITH THE BEST GP PRACTICES

I am tired of all this nonsense about beauty being only skin deep. That's deep enough. What do you want, an adorable pancreas?
-Jane Kerr

As you might have realised, no two GP practices are the same. Below are a few pointers that might help you to choose wisely.

Google
The easiest way to find practices in your area is simply to google "GP Practices near me." A list of surgeries will usually come up, but the first page is usually *Find GP Services-NHS*. Clicking this link brings up a page where you simply insert your postcode to bring up the list of practices.

Until recently, the concept of a *catchment area* applied when registering with a GP practice. (A catchment area is a set distance within which inhabitants can register with a particular practice.)

Presently, you can register with any practice of your choice irrespective of distance. However, if you were to register with a practice considerably far away, you might have limited care in the way of home visits.

If you live in a small village or town with only one practice, you probably have no choice (assuming you don't wish to travel). However, if you live in an area with many practices, there are a few general points to consider when making your choice.

Training Practice?

The first point worth finding out is whether the practice is a *training* or *non-training practice.*

A training practice is one that has been accredited by the Royal College of General Practitioners (RCGP) for the purpose of training doctors and medical students. A named *GP Trainer*, who has undergone further training, mainly does the job of mentoring doctors in the early years of training (F1 and F2) or prospective GPs in their training years (GP registrars).

In practice, most GPs in the practice take turns in daily debriefs with the trainee doctors. What this means for you is the quality of medicine is most likely to be high in a training practice. This is not to say the quality of medicine in a non-training practice is low. However, the educational environment in a training practice is an added advantage.

It is worth noting at a training practice you might occasionally get an appointment booked with a trainee doctor who might be less experienced in certain areas. This is not something to worry about, however, as help is always available to them at the end of the phone line.

The only potential drawback of a training practice might be a slightly dogmatic approach in certain areas of care. This might be a disadvantage to you, especially if your symptoms don't quite fit the textbook pathologies taught in medical school.

Patient to Doctor Ratio

The next thing to work out is the *patient to doctor ratio.*
This is, in other words, the number of patients each doctor would have if you were to divide the practice population by the number of doctors in the practice.

You can easily work out this number as both the practice population size and number of doctors in the practice are available on the practice website.

To get an accurate number, it is worth noting the number of full- and part-time GPs. Once you get the final figure, bear in mind some practices have on board advanced nurse practitioners, nurse practitioners and practice nurses who also see patients.

During my training, there was a widely quoted figure of patients per whole time equivalent (WTE) GP of 1600. Having said this, there is huge variation in this number, depending on what part of the country you live in.

In the current recruitment climate, you might find the number you get is quite high; however, most practices use locums to supplement their workforce.

A struggling practice that refuses to use locums despite a workforce shortage is one you should probably avoid as there is a high chance of finding burned-out doctors probably practising what I call *fast food medicine.*

It is not uncommon these days to find practices staffed entirely by locum doctors, for one reason or another. If such a practice is in your locality, and you can't stand seeing different doctors each time, it might be worth asking to see a *long-term locum* who might have a contract to work for many months or even years.

Having said this, if you have mastered the art of giving a history and have a clear summary of your medical conditions, you really would have nothing to worry about if you were to see a locum doctor.

Parking

The next thing to consider is availability and cost of onsite and offsite car parking.

A practice with a large practice population should ideally have ample parking space. This does minimise the stress of driving around in circles in search of an available spot and eventually arriving late.

Gender Mix

If you feel uncomfortable with the opposite sex, no matter the circumstance, you might want to choose a practice with a mix of male and female doctors. This might seem a minor point, but I have known patients cancel appointments after realising it was a male or female doctor depending.

CQC Rating

Last but not least, find out about the practice's Care Quality Commission (CQC) rating score.

The CQC is a branch of the Department of Health in England, whose role is to inspect and regulate health and social care services. How this works is a practice is communicated a date for inspections, usually a month or so in advance. During this period, most practices try to get various things in order, from written protocols to visible signs on noticeboards, general hygiene, equipment inspection, and so on. It is usually a nerve-racking business for the average practice, with some being better at preparing than others.

Most practices have a CQC rating somewhere on their website, but if it's not available you can search directly on the CQC website (www.cqc.org.uk) or just phone the practice and ask.

The CQC grades practices into four categories, namely *Outstanding, Good, Requires Improvement,* and *Inadequate.*

Like any human-based survey, the CQC inspection is potentially good at picking up glaring faults and weeding out extremely bad elements.

However, there are some areas that could be present but difficult to pick up.

As such, it is possible for an average practice to score high with the right preparation and presentation.

The take home message here for you is to keep a practice's rating in mind but don't be blinded by it.

A few years ago, a colleague of mine mentioned he got *depressed* each morning he arrived at his practice due to its rather derelict building. If you belong to the category of people who get easily affected by their surroundings, then your best bet for a plush environment is one operating in an NHS Local

Improvement Finance Trust initiative (LIFT) building. These buildings tend to be relatively new, complete with modern furnishings, compared to the traditional GP premises.

Most practices now ask for some form of identification like a driver's license, utility bill or passport as part of the registration process. A copy of a visa or relevant document from the Home Office is also sometimes required in applicable cases.

Finally, if you realise you have made the wrong decision in choosing a practice, just switch like you would an energy provider.

CHAPTER 8

UNDERSTANDING GP APPOINTMENT SYSTEMS

I failed to make the chess club because of my height.
-Woody Allen

Having registered with a practice, the next battle is trying to secure an appointment.

If you are reading this and have tried at some point to book an appointment for yourself, you will agree this is not always the easiest of tasks. Patients generally register under a *named GP*, but, practically speaking, this is mostly just a label.

Gone are the days when you could book to always see your named or regular GP, even though I am reminded of this on a daily basis by elderly patients who muse about the good old days.

In this section, I will attempt to explain how appointments are allocated and offer some tips on how to secure an appointment for yourself more efficiently in the next section.

Many years ago, I witnessed a rather hilarious chain of events.

A skinny, bony-faced man in a tracksuit and gleaming white trainers had come up to the receptionist to book an appointment early in the morning. He was immediately told by a rather austere receptionist that appointments could only be booked by phone and were not available to be booked at the desk!

There was a brief pause as the man looked at the receptionist, who at this point was now staring down at her computer screen disinterested.

In an epic move, the man stepped to the side, pulled out his mobile phone from his pocket and dialled the practice number there and then.

It was a monumental moment, and chuckles could be heard from fed-up patients in the queue who had found their new hero.

"Bring, bring, bring...... ...."

Ten-minute appointments are the average time slots for NHS GPs, with different surgeries operating different *appointment systems.*

Open Appointment System (First Come First Served)

The first system is an *open appointment system* where patients turn up to the surgery with no appointment times and get seen on a first come first served basis.

Some surgeries set time limits for morning or afternoon sessions, while some don't.

If you are not in a rush and don't mind waiting, this system might suit you.

Same-Day Release

In this system, a set number of *appointment slots* are all *blocked* and can only be *released* on the day.

Patients can only book these slots once they are *released,* usually by the IT department, receptionist or practice manager.

With this system, a future appointment cannot be booked, although in some cases someone with *admin rights* can override this.

Same-Day and Future Release

A third system uses a set number of same-day appointments, while the rest can be booked up to a predefined period in the future. As an example, a practice might allocate 30% of same-day appointments, and 70% *bookable* up to a month ahead.

If you were to phone for an appointment in say two months, you would be told appointments aren't available.

This system is probably the most widely used by surgeries, the only difference being the proportion of *same-day* and *future-booked* appointments.

Telephone Triage System

The word *triage* in the medical context simply means prioritising whatever cases one has according to need.

As the name implies, a telephone triage system uses the phone to prioritise patient cases. In practice, doctors, nurses or even experienced receptionists call patients from a list. Straightforward issues are dealt with over the phone, while less straightforward ones are booked in later for an appointment.

An example of a case not requiring an appointment could be a patient mentioning a side effect of a newly prescribed tablet. A suitable alternative is prescribed, if found to be a true allergy, without the need for an appointment.

Although a purely telephone triage system has advantages for minor issues or requests, it does pose a few challenges:

Some patients might feel they prefer to always see a clinician, rather than calling first.

Secondly, a diagnosis might be missed, as the added advantage of seeing the patient face-to-face is missing.

Last but not least, the volume of calls made by GPs or nurses can be exceedingly high.

A colleague of mine mentioned that he and his colleagues frequently made over 100 calls per day!

Combo Systems

Some practices use a combination of all the above appointment systems described above. For example, a named doctor might have a proportion of same-day appointments, future-booked appointments, and a small number of telephone appointments.

There are advantages and disadvantages with whichever appointment system a surgery uses, and it can be an extremely arduous task to strike the right balance.

Unfortunately, the bottom line is simple—all patients could never be seen when they want to be seen, irrespective of the system a practice operates. This is simply due to high patient demand alongside chronic GP shortages.

A patient once started their consultation by asking me why all appointments were not open for everyone to book. (Same-day release) According to him, this was the solution to the difficulty he and other patients experienced day in and day out in trying to book appointments.

I listened patiently, and at the end of the consultation, I asked him to book in two weeks to be seen for a review.

"No worries; will make it outside at the desk on my way out."

As he stood up, I then reminded him with a smile that in two weeks there would be one less appointment for everyone else.

Working somewhat independently alongside the above appointment systems is the *on call* or *duty doctor.*

The appointment system used by the *on call doctor* varies from one practice to another but they generally use one or a combination of the above systems.

The on call doctor mostly sees patients while also being on standby for any work required.

There is more on the on call doctor's role in Chapter 12.

CHAPTER 9

SEVEN TIPS ON HOW TO SECURE THE APPOINTMENT YOU WANT

"Do I need bring Kalashnikov to get appointment here?"
-Ukrainian Patient

Think Broader Primary Care

Before you embark on the epic battle of trying to get a GP appointment, with a bit of knowledge you might find you don't need one in the first place.

The chemist is a good place to start if you were to suffer from a minor ailment.

They might occasionally send you back to your GP, but most of the time they are of great help.

In fact, there exists a minor ailments scheme launched in England as far back as 2008.

It is worth mentioning that not all these areas operate this scheme, and, in addition, the conditions covered vary. Common ailments covered by this include upper respiratory tract infections (coughs, colds and sore throats), diarrhoea and vomiting, mild indigestion and so on.

Any eye problems can be tackled by your local high street optician, who might occasionally refer you further to a consultant ophthalmologist directly or via your GP.

Needless to say, toothache, painful or bleeding gums, and problems with dentures are for the dentist.

There are numerous self-referral services available if you do a bit of research.

CRUSE offers bereavement services, RELATE offers relationship counselling and various organisations deal with drug and alcohol abuse.

Anyone feeling suicidal can easily call the *crisis team.*

Is It an Emergency?

It is fair to say you might not know your condition is an emergency; however, I am sure you would agree a case of chest pain and a suspected stroke are emergencies.

Most GP automated systems usually advise dialling the 999 emergency number if suffering from chest pain.

I have occasionally seen patients who knew their condition was an emergency but thought they would book an appointment anyway to avoid the queue at A&E! On one occasion, it was a baby who was extremely breathless but settled after the practice nurse and I administered *back-to-back* nebulisers.

Online Appointments

Online appointments are a convenient way to book appointments for those who want to avoid hanging about at the end of a phone line. Different practices have varying numbers of appointments accessible online, but, as discussed above, the same pressures apply.

If you feel that the number of online appointments could be increased, bring it up with your doctor or practice manager. They will most likely gladly take this feedback on board—unless your practice is run by mostly old-fashioned doctors.

Being proactive in this manner helps to shape a service that best suits you.

Some practices now also offer Skype appointments.

The Practice Website

Probably every GP practice in the UK has a website with a list of practice staff, services offered and even general health information on common ailments. Some websites might include additional services offered, which could range from physiotherapy and smoking cessation to mental health services. Accessing some of these services does not require a GP referral, so in effect you bypass the queue for appointments.

The practice website will invariably have information on GPs with a *special interest.* A *special interest* is an area in which a GP has specialised, either in the way of diplomas, courses, and training days or just from lots of reading and practice.

Some areas of special interest are women's health, minor surgery, joint injections, diabetes, and dermatology, to name a few.

Some procedures like joint injections, cryotherapy, minor surgery and implant and coil fitting are not done by all GPs. Knowledge of a doctor's special interest allows you to book with the right GP and avoids the scenario of you turning up for say a joint injection only to be told by the GP they don't do the procedure.

Digital Triage Services

In order to help the growing access problems, some surgeries have adopted digital triage services to ease the burden.

Here is how it works. Instead of calling the surgery to get an appointment, the patient logs on to the system and inputs their symptoms. A smart-based computer algorithm then directs you to a course of action, which is not necessary always seeing a doctor.

This is similar to calling NHS 111, only you aren't talking to a human being.

Could Anyone Else Do?

Most GP surgeries have a mix of GPs, nurse practitioners, advanced nurse practitioners and practice nurses who all see patients. Occasionally, health care assistants (HCA) will see patients as well, although more for limited roles within *chronic disease management.*

Some practices also have an in-house pharmacist that sees selected cases. In some parts of the country, some practices are entirely manned by pharmacists.

Some practices have also started to employ physician assistants (PAs) who also see patients but are unable to prescribe at present.

The PA role is a relatively new one in the UK but has been present in the American healthcare system since the 1960s.

Nurse practitioners or physician assistants, like any other group of clinicians, vary in experience but do a great job overall. However, some medical problems are best served by a qualified doctor, who will most likely have a better perspective of pathology in general.

Booking to see a doctor might not be possible, but a nurse practitioner can always ask for help from a GP, usually the *on call or duty doctor.* This is one indirect way of seeing a doctor, if GP appointments are scarce. However, it would be inappropriate to undermine a competent nurse just because you want to see a doctor.

Work with the Receptionist

Due to the pressures of appointments, the role of GP receptionists has somewhat evolved from simply answering the phone to also prioritising calls.

To be efficient, most GP receptionists go on courses where they improve their medical knowledge.

Looking at things from this perspective, receptionists do an extremely difficult task of answering the phone, getting a gist of the problem and booking appointments accordingly. In doing this they might sometimes come across as rude, but this is mostly due to pressures of the job. Receptionists are only human and if you tell them off because you've been waiting on the phone line for a long time, they will be less likely to go the extra mile to help you.

I do admit some receptionists are *difficult* and are sometimes unable to use common sense. Some potential reasons for this are lack of experience, fear of thinking outside the box, poor management by senior staff or a *toxic culture* within the practice. In some cases, they might simply just not be a nice person!

As part of the appointment allocation process, receptionists sometimes enquire about your complaint, something not always so welcome from some patients understandably.

If you feel strongly against disclosing the reason for your appointment, just say, "It is of a private nature."

The comedian Catherine Tate has a hilarious skit involving her Nan character who turns up at a GP practice to be asked by a receptionist if her problem is an emergency.

"What has it got to do with you?" she initially responds, but later she agrees her problem is indeed an emergency after the receptionist pushes further. "Yes, it is an emergency—my head is hanging off!"

Avoid Mondays and Fridays if Possible

It is one thing to get an appointment, but you also want to get the best out of your appointment too. If you have the option, I recommend you avoid Mondays and Fridays. These are traditionally busy days and, as such, clinician stress levels are high. High stress levels occasionally make for grumpy clinicians and even occasional mistakes.

CHAPTER 10

I STILL CAN'T GET AN APPOINTMENT!

So, you have seen the chemist who has advised an appointment with your GP. You manage to get through to a friendly receptionist who tells you in the most empathetic tone there are no appointments left. The familiar words ring through your ears like the village church bells. *Don't despair; you have one more option—go private.*

I know what you are thinking—you can't afford it, but there are a variety of cost-effective options now available for almost everyone.

Over the last few years, many private GP providers have blossomed, probably as a result of rising patient demand and the frustration of not being able to secure GP appointments.

The first of such services was *Babylon*, created in 2013 by Ali Parsa, an industrious former investment banker turned healthcare entrepreneur.

Since then, many other companies with a similar *online presence* have taken off.

These services operate in a similar manner, using virtual consultations with doctors on a personal computer or smartphone.

The user can access them as a one-off consultation or subscribe to the service on a monthly basis.

All you need is a smartphone or PC and you are ready to go after a few minutes of registration. Typically, you are offered an appointment within an hour or so the same day.

About three years ago or so, a patient of mine mentioned he had paid just £10 for a consultation a few weeks before.

The main advantage of these online providers is their flexibility of working around you, rather than the opposite. It is therefore fantastic for the busy professional who hasn't got the time to hang about on the phone or leave work for an appointment.

There a few drawbacks, which include difficulty dealing with complex cases and the lack of clinical examination.

Overall, this is a promising step towards the future of medicine in my opinion.

The disadvantage from a selfish NHS GP point of view is the added workload a consultation like this can suddenly generate.

About a year ago, a patient at a practice I worked in consulted a GP on an online healthcare provider. He was subsequently referred to see a rheumatologist, who in turn requested a considerable number of tests to be done. Given it would have cost a fortune to have it done privately the patient chose the NHS route. The letter ended up with a colleague at the time who spent at least half an hour finding and arranging these tests.

"So what's the problem?" you might ask.

Imagine you are a chef at a reservation-only restaurant, cooking for the restaurant's capacity of say 50 people. Now also imagine you are suddenly told to make ten additional meals for some guests who arrive without booking.

This is exactly what happens when non-NHS work is piled onto work generated from your GP's own consultations.

This is the way the system functions, and I am not blaming you, the patient.

If you need an appointment, you need an appointment.

CHAPTER 11

GENERAL PRACTICE AS A BUSINESS

If someone offers you an amazing opportunity and you're not sure you can do it, say yes—then learn how to do it later.
-Sir Richard Branson

The term *businessman* never brings to mind the image of a GP, and although some might be reluctant to make this assertion, this is what they essentially are.

Unlike hospital doctors who are employees of the NHS, GPs technically aren't and instead sign a contract with the government to treat NHS patients. The appropriate term for this arrangement is *independent contractor*, an arrangement that has carried on since the inception of the NHS in 1948.

To deliver services, a doctor (single-handed GP) or group of doctors (GP partners) acquire premises to operate from. They then hire staff, including other GPs (salaried GPs), a practice manager, nurses, receptionists, an IT team and so on.

In simple terms, the GP's income is thus the amount received from the NHS in line with the contract, minus staff salaries, utility bills, phone bills and more.

As mentioned above, GPs are independent contractors who work under a contract.

There are generally three contracts under which GPs work: General Medical Services (GMS), Personal Medical Services (PMS) and an Alternative Provider of Medical Services (APMS). These contracts broadly cover similar core work but vary in the types of additional work contracted, as well as remuneration.

Some GPs own the building from which they operate and in practice would have taken out a mortgage to cover the cost of this expense. Because GPs treat NHS patients, the government has different schemes by which this amount is reimbursed to them. One scheme is called notional rent, where the practice is paid a monthly amount based on the current market rent rate. Most often than not, this amount is more than the monthly mortgage, and thus a profit is made by the GPs (partners only). This is one of the ways a practice building can generate money for the partners in the practice.

Occasionally, the value of the building might depreciate, and the GPs involved would be operating at a loss so to speak.

A GP premises or building can sometimes be owned by a private company who then lease it to the GPs involved. The GPs then receive a monthly amount (just like if they owned the building) and then pay the company who own the building. The only difference here is the GPs involved cannot make a profit from the building.

The government pays GP practices a fee per patient registered, currently about £75/patient (capitation fee). So, by registering you and your family, you are contributing to the practice pot of money.

In addition, GPs get paid for various other *services* they offer the population.

All GP practices provide core services, which include maternity services, child vaccinations and chronic disease management.

About 12 years ago, the Quality and Outcomes Framework (QOF) was devised as a tool to improve patient care. The thinking behind this was to remunerate

GPs for practising good quality medicine. Each criterion on the QOF attained generates a fee for the GP practice.

An example of a QOF criteria is that 90% of patients need their BP within a target of 140/80. Should 90% of a practice's registered patients achieve this, then they get a lump sum of money from NHS England.

Other aspects like smoking status and documenting you have advised a patient against smoking, for example, also attract a lump sum for the practice. There are numerous QOF criteria, but I am sure you get the idea.

In addition to core services provided by all GP practices are additional services called enhanced services. These are national enhanced services (NES), direct enhanced services (DES) and local enhanced services (LES)

Examples of NES are some child vaccinations, shingles vaccinations and the flu vaccinations. All GP practices are expected to provide these.

Examples of DES are extended opening hours or provision of minor surgery. This is entirely optional.

LES vary from area to area as they are based on local needs. Examples include minor injury management.

All the services you get from your GP are commissioned or bought from various organizations like NHS Trusts (hospitals), community mental health organizations, and other providers of services.

Recently, GP practices have also been able to bid for service provision. These services are bought by the various clinical commissioning groups (CCGs), to which all GP practices belong.

CCGs get money from the Department of Health's budget, ultimately funded by taxation, and National Insurance contributions.

For any of this to make any sense, it's important to explain the *internal market* at this point. The concept of the NHS internal market was conceived in the 1990s. Under this model, the NHS was divided into provider services, like hospitals and purchaser services, like GP practices.

As in any market, contracts are signed, and services can be bought and sold at a price. NHS Trusts (hospitals) and other provider organizations set prices for their services, while purchasers like GP practices buy them. Some contracts are block contracts (set amount paid irrespective of activity), while some contracts are activity based.

An example of a block contract could be a phlebotomy (blood taking) service.

In other words, the provider service gets a set fee, irrespective of how many blood tests the GP requests.

An example of a fee per service could be a hospital orthopaedic department that sets the cost of a hip replacement at say £300 per hip. The more GP referrals they get for hip replacements, the more money the hospital trust *makes.*

All GP Practices have a referral budget, however, which they generally aim to stay within.

Last but not least, we have the prescribing incentive scheme (PIS), initiated to help address variation in prescribing across various CCGs—in other words prescribe efficiently.

Each GP practice has an indicative budget set by the CCG prescribing team.

This is the reason why the practice in-house chemist or GP might swap your current medication to a cheaper alternative.

In practice the CCG prescribing team focuses on certain prescribing areas, say, for example, controlled drugs, special formulation drugs, tranquilisers, etc. with various set targets.

Practices that stay within budget are remunerated according to the number of targets achieved. There isn't any punitive action for practices that fail to attain their targets, apart from naming and shaming!

I have only just touched the surface in trying to explain what is a rather confusing area of the NHS.

General practice, and the NHS for that matter, is in constant evolution, and at the time of writing there is major reform underway in its organisational structure.

For example, as part of the new *five-year sustainability and transformation plans* (STPs), local CCGs have been grouped into 44 zones. The aim of STPs is to introduce new models of care, with emphasis on social care integration and other services provided by local authorities. The overall aim is to improve patient care.

CHAPTER 12

A DAY IN THE LIFE OF A GP

If you hear how wonderful you are often enough, you begin to believe it, no matter how you try to resist it.

-Dr Ben Carson

A few years ago, while waiting for a show to start at the theatre with some friends, I was challenged by a gentleman who found out I was a GP—he was furious.

He mentioned how his father's GP of many years knew his medical history thoroughly and actually took the time to listen on each visit. These days, his father just saw *a random* doctor; that is if he even managed to get an appointment.

I tried to explain how things had changed, but he wouldn't listen—there was simply no defence according to him.

The image of the GP on the golf course somehow seems to stick in the minds of people, despite relentless hours at surgery seeing patients. I am beginning to suspect it might have something to do with golf courses, in which case I think I have found a new location for my next surgery.

I once saw a nice man who had just had his third stroke. He limped into my room on crutches and asked what the chance of having another stroke was.

More importantly, he was worried he might not achieve his company targets for the year, given his company was quite strict, and he risked redundancy if he didn't perform.

This got me thinking about the different jobs I had heard about from patients over the years, and wondered what the most difficult one was: Was it the sandwich worker who stood for 12 hours plus, performing a monotonous task that was timed? The berry picker who worked 14 hours in the fields? The chicken catcher, complete with peck wounds? The heavy goods vehicle driver who woke up at 3:00 a.m. and got back home at 8:00 p.m.? The stressed investment banker who constantly carried a box of paracetamols in his pocket, who worried about the thought of losing millions in a heartbeat? The teacher who took all their work back home and couldn't cope due to unruly children and government diktat? The soldier who had been deployed to Afghanistan, who knew any day could be his last? I could go on and on, but you get the picture.

So, what's the most difficult job in the world? *I don't know*, but what I do know is that general practice is a tough job. There is something about listening to emotionally charged stories from a huge number of people on a daily basis, constantly making countless decisions that can have huge consequences, and knowing full well your career could depend on the one decision you got wrong.

While customer expectations rise, many industries have adapted to change:

24-hour services in some, same-day delivery with regards to physical products (Amazon), applications (Apps), innovations in IT, and so on. As a result, more and more customers want things *now*.

While I must admit the IT systems in the NHS could be better, healthcare delivery can't quite be compared to other industries. There is therefore a disconnection between what can be offered and what in reality is often expected.

The average GP therefore faces the dilemma of trying to keep up with patient need while also trying to do the right thing—in other words practise good quality, safe medicine.

What you might *want* might not be what you necessarily *need*, but after a while some GPs just cave in and assume a secretarial role of just doing what you ask for. At face value this might sound attractive, but some decisions might have long-standing consequences for your health.

A huge percentage of patient interactions in the NHS occur in general practice, and the GP's role is often thought of as being a gatekeeper.

Generally speaking, a GP's day is divided into a morning and an afternoon phase called *sessions*. Each session lasts from about two and a half to three hours, during which the typical GP probably sees between 15 and 18 patients in 10-minute intervals.

Using the lower average of 15 patients per session and two home visits per day, one gets to a total of 32 patients per day.

Of these 32 patients, think of any medical and non-medical complaint you could imagine, and you will be correct-Really.

Here is a list of the obvious conditions GPs deal with:

Rashes, anxiety, depression, post-traumatic stress disorder, strokes, Parkinson's disease, Alzheimer's disease, multiple sclerosis, asthma, emphysema (COPD), chest infections, hypertension, chest pain, heart failure, diabetes, thyroid disorders, reflux, irritable bowel syndrome (IBS), diarrhoea, constipation, diverticulitis, menstrual period irregularities, infertility, prolapse, fibroids, urinary incontinence, erectile problems in men, prostate enlargement, overactive bladder, joint pain, including back, knees, shoulders, various cancers and more.

Other conditions you might not immediately have thought of include:

Bereavement, domestic abuse, sexual abuse, gender reassignment (women hoping to transition to male and vice versa) alcoholic dependents, gambling addiction, pornographic addiction, problem behaviour in children, learning difficulties, autism, attention deficit hyperactivity disorder (ADHD) those in serious financial debt, family disputes, marital problems, child abuse and much more.

On average, most full-time GPs work eight sessions over four days, but some stretch to nine sessions over five days. Most GPs start surgery between 8:00

a.m. and 9:00 a.m., but some might start as early as 7:00 a.m. in practices that have opted into the *extended hours* scheme.

There is a variable interval between the morning and afternoon sessions, which depends on the end of morning and start of the afternoon surgeries. During this interval, most GPs do home visits, with the typical GP visiting an average of two patients per day. In addition, some GPs also use this time to check blood test results, sign previous prescription requests, check or dictate letters for the hospital, and any other additional work. As you can see, your GP might not be seeing patients, but they have their hands full. However, some practices have a so-called a*dmin session* (a session dedicated to paperwork only), and some just come in on their days off.

The number of blood tests to comb through is also variable and depends on the tendencies of the GPs in the practice, in other words their threshold for requesting blood tests during consultations.

On a typical day most GPs probably check between 25 and 30 blood test results per day by clicking on electronic links from the lab on the computer screen.

Once checked, a blood test result is either filed as *normal* or a message is sent electronically to the reception team for a repeat test or an appointment to discuss the results. This message is called a *task,* which is similar to a short message system (SMS) you receive on your phone.

The task system is the form of communication most surgeries use and on a typical day a GP might get from between 10 and 20 tasks that need some form of action—the number is highly variable from practice to practice.

When you phone a surgery to relay a message to your GP, for example, this message gets sent in the form of task. Throughout the day, both GP and receptionist keep a close eye on their *task screen* as some tasks are marked *urgent.*

Prescription signing is another huge part of a GP's day and when done properly involves meticulously checking each prescription before signing. Typically, most GPs include a note on the script or send a task to a receptionist for you to book an appointment if they feel you need a medication review of some kind or are questioning your request.

Common reasons to be asked to book an appointment with your GP are extremely frequent requests for controlled drugs like opioids, wrong doses of drugs, or a confusing request that makes more sense to be discussed face-to-face. This can occasionally be a nuisance, but if your GP were to do all the work via tasks, they simply wouldn't be able to cope with their list of booked patients.

While GPs often use the word *paperwork* as part of their workload, I suspect you might not know exactly what it entails. Paperwork by GPs can be divided into NHS and non-NHS (private) paperwork work for which they get extra remuneration.

Referrals make up the bulk of GP NHS paperwork, and typically letters are dictated or sent via a task to the secretaries, who book your appointment in hospital.

As referral letters leave the practice to hospital, new discharge letters from hospital arrive at the surgery. On a daily basis, the *administration staff* then distributes the letters to the various GPs, who get them in their *communications inbox*.

Similar to checking blood test results, discharge letters are actioned with an appropriate task sent to the reception staff. Medication changes on recommendation by consultants are typical, and these are amended on your records accordingly ready for your repeat medication request.

Other NHS paperwork includes coroner reports, requests from the Department of Work and Pensions (DWP), medical exemption forms, maternity exemption forms, forms from social services and much more.

Non-NHS paperwork constitutes requests from insurance companies, banks/mortgage companies, holiday cancellation forms, heavy goods vehicles (HGV) medical forms, medical reports for employees with long absences from work, government agencies like the Driver and Vehicle Licensing Agency (DVLA), DWP, police reports, and even the Home Office.

Over the last few years, there has been a tendency for hospital consultants and other staff to delegate a huge chunk of their work to the GP. This is colloquially known as a *hospital dump* and is an area of great frustration among GPs. Many GPs have now got fed up and are sending letters back to the involved departments to complete their own work.

Examples of a hospital dump are: A hospital doctor asking the GP to prescribe a drug that they themselves could have done, a request for a scan sent to the GP, a scan done by the hospital and then asking the GP to *chase* the results, being asked to refer a patent from one department to another and so on.

I once admitted a diabetic patient to hospital only to get a call from one of the nurses asking me to refer the patient to the consultant using the *choose and book system.* This was despite the fact that the consultant was right there with the patient!

Part of *hospital dumping* is due to the funding system in place. A referral from a GP debits the GP practice's referral budget, while a referral from hospital debits the hospital budget.

There is also an increasingly popular category of requests for which some GPs have coined the name GANFYD, an acronym standing for *Get A Note From Your Doctor.* For some reason, partly litigation-driven, these requests are increasingly common and add a burden to the already huge pile of paperwork.

Examples of GANFYD requests include: An employer asking a patient with an overactive bladder to get a note to enable them to go to the bathroom during a shift, a charity requesting a note to affirm fitness for bungee jumping, a school or nursery asking for a note to allow Calpol to be administered on the premises, an airline requesting a fit-to-fly note, a patient requesting a note for the council to move them into a bungalow and so on. The list is endless, and, needless to say, most GPs are irritated by these mundane requests.

The adage art imitates life is probably true, as I almost forgot to mention lunch as I write this. On a lucky day, you might have maybe 15 minutes to catch up with colleagues depending on the practice. I remember some good chats I would have with Aaron, a GP colleague at the time. We talked about diet, world affairs, economics and much more.

With blood test results all checked, prescriptions (scripts) all signed and some paperwork cleared, your GP starts off the afternoon surgery, which lasts again from two and a half to three hours. During this time, the laboratories and hospitals are also working, and, as a result, more blood test results and discharge letters continue to drip into their *inbox.* After seeing another fifteen to eighteen patients, it is the end of the afternoon session. At this time, your GP will either finish off outstanding blood test results, referrals and other paperwork or stagger into their car and head home, with a view to finishing off leftover work the morning after. Some continue their work on a laptop after logging onto the computer system.

If you are thinking the day described so far sounds tedious, you will be glad to know I have just described an uneventful surgery so to speak.

As I have mentioned, most appointment slots last ten minutes, during which your GP is expected to listen to your complaint, examine you and then prescribe appropriately.

As you know, most patients don't come with a single medical complaint, with the average number of complaints these days being three.

I have seen signs in some practices where patients are told to please come with one complaint only. The concept of *one problem per consultation* is an interesting one, which assumes each *problem* or complaint is a separate entity.

A 10-minute consultation also reflects this notion, thus consciously or unconsciously forcing the clinician to compartmentalise symptoms. Given the average GP sees 30 patients or so per day, the only practical way left to manage one's workload is indeed resort to *one problem per consultation.*

It is a quandary I am sure most GPs face on a day-to-day basis and pushing boundaries has led to burnout in quite a few colleagues.

To put things into perspective, a recent Medscape Global Physicians' Burnout and Lifestyle Comparison showed 1/3 of GPs in the UK suffer from burnout.

I mentioned things could get exciting in surgery, what did I mean?

Sometimes, after assessment, your GP might feel you are too sick and need a hospital admission. Typically, they will call the local hospital switchboard and ask for a member of the relevant specialty who takes *admissions.* This is usually a junior doctor or in some hospitals a nurse designated with the role of taking GP hospital admissions. The process of getting hold of someone in hospital can sometimes be tricky business as they too might be busy on another case. The GP will then present the case over the phone to whoever takes the call, and more likely than not you will be *accepted.*

Sometimes, the case might be beyond the remit of the hospital at hand, or whoever answers the phone might feel this is not a case that falls under the particular specialty. In cases like this, the process might have to be repeated all over by asking for another department through *switchboard* or calling a different hospital altogether.

Occasionally squabbles ensue, as to which department the patient at hand belongs to. The surgical or orthopaedic team might think a patient is *medical* or the urologists might think a case is gynaecological and so on.

In the end, your GP hands you an admission letter to take to hospital where the team will be waiting. Sometimes the now frequent statement of, "We have no beds, could you send the patient to A&E and we will see them there?" follows.

On some occasions, after assessment in surgery, your GP might feel your case is an emergency, in which case a 999 call is made.

Some cases like asthma attacks, myocardial infarctions (heart attack) or strokes fall into this category.

Another emergency, which you might be surprised to read, is suicidal patients.

I have seen a fair number of cases where the patient's opening statement is, "I want to kill myself." In cases like this, your GP will take a good history and call the *Crisis Team* who will typically ask staggering numbers of questions about the patient. In genuine cases, a member of the Crisis Team is sent out, usually to the patient's home, within a short time frame.

A few days into my training many years ago, a man walked into my room with rustling supermarket shopping bags. He looked at me stone eyed and uttered the words, "I feel like killing myself, doctor."

On hearing those words, I immediately picked up the phone and called the Crisis Team after asking a few more questions. The gentleman at the end of the line was quite professional and seemed to recognise the patient's name, and he asked me how long the patient had felt suicidal.

I had forgotten to ask. "How long have you felt this way, sir?"

"Twenty years," the man replied!

Apart from unpredictable cases during routine surgery, there is a constant stream of phone calls from Accident and Emergency, hospital departments, and medical secretaries, all wanting information on a patient, pathology laboratories ringing in urgent blood test results, and even cold callers! Most surgeries have an *on call* or *duty doctor* who deals with these requests, in addition to seeing emergency appointments and doing home visits if needed. I have had my share of duty doctor days, with some entertaining experiences and some challenging ones.

I remember a fateful *on call* day when the practice manager walked into my room and said she had some bad news for me. There had been a flu outbreak in one of the local care homes, and the guidance was to prescribe the drug Tamiflu to all the residents. She handed me the pile of papers with the patients on and left. I had to look through every patient, check their kidney function and prescribe the right dose of the drug—all this while patients were continuously being booked.

With the sheer amount of patient contacts and general work load, it is not humanly possible to consistently maintain a high quality of care. This is a reality of the job and can cause a huge amount of stress to the high achiever or perfectionist.

Finally, it's not enough to have done all the above work—you also have to show you are doing it. This comes in the form of appraisals, which most professionals also have to undergo. GPs have a yearly appraisal and a five yearly revalidation, which maintains their *license to practise.* This system was initiated after the infamous GP Harold Shipman killed over 200 of his patients. He was sentenced to life imprisonment and eventually committed suicide in his cell by hanging.

The appraisal system can be onerous and requires details and reflections about courses one has attended, complaints, compliments, interesting cases, significant events, feedback forms from patients, and so on. All this information is entered onto a website, ready for an appraisal meeting with GP and appraiser (another GP).

It might seem rather straightforward, but trying to collate a year's worth of information is quite challenging due to time constraints. Typically, what most GPs do is start preparation a few weeks before their appraisal date. During this period, stress levels are extremely high to say the least.

Almost on a weekly basis, patients are left without a practice as GPs hand their contracts back to the CCG.

I hope you now have a clearer picture of a GP's day. However, your priority is to get the best care under any given circumstances. To do this, you need to make the GP's day as easy as you can by doing some of the *work* yourself. This includes eating a healthy diet, exercising, listening to your body, researching your symptoms and learning to give a good history. This is the smart way to work with your GP to get the best health outcomes for yourself.

CHAPTER 13

WHAT YOUR GP SECRETLY WISHES YOU KNEW

If they can make penicillin out of mouldy bread, they can sure make something out of you.

-Muhammad Ali

Like any job, I think it is fair to say that most GPs spend a proportion of their time complaining about *you*—the patient! Some have the courage to tell you, while the majority vent their frustrations behind closed doors. Below are some of the most commonly discussed aspects of your behaviour.

Arrive in Good Time

If you are five minutes late, you have five minutes left for your consultation.

It might seem harsh, but that's the reality of the situation. If you're running late due to unforeseen circumstances like traffic from roadblocks, having to cater for your baby en route, or other issues, a simple phone call to the practice to let them know you will be late goes a long way.

However, ringing three hours before your appointment to say you will be late simply means you can't make your appointment time and rescheduling is advised.

I once told a patient he was seven minutes late, and he asked why a GP could not wait for him for once—after all, he had waited for GPs for years!

Cancel If Need Be

Appointments cost money, something that many patients don't seem to realize due to the funding structure of the NHS. If we all had to pay directly by cash or credit card for an appointment, I guarantee the percentage of non-attenders would significantly reduce. If you can't make it for your appointment, simply phone in good time and cancel so your slot can be allocated to someone else.

Be Respectful

In the old days people dressed up to see the doctor and were on their best behaviour. Sadly, things have changed, and the *anything goes mentality* has somehow crept in. Countless times I have had patients walk in while talking on their mobile phones, answering their phones in the middle of a consultation or just being frankly rude for no reason.

I know of a colleague who jumped out of his window after he was attacked with a fork.

Being polite and respectful does not cost a thing. Respect is also earned, and if a doctor is rude, politely tell him so with the aim of possibly getting the consultation back on track. A doctor might be unaware they are rude but perceived as so from the use of wrong words in sentences. This is particularly true if English is not their first language or they have unique body language.

Organise and Rehearse Your Symptoms

Before your appointment, it is a good habit to rehearse your symptoms or even write them down on a piece of paper so you don't forget. You will be surprised the amount of details you might forget if you do not do this. Ten-minute appointments are not the longest in the world, so giving a thorough history significantly eases your GP's job.

A mnemonic we have already discussed, which helps organise your symptoms, is SOCRATES, where:

S stands for Site, O-Onset, C-Character, R-Radiation, A-Associated symptoms, T-Timing, E-Exacerbating/alleviating symptoms, S-Severity.

Using such a system is incredibly useful and eases the diagnostic process. This prevents making a seemingly innocent throwaway statement towards the end of the consultation along the lines of, “Is that why I am also getting diarrhoea?”

A statement like this might suddenly change the diagnosis, potentially restarting the whole consultation.

I once went to see an ophthalmologist and had not rehearsed my history, only to find myself amending some of what I had initially said when she was summarising.

Few Complaints per Consultation

My good neighbour once joked about a hypothetical patient who turns up to his GP with a broken arm and leg. His GP then asks him which problem he wants attending to on that day.

It is incredibly frustrating as a patient to be restricted to one problem per consultation. This is especially the case when you might simply not have been able to secure an appointment in time and you then developed more ailments along the way. In some instances, you might be unsure whether a group of symptoms are related to particular condition or not.

Quite frequently, I hear patients bring a long list of problems and justify themselves by stating how rarely they ever attend. The bottom line is you have ten minutes per consultation, and a balance has to be struck to ensure your doctor can safely see each patient and address their concerns satisfactorily.

GPs are only human, and the more patients they see, the more scope for error.

Following this, if you were to present with too many problems in one consultation, they might try to fit everything into one consultation, potentially leading to a lapse in judgement. Mistakes can be detrimental to your care and knock your doctor’s confidence. To avoid this scenario, it is worth asking for a double appointment if possible when you do book.

Antibiotics Are Not a Panacea

The world has never been the same ever since the discovery of the first antibiotic, penicillin G, by Sir Alexander Fleming in 1928. However, it is important to realise antibiotics aren't a universal panacea, and prescribing them for every ailment is simply not good quality medicine. Countless times I see antibiotics prescribed for uncomplicated outer ear infections, viral infections, slight skin blemishes, and so on.

Today, however, antibiotic overuse has led to resistant species of bacteria (superbugs) like Clostridium difficile (C diff) and Methicillin resistant Staphyloccal Aureus (MRSA).

In addition, antibiotic overuse also potentially kills off your gut *friendly bacteria*, leading to an imbalance in your gut's microbiome. This imbalance of gut microorganisms is termed dysbiosis [1] and it can lead to gut inflammation [2].

Symptoms from the above potentially include less severe issues like food cravings [3], obesity, chronic diseases like inflammatory bowel diseases, autoimmune disorders, diabetes [4] and even mood changes. [5]

Wear Appropriate Attire

This isn't about how smartly dressed you are, although I consider this to be in keeping with good manners. The term appropriate here alludes to *dressing for the occasion*, if you like.

Michael Jackson and the band *One Direction* might be able to pull off slim fit trousers on stage, but if you were to present with knee pain wearing tight jeans, you would literally struggle to pull them off.

It can occasionally take up to three minutes to take off a shirt, tank top, jacket and coat—this leaves seven minutes for a history and examination. If you have a cough, I suggest stripping some layers off a few minutes before your appointment time while in the warm waiting room.

Most GPs Are Stressed

Many years ago, just after qualifying as a GP, I went for a partnership interview but did not get the job. I called back for feedback, and the practice manager said I had not answered one of the questions satisfactorily. The question asked was what I did when stressed.

I knew I hadn't done the question justice—the thing was I had never been stressed so didn't know the answer! It probably sounds untrue, but I honestly never had ben stressed before. In fact, my GP trainer would testify that the only problem he had with me was I would not go on holiday. Little did I know what was in store for me years later…

GPs are constantly multitasking; from seeing patients and making decisions to continuously being interrupted by phone calls, knocks on the door ("Can you just sign this?"), responding to messages, and much more, all within a tight time frame.

This is the perfect recipe for *burnout* and explains why some GPs might be off for a reason unknown to you. As already mentioned, most if not all GPs see a huge number of patients, ranging from 30 to 70 per day within a limited time frame. I know of a GP who saw 80 patients per day over many months due to issues with his NHS merger contract, which seemed to have fallen through. There is also the huge amount of paperwork to follow after consultations, as well as checking blood test results and other *tasks.*

The resulting high work and emotional load can sometimes a take a toll on your GP's mood, resulting in a rare lapse in character (a bad day at the office). Factor in the occasional added load of family life, government policy and other factors and you start to get a better picture.

The public sometimes forget the strain under which GPs operate, partly due to the *instant gratification culture* we live in as well as the constant unfavourable coverage of GPs in the press. Acknowledging the stress element in general practice is in no way saying it is the most stressful job in the world or playing down the stress in other industries, which is also huge.

I always catch a glimpse of stress in action when I am at a supermarket and see the look on the checkout assistant's face at about 9:45 p.m. when a customer comes with a trolley full of a month's worth of shopping. I usually try to make small talk by telling them the shift will soon be over or by cracking a joke or two to liven them up.

I once came to work exhausted about four years ago and a patient of mine picked this up. She asked what was wrong, and I told her I had not slept at all because my newly born daughter had cried all night. She ended up spending the rest of the consultation giving me parenting tips.

Like any job, it is important to note that not all members of staff get along. Just because a group of GPs work together does not mean they get along.

Personalities and ideologies can clash, sometimes leading to a tense work environment and acrimonious disputes.

I remember showing up at a practice for work only to be told the practice had split into two. It turned out the partners had called a representative of the doctors' trade union, the British Medical Association (BMA), in a bid to resolve the dispute. After a few days of negotiations, he ran for the hills.

---

1) Hawrelak JA, Myers SP. "The causes of intestinal dysbiosis: A review." *Alternative Medicine Review.* 2004 Jun;9 (2): 180-97

1) Li Q, Wang C et al, "Dysbiosis of Gut Fungal Microbiota is Associated with Mucosal Inflammation in Crohn's Disease." *J Clin gastroenterol.* 2004 Jul;46 (6): 513-23

3) Joe Alcock et al, "Is eating behaviour manipulated by the gastrointestinal microbiota? Evolutionary pressures and potential mechanisms." *Bioessays* 2014 Oct; 36(10): 940–949.

4) Carding S, Verbeke K, Vipond DT, et al. "Dysbiosis of the gut microbiota in disease." *Microb Ecol Health Dis.*2015;26(10):3402-3411.

5) Dinan TG, Cryan JF., "The Microbiome-Gut-Brain Axis in Health and Disease." *Gastroenterol Clin North Am.* 2017 Mar;46(1):77-89. doi: 10.1016/j.gtc.2016.09.007. Epub 2017 Jan 4.

CHAPTER 14

HOW TO PICK THE BEST GP FOR YOUR NEEDS

Mediocrity knows nothing higher than itself, but talent instantly recognizes genius.

-Arthur Conan Doyle

While it is easy for a good doctor to recognise an equally good one, it might not be so easy for you the patient. Anyone who has consulted with different doctors in a practice knows how varied their attitudes, personalities, and approaches are. It is common in a practice these days to find a mix of older and young GPs, as the older ones go on retirement.

Many years ago, any doctor could start a career in general practice immediately after medical school. It wasn't until the late 1970s when doctors had to embark on a vocational training scheme (VTS). In1965, the Royal College of General Practitioners (RCGP) offered an optional membership exam, the MRCGP (Member of the Royal College of General Practitioners). In 2007, this exam was made compulsory for any doctor hoping to embark on a career in general practice.

Some GPs might have the letters FRCGP (Fellow of the Royal College of General Practitioners) awarded by the Royal Collage based on some form of contribution to medicine or achievement in the community as a whole.

At face value, an experienced VTS trained GP with the MRCGP qualification is the ideal; however, just because a doctor hasn't got the letters MRCGP at the end of their name does not mean they are not up to the task. In fact, the older GPs tend to have a wealth of experience that is unparalleled.

Other abbreviations at the end of a doctor's name you might see and what they stand for include: MBBS/MBChB (Bachelor of Medicine, Bachelor of Surgery), MD (Medical Doctor), DRCOG (Diploma of the Royal College of Obstetrics and Gynaecologists), DFFP (Diploma of the Faculty of Family Planning), and DOccMed (Diploma in Occupational Medicine).

With qualifications out of the way, here are some points that might help you pick a good doctor. I don't claim to be the best GP around and in fact have experienced some of the very points I mention at some point in time.

The Named GP

Even though you might have a "named GP" once you register, there is no harm in seeing another doctor. If you are new to a practice, it is worth shopping around if you are not happy with the service you get. Once you find a doctor you are satisfied with, try as much as possible to stick with them. Of course, this is not always easy, so it pays to have a handful of doctors you trust.

Loyalty Might Not Always Pay

Just because a particular doctor was your grandma's or dad's GP does not mean you have to carry on with the family tradition. If they have served the family well for all those years, then it would be unreasonable to go elsewhere. However, do not feel you have to keep seeing them out of loyalty, especially if you realize you are not getting the best service. Your criteria in choosing the right doctor for you should really be one who listens empathetically, explains thoroughly what they feel the problem(s) is/are, and deals with them effectively with a sense of urgency.

Interestingly, I have witnessed scenarios where a patient had previously seen their *regular GP* only to book an appointment a few days later with another doctor regarding the same ailment. I once enquired from a patient why they hadn't posed the question they were asking me to their regular

GP just two days before. The answer was they did not want to upset the said doctor—very British.

Does Your GP *Know His Stuff*?

I once had a laptop that seemed to develop a new set of problems every month.

I *googled* a laptop repair man, as you do, and took it down for repairs. The gentleman was very pleasant and seemed extremely knowledgeable in computers. He told me about all the work he had done over the years and explained what exactly he thought was wrong—the entire system had to be cleaned out and rebooted; I agreed. He went further to give me a few minutes' crash course on how computers worked.

After a few days I took it home and within a day or so the problem cropped up again. I took it down for repairs again and this time it was a small part that needed replacing. The gentleman explained what the part was and showed me its reference number in a thick folder on his table. Again, very impressive, but after only two days in my possession the same problem cropped up.

I took it back again and got told it was yet another chip that had to be replaced.

That didn't work out either, and at this point I was slightly hot under the collar.

This time I phoned to ask him why the laptop was still not working given we had replaced two parts so far and "cleaned the entire system". His *advice* to me at this point was to buy a new laptop!

Why am I telling you a story about my laptop you probably don't care about? The reason is to illustrate the perils of a false sense of trust we develop from people we think are experts. Despite not getting any results a few times, I persisted due to my perception of him being an expert in his field. So, don't let this happen to you with regards to your health.

A few years ago, I got to talk with a receptionist at a practice I worked in. She had a dentist appointment in a few days and, as ever, was terrified. I remember asking her if the dentist she was seeing was good, given my experience of incompetent dentists in the past. She agreed that her dentist was good and recounted how nice he had been on her first visit—he had also managed to calm her down from a hysterical state while offering her a glass of water.

Even though my initial question was one of competence, the receptionist had given me an answer about character, something easily confused although not necessarily mutually exclusive.

I am not suggesting being pleasant is not a good quality to have, I mean you don't exactly want the *Terminator* as your GP—I don't mean Arnie the man, who is a nice person.

That said, a pleasant incompetent doctor is the worst you could wish for, as despite their failings you risk keep being drawn to them based on their character, which could be contrived in some cases for all you know.

Medicine is an evolving field, making a career in medicine a dedication to lifelong learning. It is therefore imperative that your doctor does not become complacent and simply coast along. A cursory approach and prescribing paracetamol for every ailment are examples for things to look out for.

Since the introduction of appraisals in the UK, most doctors will have done some sort of learning, be it online or on a course. The bottom line is easy; if after multiple visits you are still no further, it might be time to look elsewhere.

If your GP is unable to explain themselves, or deliberately makes simple things complicated, it might mean they don't understand it themselves.

Countless times, I see patients disputing a colleague's diagnosis from a few days before, citing an internet source. Before rushing to *Google* or to get a second opinion, remember diseases do not present in the text book or internet manner all the time. Some ailments are self-limiting, while others require a bit of time and patience.

Bar extreme circumstances, I would say the process of realistically rating your doctor's clinical acumen is a long one that requires multiple visits over time, rather than a spot assessment after a single encounter.

Is Your GP Willing to Learn?

The pace of research in medicine is advancing at a fast rate, so don't be surprised if your GP is clueless about a medical fact you bring up. Simply put, your GP can't know everything; however it is their ability to take on board what you have said and look into it that is important.

I usually say, "I don't know, but I will have a read on it."

However, if you get dismissed frequently on things you know are facts then your GP is not ready to learn.

An unwillingness to learn is also a sign of narrow-mindedness. Some doctors refuse to acknowledge the power of diet, lifestyle changes and so-called alternative therapies. I met a lovely lady at a healthcare conference who decided to take her care into her own hands. She radically changed her diet and lifestyle and, together with some supplements, completely came off her medication for rheumatoid arthritis. She even had blood tests that showed all markers for inflammation were down. Her rheumatologist wrote to say she would only be seen again in clinic on condition she restarted her medication!

An opportunity to learn sadly missed.

Beware of False Reassurance

I would be wary of a doctor who kept reassuring you on every visit with a pat on the back—unless you are a hypochondriac. It might sound and feel good to be reassured on every occasion, but the question you should be asking yourself down the line is if you are any better than you were before you made the appointment. If the answer is consistently no, then my advice is run like Usain Bolt.

Consistent Absence of Examination

I once met a drug rep at a meeting who was extremely annoyed with his GP.

He and his wife had presented with their three-month-old baby who had a high temperature. As soon as they walked through the door, his GP said three times, "It's a virus, it's a virus, it's a virus," before they even sat down, without so much as casting an eye on the baby.

I would say the majority of GPs I know would not risk this sort of behaviour though.

The Fallacy of Blood Tests & Scans

It is a common misconception to think the more tests a doctor requests, the more thorough they are. This is not necessarily the case as blood tests should be requested tailored to the history provided.

In some unclear cases, a blanket set of blood tests might be required to try to pick up any clues, but, generally speaking, blood test requests should not precede the history, and should be tailored to the case at hand. This concept applies equally for X rays and scans, which are not always required. More on this later in the Investigations section.

An exception to the above rule is investigations done for screening purposes, where tests are done to look for pathologies in the healthy general population.

Lack of Decision Making

If you find yourself repeating numerous blood tests to no end, especially without any explanation, chances are your GP might not have a clue what they are doing. I have seen this happen numerous times, with some repeating tests for more than a year. The reason for repeating a blood test or scan is usually to monitor any trends with time. In many cases the blood level of a particular test might normalize after a month or so. However, if the level increases instead, then further investigation might be needed to find the cause.

Resistance to Change

By now, you are probably aware medicine is an art. Sometimes a treatment plan might work, sometimes it might not. Your GP should ideally be flexible enough to change his reasoning and consequently your management plan. If you aren't getting better, but your GP refuses to consider an alternative approach, you risk remaining in the same situation for months or even years to come.

Speed & Efficiency

We all live in a fast-paced society, and speed and efficiency go a long way.

Getting a phone call a day or two later to discuss the results of a blood test you just had, receiving an appointment quickly for a recent referral by your GP, or acting on whatever they promised to do quickly, all demonstrate good organisational and time-keeping skills. It is, however, not always easy to keep up, especially if your practice has a shortage of GPs.

The Expensive Cost of Leniency

Beware of sleeping tablets and sedatives like benzodiazepines (Diazepam, Lorazepam, Temazepam, Nitrazepam) and other related drugs. They might serve a short-term purpose but are not to be prescribed long term due to their high rate of dependency.

Some patients are not aware of the long-term harm of these drugs, but some are aware and keep requesting them. If your GP has never had a frank chat with you about thus category of drugs, then their perceived leniency might be to the detriment of your health.

I have had numerous difficult consultations in dealing with this issue, and on a few occasions, I am pleased to say some patients have come back many years later to thank me for being firm and giving them good advice.

Many years ago, some law firms (Sue, Grabbit and Runne) had a field day suing GPs on the premise they had not told their patients tranquilisers were addictive!

Another area of perceived leniency is antidepressants. Prescribing antidepressants is also an area I take very seriously. Quite often patients request antidepressants because they have just broken up with their partner a few days before and are feeling low and want a tablet to *pick them up*. On other occasions they might have recently started a job they don't like or are worried they might not succeed in a new venture they have just embarked on.

I usually explain that although the easiest thing for me is to prescribe an antidepressant, I feel it is not the appropriate thing to do in such circumstances.

I usually go further to explain it is perfectly normal to feel the way they feel in difficult life situations. The situations described above are life's stresses, which eventually adjust themselves with a bit of time and perseverance.

It is an entirely different matter if a patient presents with a low mood and sleeplessness six months after of the breakdown of their 30-year relationship.

This is an example of a genuine case of depression for which antidepressants are appropriate.

I once saw a man who cried throughout his consultation with his wife. He had not been sleeping and was tearful throughout the day. His wife was at her wits' end. I prescribed a course of antidepressants, and two weeks later, he came in happier than Meghan and Harry on their first date, affirming the fact that he had never felt so good in his life.

Another area of leniency goes for sickness certificates/fit notes, commonly called *club notes.* We all know some people who are able and fit to work but keep requesting sick notes to collect government *benefits.*

The longer one stays off work, the more difficult it is to eventually take up some form of employment. In essence, you become dependent on the state, missing out on any personal development or prospective career.

I try to offer advice as often as I can, but, sadly, some patients just shop around till they find a GP who will issue one.

Typing While Listening

I have heard many patients complain about doctors who apparently were not listening to them while typing away. This is a sensible conclusion to make, as the act of typing invariably curtails eye contact, unless your GP is extremely versed with the computer keyboard.

However, GPs are known to multitask and *active typing* does not equate to a deaf ear. I usually type about half the time the patient is talking then pause to listen the other half.

While some might say it is best to focus on listening to all of the history from a patient before typing the consultation, it does have its disadvantages. Firstly, the chances your GP might forget some of what you did say as soon as you leave the room are high. This is an extremely important point as we all know 80% of any diagnosis is made by examining the history.

I have on occasions had to read through notes going back a few months to years in an attempt to try to make sense of a case. A thorough set of notes are not only important for your GP but for any other GPs you might happen to see subsequently. Locum doctors are often very grateful to work in a practice where the doctors practice meticulous note-keeping.

Secondly, in the rare event of a medicolegal claim, lawyers would stress: *If you did not write it, it did not happen.*

I know of colleagues who vehemently denied a patient's narrative stated in their solicitor's letter. The only problem was they were now relying on their memory and not on what was documented.

Looking Up Information Does Not Necessarily Equate to Lack of Knowledge

An 80-year-old lady once remarked she was "a little worried" I had to look up a drug in the British National Formulary (BNF) I hoped to prescribe for her. She mentioned that her doctor always just wrote out the drug needed without having to check. I have also heard some friends muse about this suggesting a doctor's incompetence. This couldn't be further from the truth as a doctor who checks to make sure they are prescribing safely shows consideration for you.

Quickly Out of the Door is Not Necessarily Poor

Interestingly, a quick prescription from your GP just after a few seconds might seem overzealous, but this is sometimes due to being highly proficient. A paediatric friend of mine once told me most of the time he diagnosed most of the children he saw after a few seconds but had to *play the consultation out* to appear more thorough.

Some diagnoses are referred to as a *spot diagnosis* and are easily made in seconds. Shingles, conjunctivitis and many others are some examples. A case involving mental health, for example, needs time and in some cases sensible lifestyle changes and counselling are better options, rather than just taking *a pill.*

Dependency Can Be a Disease

Some doctors seem to like to *review* their patients at very short intervals over an awfully long period of time. While some medical conditions might require this, others do not. Very frequent reviews tend to make you, the patient, dependent, not a very desirable quality if you really want to assert some independence in managing your own health. Extreme dependency on your GP might sometimes lead to anxiety in the event you are unable to see them.

In my opinion, a good GP should empower you to make good decisions about your health, rather than making you depend on them for every bit of your care.

If your GP needs your blood pressure taking frequently, invest in a good quality machine at do it at home. If you are feeling better, you can ask for less frequent reviews.

Don't Dismiss the Locum Doctor

Ironically, locum doctors inadvertently shoot themselves in the foot with the phrase, "I am *just* a locum," when asked if they are a regular doctor in a practice. Patients automatically often despair when they see a new doctor because they have to explain all their problems from the beginning. While this might be true in some complex cases, your medical records do contain all the info needed, including a list of diagnoses and medications taken.

A problem arises if your doctor's note-keeping is not up to standard, meaning a locum or any doctor you see will have no knowledge of what was discussed. The advantage of seeing a locum is they might cast a fresh eye on your condition, with the possibly of some progress being made.

In an *under-doctored* practice, there is a high chance of stressed doctors who inevitably spend little time with patients given the circumstances. It therefore comes as a pleasant surprise when you see the locum doctor, who is most likely less stressed and takes the time to listen.

Word of Mouth and Online Reviews

The best reviews in any business are via word of mouth. If someone you trust recommends a service, chances are you won't go wrong. When reading online reviews, it is important to separate the genuine reviews from the bunch. If many reviewers highlight a particular issue, then chances are the problem might exist. However, it is worth looking at the dates of the reviews, as practices continuously update their policies and make changes.

I remember listening to a hotel manager on a radio program many years ago complaining about the deleterious effect reviews on the website *TripAdvisor* were having on the industry. He was specifically discussing an increasing trend of customers blackmailing hotels with threats of writing negative reviews if their unreasonable concessions weren't met.

In the present social media culture we live in, it is not uncommon for patients to post rude, disrespectful and false statements on Facebook, Twitter or other platforms.

A patient once took a picture of a practice manager and receptionist discussing an important matter and posted it on Facebook with the words *Standing about doing nothing—No wonder we can't get through on the phones.*

Some patients are annoyed they did not get what they wanted and go on to make slandering remarks about the GPs or practice as a whole.

If you are not happy about the care you receive, the most appropriate way to approach this would be to write to the practice or request a meeting to discuss the issues you may have.

It is therefore important to take such reviews with a pinch of salt and instead concentrate on the valuable ones so to speak.

Appearance Is Not Everything but Worth Considering

If you are familiar with the TV series *Dragon's Den*, you will have noticed Peter Jones' irritation each time a prospective candidate turns up for a pitch in casual attire, having made no effort whatsoever.

The image of the village GP in a tweed jacket, complete with elbow pads, is probably almost extinct; nonetheless, a smartly dressed doctor portrays a good impression.

I know of a doctor who had been noted by patients to have dirty fingernails, and who would occasionally turn up in scruffy jeans.

There is something to be said about a well-groomed doctor who turns up in time for work on a consistent basis.

Character & Integrity

Do not trust a doctor who talks ill of another colleague's approach. Sadly, this happens more often than you would think and takes different forms.

Typically, a colleague from the same practice, clinician from another setting like a walk-in centre, A&E or other healthcare professional might make a throwaway comment like, "Your GP did not do X?" or, "Your GP should have done Y." Most of the time, snap judgements like these are unhelpful as the intricacies of the case are not generally known by the commenter and can cause unnecessary tension between patient and GP.

Character assassination on a doctor's part towards another colleague is even worse; phrases like, "No one likes him/her," or, "She is a difficult doctor to work with." Slandering another clinician is simply not professional and reflects a lack of integrity on the doctor's part.

A doctor who makes derogatory comments about other colleagues is most likely to also make similar comments about you behind your back. "Oh no! Not that patient again!" As a general rule, anyone who makes derogatory comments about others in an attempt to look good suffers from a lack of self-confidence.

I have described above the *hard* factors in choosing the right GP. However, there are other *soft* factors that are equally important and more likely to influence your decision. Examples include a female patient preferring a female GP for a gynaecological problem or a patient preferring a GP with a similar personality, cultural or social background.

CHAPTER 15

WHEN THINGS GO WRONG

Not happy with my driving? Call my boss, he doesn't give a toss either.

-Writing on a van

Doctors are not infallible and, despite their best intentions and efforts, mistakes do unfortunately happen. If you or a family member have ever been misdiagnosed or mismanaged, you will agree the feeling is distressing. I speak here for most in saying the feeling is mutual for most hardworking doctors, who might have sleepless nights ruminating on the events and how they got it wrong. This feeling is further worsened with the prospect of litigation, a trend that is becoming more and more commonplace.

Mistakes in general practice occur from a myriad of reasons, including a lack of knowledge on the doctor's part (Incompetence), lack of examination, which would have revealed important findings, frequent interruptions in surgery for one reason or another, tiredness/burnout from overworking, human error, laziness or a lack of communication to name a few.

In my opinion, there are three factors that are often overlooked with regards to medical negligence in primary care.

The first point is the fact GPs get to see many diseases in their early stages.

In practice, this means many of the characteristic signs and symptoms might be absent.

The second point worth noting is the *unpredictability of disease.* This simply means the typical signs and symptoms of a pathology might be absent and instead present in a rather unfamiliar manner. Both these factors lead to misdiagnosis, and hence mismanagement in some cases.

Thirdly, GPs haven't got the luxury of blood test and scan results within hours, similar to hospitals. You could argue why don't GPs just request blood tests and scans for all cases, just in case they pick up a pathology? While it might sound reasonable, in practice it isn't. If GPs were to send every patient they saw for further tests, the system would crash within days—we simply haven't got the capacity.

Fourthly, there is a chance you might pick something up unrelated to the pathology at hand. You then end up with a scenario of requesting even more tests to no end.

I once remarked to a colleague after reading an alleged medical negligence claim that it seemed GPs were expected to work with the efficiency of German or Japanese engineering but with the speed of a 200-meter runner.

Some negligence cases are straightforward and don't need an expert to point this out. In cases like this it is only fair for the doctor(s) involved to be as truthful and honest as possible with the patient and family where relevant.

The commonest way of signalling dissatisfaction with an aspect of your doctor's care is usually in the way of a complaint letter or email to the practice manager, who then hands it to your doctor. While some complaints are expected, interestingly, a huge number seem to come as a shock to the doctor involved.

In my opinion, just being open and upfront with your doctor if you are unsatisfied with your care is the ideal approach.

This way any issues or misunderstandings get ironed out there and then.

This might seem awkward for patients, but most GPs would really appreciate this if done constructively.

Most practices have a *complaints procedure* and a *complaints lead*, usually a GP, who will help draft a reply, usually with the doctor involved.

A GP friend of mine recently mentioned in his practice they promoted a face-to-face approach to resolve all issues. In other words, if a patient had a complaint, they were invited to sit face-to-face with the doctor involved and talk about it over a hot drink—quite refreshing I thought.

Generally, most complaints are resolved in a space of days or weeks and nothing is ever heard from the patient again, following a reply from the GP involved.

In cases where the complaint letter highlights some difficult medical, ethical or generally complex issues, the doctor involved will most likely need some advice on how to proceed. This advice is usually in the way of a medical defence organisation, which provides medical indemnity (insurance) for all registered clinicians against malpractice. Should a complaint letter come via a solicitor acting on behalf of a patient, calling their medical defence organisation is mandatory and usually done at the speed of light.

Litigation claims can potentially take years to resolve, with solicitors from both the *claimant* (patient) and the defendant (GP) writing back and forth, with possible days in court.

Some cases are successfully defended, while some are not, with the GP advised to accept liability, resulting in payouts (compensation) to the patient or family.

Litigation cases can be complicated, but to keep it simple, the claimant (patient) will have to prove *causation*.

Simply put, the concept of causation means you now have Y because your GP did not do X. For example, you ended up in A&E with severe abdominal pain, leading to your appendix being removed, because your doctor failed to diagnose appendicitis earlier.

To prove this, both legal teams will look at your medical records, consult any medical guidelines on the condition if available, and possibly consult an expert witness, usually a GP or specialist in the relevant specialty.

Depending on the case, compensation amounts could range from a few thousand to millions of pounds. The *blame culture* and resulting huge pay-outs are one of the reasons for the rising medical indemnity costs and the draining NHS budget. Up to a few months ago, a full-time GP would expect to pay about £10,000 or so per year on average for medical indemnity.

A GP in her 50s at a meeting I attended a few years ago, who was thinking of working an extra half day, was quoted £1500 worth of cover for an out-of-hours (OOH) shift. Needless to say, she dismissed the idea as it just wasn't worth her while.

As this book goes out to publish, the government has launched a *state backed indemnity scheme* for GPs. This means in essence the money paid out to successful claimants comes from a government pot and not directly via doctor subscription fees. This scheme has thus resulted in a marked reduction in subscription fees.

Complaints ideally shouldn't be made because your GP didn't do what you wanted, as what you *want* might not be what you *need*. To avoid complaints, some doctors now just succumb to whatever a patient demands in some cases, knowing full well it won't be of any additional value. To them, arguing with an already convinced patient armed with a Google search isn't worth the hassle from experience.

A colleague of mine once told me he refers patients to hospital irrespective of the request. It could well be something within his competency or something a referral would unlikely resolve—however it didn't matter. The way he looked at it was simple: He was better off being told off by the local clinical commissioning group (CCG) for being a *high referrer* than getting an unnecessary complaint from a patient—something that could easily take more of his time to respond to.

The fear of complaints also leads to overprescribing by doctors in cases they know fully well are unlikely to be beneficial. A similar argument holds for investigations like X-rays, CT scans and others, which lead to unnecessary radiation in many cases.

I once saw a 17-year-old lady who had been to A&E the previous day with abdominal bloating and pain. She was told by the A&E doctor to see her GP the day after for an endoscopy to rule out the bacteria Helicobacter Pylori (H Pylori). I tried to explain to this lady that a stool test would suffice for this, and there was really no need to put her through an invasive test like an endoscopy.

My explanation was futile; I gave in and referred her.

In many cases, it isn't that your GP does not wish to pursue your request; it is that they don't realize it is what you wanted. It therefore pays to be direct in your approach, and in my opinion this is the best way forward to avoid misunderstandings. This is especially true when dealing with doctors who haven't entirely mastered the nuances of British culture and are more familiar with other cultures that tend to have a more direct approach.

A case that rocked the medical establishment was that of Dr Bawa Garba, a paediatrician who was convicted of manslaughter after a six-year-old boy, Jack Alcock, under her care died of sepsis. Dr Bawa Garba had just recently come back from maternity leave, working flat out while covering six wards by herself as the other registrar and consultant were unavailable.

Errors resulted from a combination of things including a *systems failure* (understaffing, hospital computer systems malfunction) and human error.

It was a complex case involving the police, the GMC (General Medical Council) and its *fitness to practice* panel.

Dr Garba was arrested by the police and struck off the medical register, causing outrage in the medical community. She has since been reinstated after winning her appeal.

Writing on the case, US-based radiologist Dr Saurabh Jha couldn't have summarised it better when he wrote: "Diagnostic medicine is a fog of uncertainty until you know what the patient had."

I recently read an article in the *British Journal of General Practice* (BJGP), which featured a fellow GP doing a marathon. After pondering how she got through the full 23 miles, she realised it was the cheering crowd that showed respect towards runners that motivated her in the end. She then made a comparison to her work as a GP, which seemed the complete opposite—her work never seemed good enough.

This might sound strange to some who feel doctors should have all the answers, but in my opinion the best way to reduce errors is to do some of the work yourself. The best way to do this is to eat a healthy diet and exercise regularly, this way you avoid coming to see a doctor in the first place. Learn to listen to your body, research your symptoms and master the art of giving a history.

Once you have done this, you can have peace of mind and allow the doctor to hopefully do the rest.

I know you do this already, but when you can, always thank your GP or healthcare team for the hard work they do.

CHAPTER 16

HOW *YOU* CAN HELP THE NHS SAVE MONEY

Total spending will continue to rise, and it will be at zero percent rise in 2013/14.

-Gordon Brown

If you have ever fallen ill abroad, then you will remember the shock you must have had after seeing your medical bill. I have friends in America who hesitate to seek medical care when they think of the potential cost.

And speaking of America, a 2015 Harvard study showed medical bills were the primary factor in the decision to file for bankruptcy in more than 50% of cases.

We are blessed with the National Health Service (NHS) in Britain, but it cannot last unless we change our behaviour.

Here are a few tips we could all use to help *save* the NHS.

Prevention Is Better Than Cure

First, you need to prevent disease by living a healthy lifestyle. Eating a healthy diet and exercising are the best ways to put your doctor out of business. Many of the common chronic diseases on the rise today like type II diabetes, some forms of hypertension, heart disease, and so on are all lifestyle-related.

Part 4 of this book focuses on this.

Self-Care

There has been a big push for self-care recently by the NHS as patients are encouraged to consult with the chemist for common ailments like coughs, colds, rashes, eye symptoms and more. Due to the fear of litigation, some chemists just refer everything back to the GP. This is most frustrating and discouraging for keen patients who have taken an initiative to manage whatever ailment they have.

Attend Your Appointments

GP and hospital appointments cost money, and thus missed appointments equate to money down the drain. If you cannot attend your appointment, please call in advance so your appointment can be given to someone else waiting. A frequent cause of missed hospital appointments is change of address.

It is thus important to always make sure the practice or hospital has your current address.

Do Not Abuse the Ambulance Service

I was once told by a paramedic they are *obliged* to bring a patient in whatever the call—I am not sure how true this is.

Every emergency department has a handful of *regulars* who call on a daily basis, sometimes more than once, for the same complaint. There was a man known to us at the time who constantly called complaining of chest pain. He came in at least twice a day, and the volume of his file caused the hospital trolley wheels to squeak under the load. Each time the paramedics brought in him, he had the full works—blood pressure, ECG and blood tests, and of course discharge back home. Ironically, I hear he eventually died of a cardiac arrest.

I know of another patient who kept claiming he had drunk bleach.

On each occasion, he was brought into the ED.

The cost of an ambulance in England is approximately £250, depending on the area. More importantly, as resources are limited, the call you have made for a trivial issue has prevented an ambulance from attending an acutely unwell elderly patient with a stroke or heart attack.

Get Drunk at Home if You Must

I don't need to make my case here. A casual stroll on a Friday or Saturday night for a few minutes tells you all. During the weekends, the emergency department is full of drunken people. If you are going to be drunk, stay at home and *sleep it off* rather than *blocking* a bed that could be used for a genuine patient in need.

I once pleaded with an irate patient who threatened to leave the ED due to the level of noise. The gentleman was unwell and deserved some peace and quiet.

I then went up to the drunken gentleman who was making all the noise and tried to reason with him. Instead of being reasonable, he threatened to sue me should he fall off the bed and injure himself. The tragedy of the situation is he might have indeed stood a chance at a negligence claim as some expert somewhere would have blamed the department for not *babysitting* him while drunk.

Buy Over-the-Counter (OTC) Medication When Possible

One way the NHS gets money is via prescription charges. At the time of printing, the NHS will charge you £9.00 per drug on a prescription. The bulk of this amount ultimately goes to the NHS coffers, minus the actual cost of the drug, a small (dispensing) fee the pharmacy charges the NHS, and other set charges.

If you are entitled to free prescriptions and need a cheap drug sold over the counter, then sacrificing a bit to save the NHS the dispensing fee plus other charges is worth considering. A box of paracetamol costs about 25p in some supermarkets for example.

Hospital Transport

If you live alone and are unable to take yourself to hospital for appointments, always try your best to arrange transport with a family member or kind neighbour. Arranging hospital transport or calling an ambulance as a means of transport is an expensive job.

Home Visits

Over the years I have seen patients go into town for shopping or other chores but call a GP out on a home visit on the pretext they are housebound. Because there is no direct billing per se, these patients fail to realize GP time equals money.

I heard a story where a patient called the surgery from the town centre requesting a GP visit within a particular time frame!

Requesting Endless Investigations

Blood tests, X-rays, ultrasound scans and more all cost money; if there is no clinical indication, then it is simply money down the drain. Many patients often ask for investigations "just for reassurance" but fail to realise such requests potentially open up a can of worms. I know of cases where a patient had five pelvic ultrasounds due to a small cyst found in the ovary, which was of no consequence.

Sue Responsibly

I remember a story told to us junior doctors during induction by a psychiatrist.

It was about a man who had unfortunately been sexually abused as a child.

Years later, in his adult life, this man had taken it upon himself to provide counselling to abused children, given he had been through it himself. He sailed through the job interview and a few months into the job unfortunately started getting flashbacks. He then sued the company for hiring him too early when he wasn't ready!

You might make yourself a fast buck by suing mindlessly, but the consequences are more far-reaching than you imagine. Malpractice claims result in escalating medical defence union fees.

Just to put things into perspective, until recently, a full time GP working four days a week on average would pay in excess of £10,000/year. Rising fees prohibit doctors from continuing to practice, resulting in many quitting the profession altogether. Ultimately, fewer doctors are available to see even more patients, causing more stress for all concerned.

As this book goes out to print, the government has launched a *state backed indemnity scheme* for GPs. This means in essence the money paid out to successful claimants comes from a government pot and not directly via doctor subscription fees. This scheme has thus resulted in a marked reduction in subscription fees. Nevertheless, the government still foots the huge bill for compensation claims of billions. This is money that could potentially be used for the much-needed essential services.

Rising medical defence fees have also led doctors to practice what is termed *defensive medicine.*

When a doctor practices defensive medicine, his main priority is his own protection against any potential malpractice claim. Interestingly, the patient might feel their doctor is being extremely patient centred, not knowing their true intentions.

An example of defensive medicine is requesting lots of bloods tests or scans, knowing full well they are unlikely to provide any additional value. Again, doing this first of all gives the impression of being thorough and, more importantly, who knows? It could be you happen to have a rare pathology that occurs in one in a million cases. What would an expert witness say if you hadn't requested this test?

Another example of defensive medicine is referring a patient at the drop of a hat.

Patient: "I have had a runny nose for three days, doctor."

Dr: "Let's refer you to a specialist."

Well, it could be cerebrospinal fluid rhinorrhoea (spinal fluid leaking from the brain into the nose).

As you can see, your doctor becomes extremely and unreasonably risk averse, with the ultimate result being increased strain on the NHS budget as referrals, blood tests, and scans cost money.

In a bid to reduce escalating referral costs, some practices use so-called *referral management centres.* Referral management centres vary in the way they operate but essentially are composed of healthcare practitioners who triage all referrals from GPs according to set guidelines. Inappropriate referrals are rejected, usually with a letter informing of the reason. Some feel this is sacrificing patient care for cost saving; either way mistakes are bound to happen.

~~Always Use Hospital Parking~~

Don't get me started ☺

PART 2

INTRODUCTION TO THE HUMAN BODY

CHAPTER 17

FROM CELLS TO THE ORGANISM

Whether an illness affects your heart, your leg or your brain, it's still an illness, and there should be no distinction.

-Michelle Obama

To start off, here are some basics and concepts for you to understand before going any further. Understanding them will make things a lot simpler as you read ahead, so please don't skip this part unless you are absolutely confident in the knowledge you possess.

Cells

By age three, many children are able to tell you the various body parts like face, eyes, ears, nose etc., and if you did biology you will also know the human body is made up of cells.

Cells are the smallest structural and functional unit of an organism and can be visualised only with a microscope. It is estimated the human body is made up of about 30 trillion cells. Think of cells like individual bricks that make up a house, the human body.

Even though cells are tiny and can be visualised only with a microscope, they contain structures in them called organelles, which perform specific organised functions. Among the numerous organelles are the mitochondria, for example, commonly known as the *power house* of the cell. When you eat a meal, chemical processes in the presence of oxygen occur in the mitochondria to produce a substance called adenosine triphosphate (ATP). These chemical processes are described by the Kreb's Cycle, named after Hans Kreb, a German biochemist and doctor. Cells use ATP as energy, hence its name as the energy currency of the body.

All cells contain a centre, also known as the nucleus. The nucleus contains the genetic blue print of the organism also known as deoxyribonucleic acid (DNA).

The total number of genes in humans (genome) is thought to be about 25000.

Surrounding the cell is the cell membrane, made mainly of cholesterol and protein. Some cells possess protein structures on their surface called receptors.

Receptors are extremely important and act as conduits through which information about the internal or external environment is relayed. While some drugs simply cross (diffuse) through the cell membrane, others act on specific receptors to have an effect.

Cells come in different shapes and sizes depending on what part of the body or organ they are found in. For example, red blood cells are cylindrical, fat cells are globular, and liver cells are polygonal or cubical in shape, to name a few.

Metabolism is the term used to describe chemical reactions that occur in cells via various pathways.

Cells grow at a set rate, a term called replication. During replication, one cell becomes two, two become four, and four become sixteen and so on.

Some cancers result when cells replicate faster than they should, thus forming abnormal structures. A primary cancer results from abnormal cells in an organ but sometimes it can spread (metastasize) to other organs. When this occurs, it is called a secondary cancer or spread. Different cancers have usual organs of spread. Prostate cancer, for example, spreads usually to the brain, liver and lungs.

Tissues

Tissues are groups of similar cells, present in different parts of the body, which collectively perform common functions. The body is made up of four different types of tissues, namely muscle tissue, epithelial tissue, connective tissue and nervous tissue.

Organs

An organ is a group of different tissues working together for a particular function. The liver, pancreas, appendix, heart, brain and so on are all organs.

Organ System

Groups of organs working together towards one function are called an organ system, for example the nervous system is made of the central nervous system (CNS) and the peripheral nervous system (PNS). The gastrointestinal system is made up of several organs for digestion, for example. Every organ has a blood supply that delivers oxygen and nutrients that keep it healthy.

Organism (Human Body)

The human body is formed from different organ systems. The human body or organism uses the concept of division of labour. Each part or organ system specialises in a particular task or function to promote efficiency. However, all the different organ systems work harmoniously within the body for a desired effect.

From Chapter 25, we will go into a bit more detail on the various organ systems.

However, before we do this, it is important to explore a few more concepts of how the human body works.

CHAPTER 18

HOW CELLS COMMUNICATE

Everyone has a plan 'till they get punched in the mouth.

-Mike Tyson

As a reminder, cells are the smallest structural and functional unit of an organism and can be visualised only with a microscope. It is estimated the human body is made up of about 30 trillion cells. Think of cells like individual bricks that make up a house, the human body.

Generally speaking, the different ways cells communicate with each other depend on how close the cells are to each other as well as the type of messages that need to be transmitted.

Cells stacked side by side sometimes communicate via tiny openings in the cell membrane called gap junctions. Gap junctions allow chemical messages to flow from one cell to another.

In cases where cells do not touch each other but are relatively close, chemical messages from one cell pass through the cell membrane of another cell, called a *target cell.*

The third way cells communicate is via the endocrine system. With this form of communication, a chemical message or hormone is formed by a cell or organ.

This hormone then travels in the blood giving its desired effect in different parts of the body farther away. There is more on the endocrine system in Chapter 28.

The fourth way cells communicate with each other is via the nervous system.

This occurs via nerves with the aid of chemicals called neurotransmitters. There is more on the nervous system in Chapter 25.

There are various neurotransmitters in the body that have different functions.

Examples of neurotransmitters include adrenaline, acetylcholine, dopamine, serotonin and more. These neurotransmitters activate special proteins on cells called receptors. Every cell in the body processes receptors, of which there are numerous types, each with a particular function. Once receptors are *activated*, chemical processes occur inside the cell. Common receptors in the human body include beta receptors in the heart (b1) and airways (b2), alpha receptors in the blood vessels and bladder, neck and so on.

Receptors are crucially important in the body, and appreciating their function is essential in understanding how the body works. Drugs generally work by either selectively activating or blocking receptor activity in different parts of the body.

Understanding basic receptors' types and function also helps understand or predict the side effects of drugs.

This explains why some eye drops might slow your heart down; some beta blockers might worsen your breathing by tightening the airways; some blood pressure tablets might increase bladder urine flow and so on.

As a learning exercise, the next time you are prescribed a drug or experience any symptoms you suspect might be drug-related you could start by *googling* receptors the said drug works on. Knowing the role of the receptor in the body or organ, you could then infer to a degree whether the symptoms are genuine side effects or not. Sure, not all side effects are receptor-related, but doing this will gradually increase your knowledge about how the body works.

CHAPTER 19

BLOOD AND ITS COMPOSITION

Yet who would have thought the old man to have so much blood in him?

-William Shakespeare

Blood is made up of cells, made largely in the bone marrow, and special liquid called plasma. Cells present in blood are the red blood cells, white blood cells and platelets, and all have different functions in the body. The blood plasma contains acids, basis and electrolytes, which maintain it at a particular pH (a measure of how acidic or basic a solution is).

Red Blood Cells (RBC)

Red blood cells carry oxygen round the body. When their numbers are low, you get less oxygen as a result. This condition is called anaemia, and, unsurprisingly, you will feel tired. You can tell someone is anaemic if they appear pale.

White Blood Cells

There are four types of white blood cells, namely neutrophils, lymphocytes, basophils and eosinophils. These cells all fight infections of different types.

The total amount of white cells increases with infection and other conditions, a little bit like an army needing to increase their troops during battle. Because we know the number of white cells that should be in the human body under normal circumstances, an increased amount found during a blood test tells us infection is present. It is that simple.

In addition, the number of white cells might increase in some cancers of the blood called leukaemia.

Platelets

Platelets help blood clotting via receptors, which they possess on their surface.

So what process is involved in the clotting process?

A tiny cut to the finger or graze to the knee stops bleeding due to the formation of a clot from platelets clumping together.

Platelets clumping together (coagulation) involve special proteins called clotting factors in a process called the coagulation cascade.

The coagulation cascade involves 13 proteins in total, mostly made in the liver and denoted by Roman numerals. Some of these clotting factors, namely factors II, VII, IX and X, require vitamin K to function effectively and are thus called vitamin K dependent clotting factors.

Some commonly known clotting factor deficiencies are haemophilia A and B.

Both are genetic diseases and can be passed on to offspring.

In 1952, haemophila B was first described in a patient by the name of Stephen Christmas, and this is why haemophila B is also called Christmas disease.

Another interesting fact is haemophilia B was common in Queen Victoria's family.

When a clot forms in a blood vessel, it is called a thrombus, e.g. deep venous thrombosis (DVT)—a clot in the deep veins of the legs. As a result, the organ or region involved dies due to lack of blood and oxygen, resulting in tissue death (Ischaemia). A heart attack or ischaemic heart disease, for example, results from a blood clot in one of the arteries that supply the heart. The result is death of that part of the heart muscle as it is robbed of oxygen and nutrients.

Some drugs like warfarin help thin the blood and prevent it from clotting fast.

It does so by inhibiting all the vitamin K coagulation factors (II, VII, IX, X) mentioned above. Warfarin is also prescribed for people who have had a blood clot in the lungs (pulmonary embolism) or the legs (deep vein thrombosis).

CHAPTER 20

BLOOD VESSELS AND THEIR FUNCTIONS

What's the fastest way to determine the sex of a chromosome? Pull down its genes.

-Biology Joke

Blood travels in blood vessels, which are made up of arteries, veins and capillaries.

Arteries

As a general rule, arteries carry oxygen-rich blood from the heart to various organs of the body, while veins carry oxygen-poor blood towards the heart.

The exceptions to the rule are the pulmonary artery, which carries oxygen-poor blood, and the pulmonary vein, which carries oxygen-rich blood.

Arteries have a thick muscular wall, which allows them to contract and relax, an important mechanism used to maintain blood pressure. Some blood pressure medications act via receptors on the artery wall to increase its diameter. This results in lower blood pressure.

Veins

As a general rule, veins carry oxygen-poor blood towards the heart. The exception to the rule is the pulmonary vein, which carries oxygen-rich blood from the lung.

Veins are thin-walled and have valves in them that allow a unidirectional flow of blood towards the heart. With walking or activity, the muscles in the lower limbs squash the blood in the veins. The valves in them ensure blood flows in one direction, from the legs towards the heart. Varicose veins, for example, result from poorly functioning venous valves, and blood then backtracks away from the heart.

On a hot day, or a long-haul flight, you might notice slight swelling of your ankles or lower legs. This happens because blood easily *pools* into the thin-walled veins with the effect of gravity in the lower extremities.

Capillaries

They are a link between the arteries and the veins. They distribute oxygen-rich blood to the tissues and take away oxygen-poor blood from the tissues towards the heart.

Oedema

Oedema is a collection of excess fluid in tissue spaces. This is generally due to increased pressure in the blood vessels. Common areas of oedema are in the legs and lungs.

Oedema of the legs is visible as ankle or leg swelling and can be demonstrated by watching the skin slowly rise after being pushed in with a finger. Some causes of leg or ankle oedema are *lifestyle related*, while others signify more serious pathology.

Lifestyle causes of leg or ankle oedema include being immobile for hours like on a long-haul flight, standing for long periods of time or excess heat.

The more serious causes of oedema include poorly functioning valves in the veins, blood clots in the leg, also known as deep venous thrombosis (DVT), kidney disease, liver disease and congestive heart failure.

Oedema in the lung cannot be seen but can present as a cough or breathlessness. Oedema in the lung is usually a result of lung infections or congestive heart failure. It can be heard with a stethoscope at the base of the lungs as *crackles*, a sound similar to Velcro being pulled apart. Oedema is generally treated with diuretics, commonly called *water tablets*, which help get rid of the excess fluid.

Oedema not improved by diuretics is sometimes due to blocked lymph vessels.

Lymph vessels are thin-walled blood vessels that carry a milky fluid called lymph.

All blood vessels are lined by a smooth lining called the endothelium, which allows for an undisturbed flow of blood. Factors like smoking, diabetes, and hypertension, to name a few, can cause damage to the endothelium, leading to pathologies like heart disease and more. This is one of the reasons why a good diet and exercise are beneficial.

CHAPTER 21

ENZYMES AND THEIR FUNCTION

Forgive your enemies but never forget their names.
-John F. Kennedy

You might be asking what enzymes are, what they do, and why you need them in the first place.

Enzymes are protein structures or molecules that help speed up different chemical reactions in the body. Without enzymes these reactions would otherwise be too slow to sustain life. A term used to describe an enzyme is a catalyst. A catalyst is any substance that speeds up a reaction without itself being changed. Enzymes are therefore biological catalysts as they work in the body.

Two important qualities of enzymes are their need for activation and their ability to remain unchanged in the reaction they catalyse. This is important as they are used over and over to catalyse similar reactions.

There are six classes of enzymes in total, and different examples are present in various organ systems.

Patients who suffer from excessive bloating or indigestion are sometimes prescribed digestive enzymes to help their food to be broken down properly before absorption.

Some lab tests measure enzyme activity in the blood and can be used to confirm or exclude pathology. When used in this way, they are called *markers of disease.*

A good example to illustrate this is the cardiac enzymes. The cardiac enzymes are normally present in the heart muscle cells but when damaged they seep into the blood. A blood test showing a high level of these enzymes might indicate heart damage or a heart attack. A frequent cardiac enzyme usually requested by doctors in the emergency department is called troponin, often shortened to *trop.*

CHAPTER 22

MICROBES (PATHOGENS)

If you don't like bacteria, you are on the wrong planet.
-Stewart Brand

The human body occasionally gets attacked by *invaders* called microbes, which include bacteria, viruses, fungi and protozoa.

Bacteria

Bacteria are tiny microorganisms that can only be visualised with a microscope.

They are simple organisms made up of a single cell, a single strand of deoxyribonucleic acid (DNA) and a cell wall. They do not contain any specialised structures (organelles) seen in human cells.

Bacteria are thought to be the oldest living organisms. They are classified according to shape, type of staining used to visualise them under the microscope, biochemical processes and so on.

Not all bacteria cause disease (pathogenic) and some live on the skin and digestive tract in harmony with other microorganisms. This community of *friendly bacteria* form part of what is termed the microbiome.

Disease-causing bacteria usually enter the human body from the air, water, food or any contaminated surfaces. With the help of tail-like projections (flagella), protective walls (capsids), production of toxins, and other mechanisms, the bacteria breach the body's immune system and start multiplying (replicating) at a fast rate.

Common pathogenic bacteria include Streptococcus, which causes a sore throat (strep throat), salmonella which causes food poisoning, staphylococcus, the flesh-eating bug and so on.

Antibiotics kill bacteria by either destroying the cell wall, structures called ribosomes, or blocking specific proteins in the bacterial cell.

Today, however, antibiotic overuse has led to resistant species of bacteria (superbugs) like Clostridium difficile (C diff) and Methicillin resistant Staphyloccal Aureus (MRSA).

In addition, antibiotic overuse also potentially kills off your gut *friendly bacteria*, leading to an imbalance in your gut's microbiome. This imbalance of gut microorganisms is termed dysbiosis. (See fungi section.)

Viruses

Viruses are tiny microscopic infectious agents. They are about 100 times smaller than bacteria on average. They contain a protein coat called a capsid, encircling their genetic material, made up of either deoxyribonucleic acid (DNA) or ribonucleic acid (RNA) Based on genetic material, there are thus two types: DNA viruses and RNA viruses.

Viruses can only replicate once inside an organism they infect, called a host.

Once in the host they multiply, causing the cell to die. Some viruses called retroviruses inject their genetic material into the host's cells and instruct it to make more copies of itself!

Viruses have many ways of evading the host's immune system. Examples include producing proteins that *disable* the host's immune system, competing with host receptors, or changing protein structures on its surface. In this way, viruses can stay dormant undisturbed for years.

Common examples of viruses include the influenza (flu) virus, chickenpox virus (varicella), measles, mumps, rubella, polio, hepatitis A, B, C, HIV and more.

While antibiotics are prescribed for bacterial infections, antivirals are prescribed for viral infections. This is why antibiotics do not work for the common cold or influenza.

Fungi

Fungi are a group of microorganisms that can be broadly divided into yeasts, moulds and mushrooms.

Yeasts made up of one cell are termed unicellular, while moulds made up of many cells are multicellular. Both yeasts and moulds can only be seen with a microscope.

Mushrooms are fleshy type of fungi that grow above the ground and are eaten as food.

Common examples of parasitic moulds include athlete's foot (tinea pedis), ringworm (tinea corporis), jock itch (tinea cruris) and fungal nail infections (tinea unguium).

Not all yeasts and fungi cause disease, and some live on the skin and gastrointestinal tract in harmony with other microorganisms. This community of *friendly yeasts* form part of the microbiome.

Saccharomyces Boulardii form part of the normal intestinal flora, as well as candida albicans. [1]

A poor diet, prolonged unnecessary antibiotics, pesticides and other toxins and more sometimes kill off the body's *friendly bacteria*. Candida Albicans can then proliferate once the balance of the microbiome is altered. This imbalance of gut microorganisms is termed dysbiosis [2] and can lead to gut inflammation [3].

Symptoms of the above potentially include less severe issues like food cravings [4] and obesity and chronic diseases like inflammatory bowel diseases, autoimmune disorders, diabetes [5] and even mood changes. [6]

Another common example of a yeast is Saccharomyces cerevisiae, also known as brewer's or baker's yeasts.

A common example of a mould is penicillium, famously used to produce the first ever antibiotic, penicillin G, by Sir Alexander Fleming in 1928.

Protozoa

Protozoa are organisms made of a single cell that contain specialised structures called organelles.

Protozoa can infect the human body via the gastrointestinal, respiratory or genitourinary tract.

Plasmodium is a common parasitic protozoan that causes malaria.

Some protozoal infections thrive in immunocompromised individuals with a low immunity (Immunocompromised) and are a sign to investigate further. Pneumocystis carinii, for example, commonly causes pneumonia in people with Acquired Immune Deficiency Syndrome (AIDS).

Pregnant women are screened for toxoplasma gondi, a protozoan that can potentially affect the foetus.

---

1) Scanlan PD, Marchesi JR. "Micro-eukaryotic Diversity of the Human Distal Gut Microbiota: Qualitative Assessment Using Culture-Dependent and Independent Analysis of faeces." *ISME* J. 2008; 2(12): 1183-93

2) Hawrelak JA, Myers SP. "The causes of intestinal dysbiosis: A review." *Alternative Medicine Review.* 2004 Jun;9 (2): 180-97

3) Li Q, Wang C et al, "Dysbiosis of Gut Fungal Microbiota is Associated with Mucosal Inflammation in Crohn's Disease." *J Clin gastroenterol.* 2004 Jul;46 (6): 513-23

4) Joe Alcock et al, "Is eating behaviour manipulated by the gastrointestinal microbiota? Evolutionary pressures and potential mechanisms." *Bioessays* 2014 Oct; 36(10): 940–949.

5) Carding S, Verbeke K, Vipond DT, et al. "Dysbiosis of the gut microbiota in disease." *Microb Ecol Health Dis.*2015;26(10):3402-3411.

6) Dinan TG, Cryan JF., "The Microbiome-Gut-Brain Axis in Health and Disease." *Gastroenterol Clin North Am.* 2017 Mar;46(1):77-89. doi: 10.1016/j.gtc.2016.09.007. Epub 2017 Jan 4.

CHAPTER 23

DISEASE PROCESSES

I don't mind that I am not necessarily a household name, because I think my characters have outshined me. That was by design. And I am not wanting for appreciation.

-Jeffrey Wright

Many diseases occur through a few common processes, which are:

Inflammation:

I am certain you have heard this word countless times, but what does inflammation really mean?

Inflammation is the body's response to local injury, be it from heat, stings, bites, radiation, infection or other modalities. Inflammation is the oldest known phenomenon in medicine, documented as far back as 30–40AD by Cornelius Celsus, a Roman encyclopaedist. He described the four classical signs of inflammation, namely pain, heat, redness and swelling.

The inflammatory process activates a chain of events via the immune system, with the aim of containing any injury that may have occurred, producing chemicals called cytokines in the body. Inflammation is a two-edged sword as in trying to contain an injury its response can harm the body.

You will know inflammation is present if a word ends in **"itis,"** e.g. Appendic**itis** (inflammation of the appendix), bronch**itis** (inflammation of the bronchus), mening**itis** (inflammation of the meninges), arthr**itis** (inflammation of the joints) and so on. As a rule, acute inflammation is a defensive mechanism, while chronic inflammation causes havoc.

Non-steroidal anti-inflammatory drugs (NSAIDS) help stop inflammation in some parts of the body. Ibuprofen is an anti-inflammatory drug used for treatment of arthritis. (Arthros – joint in Greek.)

Infection:

Microbes cause infection and can be either viruses, bacteria, fungi or protozoa.

Infections can cause inflammation, although this is not necessarily always the case.

Thrombosis

Thrombosis is a word that describes the formation of a blood clot. Blood cells called platelets clump together in the presence of tissue damage to prevent further bleeding. The whole process requires 13 proteins, called clotting factors, which are activated in a step-by-step fashion, hence the name clotting cascade.

A common pathology you may have heard of is deep vein thrombosis (DVT).

This is a blood clot or thrombus that forms in the deep veins of the body, most commonly the leg.

A DVT usually causes leg pain and swelling.

I have had a few consultations over the years from worried patients with varicose veins who thought they had a DVT.

Varicose veins are due to poorly functioning valves in the superficial veins of the limbs. A DVT, as the name implies, is a pathology that affects the deep veins.

Another related condition is pulmonary embolus (PE). This is also a blood clot or thrombus—in the pulmonary artery, mind you, not vein.

A PE is mostly formed from a dislodged clot, usually from the leg, which might have been painful. This is why if you present to your doctor with sudden breathlessness, they may enquire about leg pain.

I once saw a claimed ex-drug user who presented with breathlessness, a classic symptom of pulmonary embolism. He became irate when I asked if he had noticed any leg pain. (Many drug users inject into their leg after tiring out their arm veins.)

"I know I am still dabbling, doc, to be fair," he retorted, thinking I was prying into his drug habit.

I found it amusing as I had thought it was obvious and didn't need any covert questioning.

Autoimmunity

Autoimmunity occurs when the body's defence mechanism, called the immune system, starts to destroy its own healthy cells.

When the body is under attack from microbes (bacteria, viruses, parasites and toxins), the immune system recognises them through structures they possess on their surface called antigens. Under normal circumstances these microbes are selected and destroyed by the white blood cells. They do this in two ways, firstly by producing protein structures called antibodies, which attach to the antigens, or by directly wrapping around them like a blanket.

It is thought that in genetic predisposed people, some agents like viruses or bacteria cause this *recognition system* to fail.

This results in the immune system attacking and destroying normal cells instead of the unwanted cells. It is analogous to a police patrol shooting indiscriminately into a crowd instead of targeting the baddies.

Some common autoimmune disorders include type I diabetes, multiple sclerosis, coeliac disease and rheumatoid arthritis.

Mutation

A mutation is any alteration that occurs in the cell DNA.As a result, abnormal proteins are coded, potentially leading to pathology. Note I used the word *potentially* as the environment has a huge part to play in the development of disease. This area is a growing field and is called epigenetics.

Factors that can cause mutations include environmental agents like radioactivity, smoking and X-rays to name a few. Some viruses referred to as oncogenic viruses can potentially cause cancer. Common examples include the human papilloma virus (HPV) that causes cervical cancer and hepatitis B causing liver cancer.

CHAPTER 24

UNDERSTANDING THE BODY SYSTEMS AND HOW TO SUPPORT THEM

Every day my Daddy told me the same thing. "Once a task is begun, never leave it till it is done. Be the labour great or small, do it well or not at all."

-Quincy Jones

The human body is formed from different organ or body systems. As we have previously mentioned, the human body or organism uses the concept of division of labour. Each part or organ system specializes in a particular task or function to promote efficiency. However, these organ systems work harmoniously within the body for a desired effect.

As a quick recap, the different body systems include: The nervous system, the respiratory system, the circulatory system, the endocrine system, the digestive system, the reproductive system, the urinary system, the immune and lymphatic system and the musculoskeletal system.

Knowing and understanding the various body systems is important for a few reasons. Firstly, you will acquire knowledge on how your body really works, leading to a sense of self-confidence. In addition, your *Google searches* will be more focused and less likely to cause alarm from the knowledge you possess.

Although it might not be initially obvious, your newly acquired knowledge will provide a guiding framework for a symptom you might develop without you even realising it.

While it is important to know how the body systems work, it is also important to know how to *support* them.

As a rule, the most important thing you can do to support your body systems is to eat a healthy diet, exercise and rest adequately. In one sentence, a healthy diet is one relatively low in calories and high in nutrients, complete with minerals, vitamins, beneficial plant substances called phytonutrients and antioxidants.

Most importantly, increase your daily intake of green leafy vegetables, which are full of nutrients.

In all cases, avoid processed foods, which are essentially *empty calories*—in other words devoid of nutrients. Processed flour in cakes and biscuits is devoid of nutrients, which are stripped away when wheat is bleached. To make matters worse, when you consume them, your body uses its own body stores of trace minerals and nutrients in order to digest these processed foods (*empty calories).* In the process, your body is robbed even more of its own nutrient stores.

At the end of each body system I will provide some helpful basic health tips to help support the system in question. These tips will hopefully make you see the relationship between healthy habits and proper function of the human body.

For a more comprehensive look at diet and nutrition, have a read of Part 4 of this book.

As you read the various body systems, don't be put off by some of the terms, which might sound difficult. Once you understand the concept, you will find it really isn't that difficult at all.

With that said, let's delve into the various body systems.

CHAPTER 25

MASTERING THE NERVOUS SYSTEM

I get nervous when I don't get nervous. If I am nervous, I know I'm going to have a good show.

-Beyonce

The nervous system collects, processes and acts on information about the inside and outside of the body. It does so via special organs called sensory organs. Examples of sensory organs include the skin, eyes, ears and joints.

One can get a little lost in the different divisions and subdivisions of the nervous system. However, keeping it simple, the nervous system is mainly divided into two parts: The central nervous system (CNS), made up of the brain and spinal cord, and peripheral nervous system (PNS).

Both the brain and spinal cord are lined by three protective tissue layers called meninges, which are in turn cushioned by a clear fluid called cerebrospinal fluid (CSF). You must have heard of the disease meningitis, which is inflammation of the meninges in the brain or spinal cord.

Let's get into bit more detail with the brain.

The human brain weighs about 1.2–1.3 kg (three pounds) and is housed in the skull or cranium. The brain is divided into two parts or hemispheres and made up of brain cells, also called neurones, which join each other at particular points called synapses. Chemicals called neurotransmitters are present at these junctions or synapses. Examples are dopamine and serotonin.

All brain cells are covered in a material called myelin and form the myelin sheath. Some diseases, like multiple sclerosis (MS), result from loss of this myelin sheath at certain areas of the nerve cell.

The brain is in turn subdivided into different sections or *areas* called Brodmann's areas, named after German anatomist Korbinian Brodmann.

Each *area* contains particular groups of nerve cells or neurons, which control different functions of the body. An example is the language-processing area also known as Brodmann area 22 or Wernicke's area.

The brain has a complex network of blood vessels that supply specific territories.

A blood clot or bleed in a particular artery of the brain is called a stroke, and one can thus deduce to a degree where the problem is, based on the distribution of the artery.

It is worth mentioning at this point that nerve pathways from the left side of the body cross over in the brain to the right side, while pathways from the right side of the body cross over to the left side of the brain. This crossing over or decussation is of vital clinical significance. This means a patient who presents with sudden left arm weakness has had a stroke in the right side of the brain.

Conversely, a person who presents with right arm weakness has had a stroke in the left side of the brain.

Just behind the brain and continuous with the spinal cord is the brainstem.

The brainstem acts like a relay centre of information between the brain and spinal cord. It controls basic body functions like breathing, heart rate, swallowing, movement, and consciousness.

Now let's have a look at the spinal cord. The spinal cord is a long, slender group of nervous tissue that extends from the brain stem through the bony vertebral column.

Nerves arising from the spine are called spinal nerves and supply your arms, trunk (chest) and lower legs. They are named according to what level they exit the spinal cord, with a letter and number. These are C for cervical, T for thoracic, L for lumbar and S for sacral. L4 and L5 are thus the 4th and 5th nerves exiting the lower back or lumbar region.

Irritation of the nerve roots in the lower lumbar area can lead to pain in the back radiating down the leg. This is commonly referred to as sciatica, a term I am sure you have heard before.

So, let's use a quick example to demonstrate how all this works.

Imagine you are sitting in one position for hours on a long-haul flight. After the fifth hour, you might notice your arms and legs aching. Information relaying pain from your arms and legs is picked up and relayed to the spinal cord. From the spinal cord, the information is relayed to the brain via special pathways that cross over in the brain as previously mentioned. The brain then processes the information and instructs you to adjust your position or stretch your body.

A goalkeeper who sees a penalty shot towards the left side of the goalpost dives in that direction to save it. If the sun is too warm in one part of your garden, you simply move into the shade. As you can see, all three examples demonstrate voluntary control—something happens and you take action.

There is another part of the nervous system, part of the peripheral nervous system, which controls involuntary actions—in other words not under our control. This part of the nervous system is called the autonomic nervous system (ANS), and you will see a lot of it in different parts of this book. The autonomic nervous system controls all the body functions that you are not consciously aware of but that are vital for life. These include control of respiration, heart rate, blood pressure, digestion, urination and more.

The autonomic nervous system is divided into the sympathetic and parasympathetic branches.

Both the sympathetic nervous system and the parasympathetic branches supply the same organs but with opposite effects.

Here are a few examples to help you get the idea:

The sympathetic nervous system increases pupil and airway size as well as heart rate and force of contraction. The parasympathetic nervous system reduces pupil and airway size as well as heart rate.

Generally speaking, the sympathetic nervous helps the body use up energy, while the parasympathetic nervous systems helps conserve it. This is clearly seen with the digestive system during highly stressful periods, where the sympathetic nervous system causes the vessels supplying the gut to constrict. Consequently, blood flow to the digestive organs is reduced, leading to reduced secretions and its general movement or motility. This is an adaptive mechanism used by the body to favour blood and energy supply to the organs immediately needed for survival like the muscles, brain and heart.

Conversely, the parasympathetic nervous system is more *calming* on the gut, increasing secretions and general motility. This is one of the reasons why relaxation techniques generally help some gut disorders.

Healthy Tips to Help Support Your Neurological System:

Increase your daily intake of green leafy vegetables, which are full of minerals like potassium and magnesium. Both minerals are essential for maintaining the electrical charge and thus function of nerve cells. Magnesium is also known as the *calming mineral* and helps relax the body.

Proteins from animal sources, nuts, seeds and beans are essential for the manufacture of neurotransmitters in the brain and gut.

Brown rice and organ meats (liver, kidney, tripe, heart etc.) are excellent sources of B vitamins, which are essential for energy production and proper nerve function.

Encourage consumption of healthy fats from nuts, seeds and avocadoes, which are essential for cell membranes and the lining of nerves.

Remember the brain is like a muscle, so remember to exercise it too! Mental exercises like Sudoku or puzzles are extremely important.

Aim to meditate when you can, as it can potentially reduce stress levels.

A good night's sleep is essential for cell repair.

CHAPTER 26

MASTERING THE RESPIRATORY SYSTEM

Forgive me for asking, doc, but are you married or are you happy?

-Patient

The respiratory system is made up of the upper airways, starting from the mouth and nose and continuing through to the lower airways, the lungs. The main function of the respiratory system is to provide the cells of your body with oxygen (O_2) while allowing carbon dioxide (CO_2) to be expelled.

The lungs themselves are a spongy organ, divided into lobes and lined by a sheet-like layer called the pleura. Inflammation of the pleura is termed pleurisy.

The lungs expand when you breathe in (inspiration) and relax when you breathe out (expiration). The airways are supplied by the sympathetic and parasympathetic nervous systems, which act on receptors on their walls.

Activation of the sympathetic nervous system increases the size of the airways, while activation of the parasympathetic nervous system reduces their size.

This is how salbutamol, *the blue inhaler,* opens up the airways, by activating the b2 receptors on the airway walls.

There is a close relationship between the respiratory and the circulatory systems, which partly explains the similar signs and symptoms of diseases they share. Blood from the body is pumped into the right side of the heart, from where it leaves via the pulmonary artery to the lungs where oxygen is added.

Blood then leaves the lungs via the pulmonary vein into the left side of the heart and then via the aorta back to the body again.

A blood clot in the pulmonary artery, called a pulmonary embolism (PE), not only causes breathlessness and sometimes pain but also has repercussions on the heart.

Healthy Tips to Help Support Your Respiratory System

Eating a healthy diet results in weight loss, which reduces strain on your lungs.

Meditation helps reduce stress levels, potentially opening up the airways.

Breathing exercises are a great way to increase your *lung capacity.*

CHAPTER 27

MASTERING THE CIRCULATORY SYSTEM

I am not a robot. I have a heart and I bleed.

-Serena Williams

The circulatory system is also known as the cardiovascular system. It comprises a four-chambered heart complete with a system of valves and blood vessels, made up of arteries, veins and capillaries. The function of the cardiovascular system is to pump and distribute nutrients, gases and hormones via the blood to various parts of the body.

Blood entering the right side of the heart gets pumped into the lungs where oxygen is added (oxygenation). From the lungs, the blood enters the left side of the heart, which pumps blood to the rest the body. The blood then returns to the right side of the heart and cycle begins again.

This intimate relationship between the heart and lung explains why they share similar symptoms like breathlessness or chest pain.

The heart is composed of special cells called cardiac muscle cells or myocytes that possess receptors called beta receptors on its walls. The sympathetic nervous system acts on these b1 receptors on the heart to increase not only the heart rate but also the strength of contraction. This is the reason why beta blockers, a class of drug, are used for palpitations and tremor amongst other things.

In the right atrium of the heart are embedded a group of cells in its wall called the Sinoatrial (SA). The SA node sets the rate of the heart, and fires at a rate of about 60-100. The SA node is therefore considered the natural *pacemaker* of the heart and sets the rhythm, if you like, of the heart.

Any disturbance in this sequence leads to rhythm abnormalities like atrial fibrillation (AF) or atrial flutter for example.

The SA node is also under the influence of the autonomic nervous system. The heart rate is slowed down by the parasympathetic nervous system's action on the SA node's b1 receptors and sped up by the sympathetic nervous system's action on it. This is another reason why beta blockers, a class of drug, are used for palpitations and tremor amongst other things.

The heart, like any other organ, also needs its own blood supply, and this is provided by the coronary arteries, of which there are three in total. A triple bypass is a procedure done by cardiac surgeons when all three of the coronary arteries are blocked.

You can take your own pulse directly on the heart using a stethoscope (centrally) or more commonly using a pulse called the radial pulse (peripherally) just a few cm from the base of the thumb. There are seven pulses in total, but the most used is the radial pulse.

With the above background information, a heart problem could result from its structure (heart muscle, valves), its nerve supply or blood supply.

Healthy Tips to Help Support Your Circulatory System

Increase your daily intake of green leafy vegetables, which are also full of minerals like potassium and magnesium, which are essential for maintaining the electrical charge and consequently function of cells. Magnesium is also known as the *calming mineral* and is important for heart function.

Encourage consumption of healthy fats from nuts, seeds and avocadoes, which are essential for cell membranes and the lining of nerves.

Eating a healthy diet results in weight loss, which reduces strain on your heart.

Strive to exercise at least three times per week as it improves circulation.

Avoid smoking and excess alcohol.

CHAPTER 28

MASTERING THE ENDOCRINE SYSTEM

Medicine is a science of uncertainty and an art of probability.
-William Osler MD

The endocrine system comprises a variety of glands that secrete chemicals into the blood called hormones. Hormones travel from these glands, via the blood, to affect their *target organs* by binding to receptors on cell membranes resulting in varied effects on the organs and hence the body.

As a general rule, the actions mediated by hormones are comparatively slower to the actions medicated by nerves. The reason is because hormones travel in the blood to the desired target organ, while nerve impulses, which are electric in nature, travel at faster speeds.

The endocrine system is controlled by an organ in the brain called the pituitary, also known as the *master gland.* It is so named because its hormones control the function of other endocrine glands via another gland in the brain called the hypothalamus. These other glands are namely the adrenal, thyroid, testes and ovary, and they in turn secrete their own hormones that affect different functions of the body.

The thyroid gland is a butterfly-shaped endocrine organ located below your Adam's apple in the neck. It secretes the thyroid hormones in conjunction with the pituitary and controls the rate of all chemical processes in the body, termed metabolism. An underactive thyroid generally results in tiredness, weight gain and other symptoms associated with *deficiency*. An overactive thyroid results in weight loss, rapid heart rate, sweating and many other symptoms related to *excess*. There is more on the thyroid and testing in Chapter 40.

The adrenal glands are two small organs located above the kidneys. They are divided into two parts, an inner *medulla* and an outer *cortex*, all of which secrete hormones.

The adrenal medulla secretes adrenaline (epinephrine), norepinephrine and dopamine. These hormones, in conjunction with the sympathetic and parasympathetic nervous systems (autonomic nervous system), are involved in the *fight*, *fright* or *flight* response.

The adrenal cortex produces four main hormones, namely cortisol, aldosterone, testosterone and dehydroepiandrosterone (DHEA), all of which have varied functions in the body.

Cortisol is a steroid hormone whose main function is to combat stress of all forms including emotional, physical, chemical and much more.

Excess cortisol production from constant (chronic) stress can potentially lead to your adrenals being overworked and in some people can lead to accumulation of fat in the middle section of the body. This explains why taking high doses of steroids like Prednisolone for long periods of times can lead to belly fat. Through other mechanisms, you might then end up with high levels of insulin, diabetes, high blood pressure and other symptoms. This is why adopting good stress-coping techniques, especially in the busy world we all live in, is vitally important. There is more on this in Part 4 of this book.

The hormone aldosterone mainly controls the blood pressure through regulating the body's sodium/salt level with the aid of the kidneys.

Testosterone and DHEA are involved in sexual development in men and women.

The testes, which also form part of the male reproductive system, are two oval-shaped glands located in the scrotum. They are also an endocrine gland and produce the sex hormone testosterone, mainly involved in development of secondary sexual male characteristics like development of the male sexual organs, body hair, deep voice, erections and much more.

The ovaries, part of the female reproductive system, are two glands located on either side of the uterus in the female pelvis. They are also an endocrine gland and produce the sex hormones progesterone and oestrogen. The ovaries also produce the egg or ovum needed for reproduction.

Healthy Tips to Help Support Your Endocrine System

Increase your daily intake of green leafy vegetables, which are full of minerals like potassium and magnesium, essential for maintaining the electrical charge and thus function of cells.

Proteins from animal sources, nuts, seeds and beans are essential for the manufacture of neurotransmitters in the brain and gut.

Encourage consumption of healthy fats from nuts, seeds and avocadoes, which are essential for cell membranes and the lining of nerves.

Seaweed and shellfish are an optimal source of iodine, necessary for the production of thyroid hormones.

Organ meats (liver, kidney, tripe, heart etc.) contain chromium, an essential mineral for insulin production.

An important and relatively unknown tip is avoiding chemicals called endocrine disruptors. There are various types of endocrine disruptors, with the xeno-oestrogens being one of them. Xeno-oestrogens are found in plastics, pesticides, perfumes, makeup, lipsticks and other hidden sources. They can mimic the body's natural oestrogen production, leading to a situation called oestrogen dominance.

Bisphenol A (BPA) is a relatively known xeno-oestrogen found in plastics, and you might have seen the phrase *BPA-Free* on a kitchen item.

Strive to exercise at least three times per week. Exercise encourages circulation and stabilises blood sugars.

Aim to meditate when you can as this can potentially reduce stress levels.

A good night's sleep is essential for the cells to repair.

CHAPTER 29

MASTERING THE DIGESTIVE SYSTEM

The most intimate relationship you would have in your life is the food you put in your mouth.

-Michael Ash

If there is one thing you could do to take care of your health and prevent disease, I would suggest you take care of your digestive system. But you don't have to take my word for it. Hippocrates said it himself: "All disease begins in the gut."

This is not to ignore the other body systems, which are also vital; however, extensive discussion of each system is beyond the scope of this book. Here is a general overview of the digestive system, which I hope will make sense after having learnt some of the basics of how the body works. There is also more on the gut in Part 4 of this book.

The digestive system comprises a group of hollow and solid organs whose principle function is breaking down the food we eat to produce energy.

Organs that make up the digestive system include: the mouth, oesophagus (gullet), stomach, first, second and third parts of the small intestine (duodenum, jejunum and ileum), gallbladder, pancreas, large intestine (colon) and anus (rectum).

The food we eat is broken down by various enzymes present in different organs of the digestive system that break down food into an absorbable form.

There is also a vast community of bacteria, fungi and protozoa present in the gastrointestinal tract, which plays a vital role in digestion among other things.

This community of microbes is known as the microbiome, it's estimated to be about 100 trillion, and, due to its importance, I have dedicated a whole section to it in Part 4.

The hollow organs of the digestive system are lined by a single row of cells that act as a barrier. The spaces between each of these cells are known as tight junctions.

Some toxins can cause the space between tight junctions to increase, leading to increased gut permeability, commonly known as leaky gut, allowing pathogens, toxins and incompletely digested food material to pass directly from the gut into the blood. This can potentially lead to a myriad of symptoms from digestive disorders to brain fog and fatigue. [(1)] There is more on this in Part 4 as well.

The hollow gut organs are also lined by smooth muscle, which helps to propel food along in a process called peristalsis.

Last but not least, the gut is supplied by a network of nerves that form the enteric nervous system as well as the tenth cranial nerve called the vagus.

To get a better idea of the digestive process, it is important to get into a bit more detail.

Digestion starts with the thought and smell of food, even before it touches your mouth, with the release of an enzyme called amylase in the saliva. Amylase mainly breaks down carbohydrates into *simple sugars*. The food then travels down the oesophagus and is propelled down aided by its muscular walls into the stomach.

Once in the stomach, *gastric juices* are secreted, containing hydrochloric acid (HCL) and the enzyme pepsin among others. HCL makes the stomach environment acidic, while the enzyme pepsin mainly breaks down proteins into smaller units called amino acids. (The term pH is usually used to denote the degree of acidity, with a low pH meaning more acidic and high pH meaning less acidic.)

Once the acidity in the stomach is high enough, two things happen: A tightening at the junction of the stomach and the oesophagus called the oesophageal sphincter closes, while another tightening at the junction of the stomach and first part of the small intestine or ileum called the pyloric sphincter opens.

This systematic opening and closing of these sphincters, dependent on the degree of acidity, prevents stomach acid and food from going in the wrong direction and irritating the oesophagus and beyond.

Once in the duodenum, the acidic contents from the stomach trigger the gall bladder to contract, releasing its stored contents called bile salts, made by the liver. The gallbladder not only stores the bile, but also concentrates it.

Concentrated bile is an efficient way for the body to use small amounts to help aid the breakdown of fats in a process called emulsification. Bile acts like a detergent, helping to make fats and water-based fluids mix and dissolve easily. This is exactly the same thing that happens when you use washing up liquid to wash a greasy plate.

It is worth noting that bile also acts like a disinfectant, which helps kill off unwanted microbes in the small intestine. A deficiency of bile can lead to bacteria not normally present in high amounts in the small intestine to overgrow. This condition is known as small intestinal bacterial overgrowth (SIBO) and is one of the reasons why people whose gallbladders have been removed sometimes suffer from this. [(2)]

As bile is released by the gallbladder, the pancreas is also triggered to secrete the enzyme lipase, among other enzymes, to help fat and protein digestion.

The digested food then progresses from the duodenum into the jejunum and ileum where important nutrients are reabsorbed back into the blood.

Finally, the digested food enters the large intestine or colon where water and other important minerals and electrolytes are reabsorbed back into the blood.

The remaining contents in the colon are eliminated as faeces.

Apart from production of bile, the liver also has numerous functions, which include metabolism of proteins, fats, carbohydrates and vitamins.

The liver is also a major detoxification organ. In other words, it converts harmful poisons, substances, drugs or chemicals into harmless ones for excretion.

In this regard, the liver can be viewed as a filter.

There are three phases to the detoxification process, denoted as phase I, phase II and phase III.

The liver enzyme cytochrome P450 (CYP 450) is largely responsible for phase I of the detoxification process.

The liver contains many enzymes that are important, namely AST, ALT and ALP, which are discussed in more detail in Chapter 40.

In addition to production of digestive enzymes, the pancreas also secretes insulin from its beta cells.

Digestive ailments are extremely common in the population and make up more than 10% of GP consultations. (3) Unfortunately, the conventional approach to treating some gastrointestinal disorders produces moderate results in a cohort of patients.

Please see Part 4 where I give you a basic framework on how to heal your gut.

If you have any questions, please contact me at www.guthealthmedic.co.uk

Healthy Tips to Help Support Your Digestive System

Part 4 of this book is dedicated to what to eat, how to eat and more. However, I would like to share one healthy tip in this section, which is eating cruciferous vegetables.

Cruciferous vegetables are a varied group of vegetables that include cabbages, broccoli, Brussels sprouts, cauliflower, kale and more. They are packed with phytonutrients called glucosinolates, which break down to form products that increase activity of liver detoxification enzymes. [4]

Last but not least, avoid smoking and excess alcohol.

---

1) Shen L, Turner JR. "Role of epithelial cells in initiation and propagation of intestinal inflammation. Eliminating the static: tight junction dynamics exposed." Am J Physiol Gastrointest Liver Physiol. 2006 Apr;290(4):G577-82.

2) Hea Jung Sung et al., "Small Intestinal Bacterial Overgrowth Diagnosed by Glucose Hydrogen Breath Test in Post-cholecystectomy Patients." *J Neurogastroenterol Motil.* 2015 Oct; 21(4): 545–551. doi: 10.5056/jnm15020

3) Jones R, et al. "Management of common gastrointestinal disorders: Quality criteria based on patients' views and practice guidelines." *Br J Gen Pract.* 2009;59(563):e199-208.

4) Nho CW, Jeffery E; "The synergistic upregulation of phase II detoxification enzymes by glucosinolate breakdown products in cruciferous vegetables." *Toxicol Appl Pharmacol.* 2001 Jul 15;174(2):146-52.

CHAPTER 30

MASTERING THE REPRODUCTIVE SYSTEM

If men went through menopause, we'd know everything about it, but we still don't even know if we should be taking hormones.
-Joycelyn Elders

The reproductive system is made up of a group of sex organs and glands whose role is sexual reproduction.

In the female, the main organs and glands are the ovaries, fallopian tubes, uterus, and vagina. In the male, the main organs and glands are the penis, testicles and prostate.

The female reproductive system is mainly made up of the uterus, cervix, vagina, ovaries and fallopian tubes. The uterus is also known as the womb and is the largest of the female reproductive organs. It is a pear-shaped organ, in which the embryo develops, and is made of smooth muscle and lined by an outer layer of cells and glands called the endometrium. The characteristics of the endometrium change with the menstrual cycle, as well as during menopause.

The lower end of the uterus forms the cervix and opens up into the vagina.

Changes in the cells of the cervix can occur due to inflammation or even cancer, and can be detected by the PAP smear, usually done by the practice nurse.

On each side of the uterus are the ovaries, whitish oval shaped glands that vary in size depending on age. They contain a ball-like collection of cells called follicles, each surrounding an egg. Development of these follicles is under the influence of the hormone follicle stimulating hormone (FSH) from part of the brain, the anterior hypothalamus.

The term ovulation describes the release of the egg from the most mature follicle at about *Day 15* of the menstrual cycle.

The ovaries are also an endocrine gland and produce the sex hormones progesterone and oestrogen.

Finally, we have a pair of narrow tubes called the fallopian tubes, which serve as a conduit between the uterus and the ovaries. The released egg from the ovary travels down the fallopian tubes into the uterus where it is fertilised.

An embryo that develops in the fallopian tube instead of in the uterus is termed an ectopic pregnancy.

Some forms of contraception prevent release of the egg from the ovary.

I once overheard a few staff members talking about a furious lady who had stormed the reception area. She didn't find it funny that she kept getting pregnant despite the pill prescribed by her GP. The obvious question that came to mind was had she missed any pills? To everyone's amazement, she hadn't taken a single pill and had been giving the pill to her boyfriend instead! According to her logic, it was *he* who needed the pills, given it was *he* who could make her pregnant.

The testicles are oval-shaped glands, housed in the scrotum, and produce the sperm. A normal sperm count is over 15 million sperm per ml of semen.

During sexual intercourse, the sperm swims up the uterus and gets fertilised in the upper third of the uterus. Fertilisation outside this area is termed an ectopic pregnancy.

The testes also secrete the hormone testosterone, which has an effect on cell growth as well as altering male secondary sexual characteristics like deepening of the voice, pubic hair and more.

As mentioned previously, the main gland of the male reproductive system is the prostate, which hugs the bottom of the urethra below the bladder. It is a muscular gland that possesses receptors on its wall. The prostate produces part of the seminal fluid, which serves as a lubricant and a medium to aid the sperm swim.

Healthy Tips to Help Support Your Reproductive System

Optimise intake of vitamin C through green leafy vegetables and fruits.

Vitamin C is an antioxidant and is necessary for cell repair.

Nuts, seeds, seafood and organ meats are great sources of zinc, a mineral important for sperm development.

Encourage consumption of healthy fats from nuts, seeds and avocadoes, which are essential for cell membranes and the lining of nerves.

An important and relatively unknown tip is avoiding chemicals called endocrine disruptors. There are various types of endocrine disruptors, with the xeno-oestrogens being one of them. Xeno-oestrogens are found in plastics, pesticides, perfumes, makeup, lipsticks and other hidden sources. They can mimic the body's natural oestrogen production, leading to a situation called oestrogen dominance.

Bisphenol A (BPA) is a relatively known xeno-oestrogen found in plastics, and you might have seen the phrase *BPA-Free* on a kitchen item.

A good night's sleep is essential for cell repair.

CHAPTER 31

MASTERING THE URINARY SYSTEM

I don't need you to remind me of my age. I have a bladder to do that for me.

-Stephen Fry

The urinary system consists of the kidneys, ureters, bladder and urethra.

The kidneys are two bean-shaped organs located to the left and right of your lower back. (Loin) They are made up of tiny functional units called nephrons, which act as filters.

The kidneys also have an important role in regulating blood pressure. They do so via three hormones, namely renin, angiotensin and aldosterone, which form the renin angiotensin aldosterone system. Blood pressure drugs belonging to the class of angiotensin-converting enzymes (ACE inhibitors like Ramipril) work precisely on this system to reduce blood pressure. There is more on blood pressure control in Chapter 44.

The ureters are a pair of narrow tubes made of smooth muscle that connect the kidneys to the bladder. The bladder acts a reservoir for urine, and its muscle wall contains receptors that respond to stretching and send signals to the brain when full and ready to void.

Sometimes, the bladder wall might contract repetitively, despite containing little urine. This condition is called irritable bladder and sometimes misdiagnosed as a urine infection. This condition is easily treated using special drugs that act on the bladder wall receptors.

Filtered products from the kidneys enter both ureters, which eventually drain into the urinary bladder as urine, consisting of ammonia, creatinine, medications, and other metabolic by-products.

Urine from the bladder eventually drains into a thin urethra, which itself passes through a small organ in males located just beneath the bladder neck called the prostate. The prostate has receptors in its muscle wall, which, when activated, cause contraction around the urethra, thus preventing urine flow.

An easy way to understand the relationship between the bladder, urethra and prostate is to imagine a short straw inserted into a water-filled balloon. The balloon represents the bladder, the straw represents the urethra, and a clenched fist around the other end of the straw represents the prostate.

If you tighten your fist, the straw gets compressed, thus letting out little urine.

A common condition in elderly men called benign prostatic hyperplasia (BPH) results when the prostate gland is enlarged. Special drugs that act on receptors on the prostate and bladder neck reduce the pressure, thus easing the flow of urine.

Healthy Tips to Help Support Your Urinary System

Drink lots of water, which helps *flush* out your urinary system.

Avoid processed foods laced with high amounts of sugars. These sugars potentially cause bacterial and fungal overgrowth in the urinary tract, leading to infections.

CHAPTER 32

MASTERING THE IMMUNE AND LYMPHATIC SYSTEMS

Solutions come through evolution. They come through asking the right questions, because the answers pre-exist. It is the questions that we must define and discover. You don't invent the answer—you reveal the answer.

-Jonas Salk

The Immune System

The immune system is made up of a diverse collection of cells, tissues, organs and chemical messengers that work together to defend the body against anything it classes as foreign. These *foreign invaders* mainly include bacteria, fungi, viruses, and parasites, called pathogens. *Foreign invaders* also include dead and cancerous cells or any foreign bodies that make their way into the body like chemicals, coins etc.

In a normal state, the immune system is fine-tuned to recognise self from non-self. This means the immune system is able to recognise its own cells from foreign invaders like bacteria, viruses and other pathogens. Sometimes, however, the body might inadvertently destroy its own cells, erroneously thinking they are foreign—this is the basis of autoimmunity.

In autoimmune diseases, special proteins called autoantibodies are produced and attack the body's own cells. In rheumatoid arthritis, for example, an antibody called IgM attacks the body's cells. This IgM autoantibody is also called rheumatoid factor.

The Lymphatic System

The lymphatic system is made of a type of thin-walled blood vessels called the lymph vessels, together with a group of glands. Metabolism or chemical processes occur in all cells of the body on a daily basis, and it is the job of the lymphatic system to clear the body of the waste products and toxins formed.

The lymphatic system also helps to defend the body against infection.

Healthy Tips to Help Support Your Immune and Lymphatic Systems

Avoid processed foods laced with high amounts of sugars. Sugary foods reduce the function of the white blood cells responsible for fighting infections.

Increase your daily intake of green leafy vegetables and fruit, packed with vitamin C. Vitamin C is an antioxidant and helps to boost immunity.

Some nuts, seeds, seafood and beans contain the mineral selenium and zinc which helps boost the immune system.

Oily fish and egg yolks contain vitamins D and E, essential for an optimal immune system. Spending time in the sunlight is the best way to increase vitamin D production.

Aim to meditate when you can as this can potentially reduce stress levels.

Stress has been shown to reduce immunity.

A good night's sleep is essential for cell repair.

CHAPTER 33

MASTERING THE MUSCULOSKELETAL SYSTEM

Milk is for babies. When you grow up you have to drink beer.
-Arnold Schwarzenegger

The musculoskeletal system is made up of muscle, bone, tendons and ligaments, which help with structure and movement of the body. There are three basic types of muscle in the body, named according to structure and location.

Voluntary or skeletal muscle is found mainly around joints, involuntary or smooth muscle is found mainly around in the hollow internal organs of the body, and lastly there is cardiac muscle, found in the heart. Muscle cells contain receptors onto which nerves relay their signals, causing them to contract or relax.

Skeletal Muscle

When we think or talk about muscles, in most cases we are referring to skeletal muscle.

Skeletal muscle is mostly found around bones of the skeleton. Examples include biceps and triceps around the forearm, quadriceps around the thigh, and deltoids around the upper arm and shoulder among many.

Movement of skeletal muscle is under voluntary control, and their actions are mediated via receptors, which enable them to contract or relax.

Smooth Muscle

Smooth muscle is found mainly in the hollow internal organs of the body like the bladder wall, ureters, stomach, intestines and more. An important fact about smooth muscle is they are not under voluntary control. In other words, they contract and relax automatically.

Smooth muscle function is under control of the autonomic nervous system.

Remember the autonomic nervous system has two branches, namely the sympathetic and parasympathetic branch. Generally speaking, the sympathetic nervous system causes smooth muscle to relax, while the parasympathetic nervous system causes smooth muscle to contract.

Cardiac Muscle

Cardiac muscle is found in the heart walls. Like any muscle, cardiac muscle can be conditioned to perform better. This is one of the reasons why exercising is good for you. They are under involuntary control, and contain receptors on their surface. Activation of receptors on the heart wall via the sympathetic branch of the autonomic nervous system helps speed the heart or increase the force with which it contracts.

Musculoskeletal issues are extremely common in primary and secondary care.

Although they might seem complicated at first, in fact they are quite simple.

Skeletal muscle issues belong to one of the following categories: Bone fractures, joint arthritis, inflammation from sprained tendons, ligaments or structures lining the joints, called bursae, as well as problems with nerves supplying these very muscles.

In some cases, fractures are obvious, usually due to significant trauma, while in others further investigation, usually in the way of X-rays, is needed. In rare cases, an MRI is needed to show tiny fractures in small bones like in the foot for example.

Joint arthritis is extremely common, especially in the elderly. Always remember a diagnosis of arthritis is mostly made based on the patient's history and not X-ray results, which occasionally *come back normal.*

Sprained tendons and ligaments also generally occur following some form of injury, although they are not always obvious. Inflammation in the bursae is a commonly missed diagnosis, as joint bursae are often forgotten. Common areas of bursitis include the shoulders, elbows, knees and thighs. So your hip pain erroneously diagnosed as arthritis could in fact be trochanteric bursitis for example.

Pain in joints with a shooting type character is often nerve-related. In most cases, the pain originates somewhere usually above and radiates further down.

A common example is sciatica, pain in the lower leg originating in the back.

Another common example is shoulder and arm pain but originating further up from the neck.

Healthy Tips to Help Support Your Musculoskeletal System

Increase your daily intake of green leafy vegetables, which are packed with minerals like potassium and magnesium, essential for maintaining the electrical charge and thus function of cells. Magnesium, known as the *calming mineral*, is important for muscle function. Green leafy vegetables also contain vitamin C, an antioxidant necessary for cell repair and providing energy.

Encourage consumption of healthy fats from nuts, seeds and avocadoes, which are essential for cell membranes and the lining of nerves.

Organ meats (liver, kidney, tripe, heart etc.) are an excellent source of B vitamins, which are essential for energy production and proper musculoskeletal function.

Eating a healthy diet results in weight loss, which reduces strain on your joints.

Strive to exercise at least three times per week, but beware of impact on the joints.

Aim to meditate when you can. This reduces stress levels, which can potentially lead to relaxed muscles.

A good night's sleep is essential for cell repair.

PART 3

THE BASIC FUNDAMENTALS OF CLINICAL MEDICINE

CHAPTER 34

DISSECTING SIGNS AND SYMPTOMS OF DISEASE

Most illness is just stress from not living in harmony.
-Bruce H. Lipton

In a disease-free body, all cells, tissues, organs and organ systems work together in harmony. When things go wrong at the cellular level and beyond, there is disharmony. As mentioned before, all the research is pointing to inflammation in different parts of the body as the root cause of many diseases.

What a person complains of or feels when they have a disease is called a symptom. In other words, a symptom is a subjective in nature. Examples of symptoms are tiredness, nausea, vomit, pain and so on.

Sometimes, despite the presence of disease, the patient feels no different from their normal self. When this happens, they are called asymptomatic, meaning the absence of symptoms. Many patients with high blood pressure (hypertension) do not know it and are therefore asymptomatic. This is why it is important to have your blood pressure checked at least once a year.

What a person or doctor can see in a patient with a disease is called a sign. A sign is therefore an objective entity and therefore it can be seen or even measured. Examples of a signs are fatty deposits usually around the eyes (xanthelasma), which is sometimes related to high cholesterol levels. Other examples are swelling at the finger joints (Bouchard and Heberden nodes) due to arthritis.

The above definition of symptoms and signs is just one classification system, and it is important to note there can be some overlap.

A high temperature, among other examples, can potentially be classified as a symptom or a sign.

Symptoms have different characteristics and features depending on the pathology at hand. Sometimes a symptom might be preceded by another symptom or warning sign. An example of this is a migraine with some patients aware they get flashing lights or feel sick before the start of their headaches.

These warning signs are important in helping to distinguish between various types of headaches.

A warning sign is an extremely important factor in cases of faints or collapses, where there might be difficulty in distinguishing cardiac (heart) from neurological causes. As a general rule, collapses from neurological causes usually are preceded by warning signs. The patient might initially feel faint or even get bizarre symptoms like tingling in a limb or face before they collapse.

A collapse from a cardiac cause is usually sudden, with no warning signs as a general rule.

Another characteristic of a symptom are the circumstances that lead to it coming on, in other words *when*. A classic example is chest pain of heart (cardiac) origin. Pain at rest points to unstable angina while pain during activity points to stable angina.

Although they both relate to the heart, there are subtle important differences.

Unstable angina occurs when plaque, made up of cholesterol, calcium, clotted blood and other substances breaks off from the artery wall. This results in a sudden blockage of the artery that supplies the heart with oxygen and nutrients, thus causing pain. With stable angina, the plaque is fixed, but the supply of oxygen to the heart is insufficient during activity, due to the narrowing of the artery.

Next, we have an important characteristic of symptoms, which is the speed of onset. In other words, how fast or slow a particular symptom comes on.

The term acute is sometime used to describe a symptom that comes on very quickly while the term chronic is used to describe one that comes on slowly.

The terms acute and chronic could also be used to describe the length of time symptoms have been present.

Knowledge of symptom onset is an important characteristic that can serve as a guide. Take, for example, a rapid heart rate, also called palpitations, which could start suddenly, like a switch turned on, or start slowly and build up to a quicker pace. This single criterion, together with other parameters, can help narrow down different heart rhythms, thereby aiding diagnosis.

The character or nature of a symptom is also important as a distinguishing feature. Pain is a good example which illustrates this, with different adjectives used pointing to a probable potential cause. Nerve pain is generally described as "burning" or "like electric shocks" while pain from internal organs is described as "contractions" or "spasm".

Another characteristic that could be discussed under the character of a symptom is symmetry. Symmetry of symptoms simply means the same symptom is present equally both on the left and right side of the body. The pain and stiffness in rheumatoid arthritis is usually symmetrical, while the pain and stiffness from osteoarthritis is more likely one-sided.

This symmetrical feature, joints involved and age of the patient help distinguish rheumatoid arthritis, an autoimmune disorder, from osteoarthritis, generally from wear and tear.

Another character of symptoms is pattern onset. Symptoms from multiple sclerosis (MS) tend to appear, disappear and reappear many months or even years after, with the patient feeling well between *attacks.* The pattern is usually only evident many years after numerous consultations. The phase *relapsing and remitting* is usually used to describe this pattern of symptoms.

The timing of a type of migraine headache called a cluster headache is so regular it is almost diagnostic. Patients would say it comes on like an alarm clock.

A stuffy or runny nose with itchy eyes and sneezing that comes on every spring is more often than not allergic rhinitis (hay fever).

Another important characteristic of a symptom is duration, best described by the example below.

Many parents usually worry their children are asthmatic, due to breathlessness on exercise. Most of the time the reason is simply explained by inactivity; however, there is an important question that can help separate the asthmatic from the non-asthmatic. Breathlessness during any sport is to be expected at varying degrees, but breathlessness that continues for more than half an hour or so after exercise might be asthma. I usually ask, “So how long do you stay breathless for after exercise?”

With regards to signs in disease, let’s start with a common symptom, a sore throat. Many patients think if they see *white spots* this means it is bacterial in origin; however, this is not always the case.

As you can see, it’s all about piecing information together to make sense of a potential diagnosis. This is the sort of reasoning you should develop to a degree but comes with time and experience as well as knowing your own body.

CHAPTER 35

HOW DOCTORS DIAGNOSE AND TREAT DISEASE

Medicine is a science of uncertainty and an art of probability.
-William Osler MD

"I am just not feeling right," is a phrase you might have used to describe your symptoms, thinking a doctor would be able to get to the bottom of the problem. Sometimes, you might have thought all you needed was a blood test or some sort of *scan* to show what you thought was wrong. This is unfortunately not the case as doctors mainly rely on the story you provide to reach a diagnosis.

A doctor is a little like Sherlock Holmes, Columbo or your favourite TV detective.

They use a logical step-by-step approach to arrive at a diagnosis based on what you tell them. This step-by-step process is called the diagnostic process and starts with a summary of your symptoms or story, called the history, followed by the examination, investigation and finally treatment, in that order.

A description of your symptoms or the history is paramount and makes up about 85% of the diagnosis. The examination and investigation make up the leftover 15%. In practice, this means the better the history, the better the chance of making the correct diagnosis.

History

Once an accurate history is taken by your doctor, they will already have started to get an idea of the diagnosis. In some cases, this is straightforward, as the history is typical for a particular condition.

A 70-year-old man who complains of breathlessness, crushing chest pain with radiation to his left arm and jaw and vomiting when he walks, for example, is most likely experiencing a heart attack (myocardial infarction).

A 35-year-old charity worker who gets a high temperature, chills and muscle pain a few days after visiting sub-Saharan Africa is most likely suffering from malaria.

A 15-year-old obese boy's months of breathlessness and chest tightness when he walks up the stairs is most likely due to inactivity or asthma.

In all three examples above, the most probable diagnosis is made based on the history and age of the patient.

However, if you find out the boy's father and uncle in the second example were diagnosed with a hole in the heart at about the same age, then the reasoning changes altogether.

This is the thinking process your doctor would use on a daily basis to arrive at the correct diagnosis.

The history therefore generates a list of possibilities (differential diagnosis) based on knowledge of the signs and symptoms of disease, age, sex and past medical history, all combined.

Examination

The next step of the diagnostic process is the examination, which helps to refine or narrow down the list of possibilities, also called the differential diagnosis.

The examination is therefore a *focused examination*, looking for these signs of disease.

Examination generally comprises four steps. These include inspection, which simply means observation, palpation (feeling), percussion (striking with the examining hand) and auscultation (listening). We will talk a bit more about this in the *Understanding the Basic Clinical Examination section,* but here are a few examples.

Inspection can give vital information on almost every organ system. The hands are a common place doctors would start to inspect after forming a general impression. Many clues to disease can be found by just looking at the hands.

An interesting finding is clubbing (not the in the *night out* sense). This is a bulbous-like enlargement of the finger ends, which is present more commonly in some diseases of the lung or heart like COPD (emphysema) and heart failure amongst others.

A quick look at the face, the position or form of a rash, the shape of a spine (Hunchback of Notre Dame), neck goitre and so on are all important clues.

The characteristic gait in a Parkinson's patient can also be gleaned from observation only.

Sometimes the smell of chemicals called ketones described as pear drops can be detected from a diabetic's breath. A colleague once told me he diagnosed a woman with diabetes as soon as she walked in the room. He claims he could smell the sweet aroma of pear drops. I admit I have never been privileged to make a diagnosis of diabetes in this way.

A 55-year-old obese lady who complains of vague abdominal pain, worse after eating, could have gallstones or gastro oesophageal reflux disease. (GORD)

Pain on palpating the right upper abdomen (right upper quadrant) suggests the diagnosis is most likely gallstone disease.

The last part of the examination is auscultation. Auscultation is basically listening to sounds produced inside the body, with the aid of an instrument called a stethoscope. Before the invention of the stethoscope, doctors would place their ear directly to the area they wanted to listen to!

Common organs listened to include the lungs, heart and abdomen.

Investigation

After the history and examination, the diagnosis might still be elusive, and this is where the investigation stage comes in.

Investigations include blood tests, urine and stool samples, X-rays, ultrasound scans (USS), computer tomography (CT) scans and other special tests.

A doctor will generally order specific blood tests depending on what pathology they suspect and not a blanket batch, although this is sometimes done.

In simple, straightforward cases, a positive test confirms a diagnosis and a negative one excludes it. However, life is never that simple as not every test is 100% sensitive and 100% specific. In simple terms, this means your test could be negative despite having a particular disease. (Sensitivity) Equally, your test could be positive despite **not** having a particular disease. (Specificity) In scenarios like this, going back to revisit the history or doing further tests is usually the way forward.

Some investigations are better equipped at looking for particular diseases.

An MRI scan, for example, is the appropriate test for suspected knee ligament damage, in preference to a USS, which gives little information on the knee joint structures. (Except a Baker's cyst)

Another important point to note is that all scans are operator dependent, with some being more skilled than others. This means in rare cases something might simply be *missed.*

A missed diagnosis following a scan could also be due to circumstance. An X-ray of a swollen hand might not show a small fracture, while a repeat X-ray two weeks after the swelling subsides later reveals it. This is one of the reasons the why history is always crucial.

Management/Treatment

Once a diagnosis is made, the next logical step is *managing* the condition, a word usually used to describe treatment. Most areas have local guidelines for managing various conditions, in addition to national guidelines like the National Institute of Clinical Excellence (NICE) in England and Scottish Intercollegiate Guidelines Network (SIGN) guidelines in Scotland.

Although some GPs rush to prescribe a tablet, partly due to patient expectations of wanting a *quick fix* and time constraints, lifestyle modification/changes are always the first thing to consider where relevant.

Unfortunately, this is not an area in which much emphasis is placed in medical school, so even if you were to ask, your GP might struggle. This is one of the reasons why you should do as much research as you can about your health as there are many ways you can help yourself.

With regards to medication, it is good practice for your GP to discuss these options for you to make an informed choice. However, don't always expect this to happen as the decision might be too complicated for you to understand.

In some cases, a diagnosis is made by first treating to see what the outcome would be. This is called a test treatment and is a useful way to diagnose certain conditions. "Let's try this cream and see how it goes."

Occasionally, your doctor might need the help of a specialist in a given field.

This can simply be in the way of a phone call or email to ask for advice. More commonly, a referral letter with details of the case is written to the hospital consultant.

So, in summary, your GP listens to your symptoms, formulates a provisional diagnosis (what they think is wrong) orders some tests or investigations if appropriate, and treats accordingly.

Diagnosing disease in general practice can be a tricky business as GPs generally see disease in its early stages. In practice this means at the onset your signs and symptoms might be non-specific and vague, making them difficult to make sense of. A few months, days or even hours down the line and you may get a diagnosis made in the emergency department, but remember in most cases it is not sheer incompetence on your doctor's part but the natural history or course of disease.

Now, despite an exhaustive diagnostic process, your doctor might still not have a clue what your diagnosis is. It might be you just have a very rare pathology, or it might be your symptoms don't fit the standard/conventional medical model.

In cases like this, it might be worth approaching things from a different perspective altogether. There is more on this in *Why Your GP Might Not Have the Answer to Your Healthcare Issues* in Part 4.

CHAPTER 36

HOW TO GIVE A HISTORY IN FIVE MINUTES OR LESS

Take your time, but hurry up!

-Avery Sharpe

It would be an ideal situation if you could spend as much time as you wished with your GP, but, as you know, the reality is far from this.

Generally speaking, you have ten minutes with your GP from start to finish, so adopting a system to present your symptoms is mandatory.

The symptom(s) you list are called the *presenting complaint*, which might or might not be related, and a doctor will generally be able to tell after listening to all symptoms presented.

While doctors learn the art of taking a history from patients in medical school, you the patient don't learn how to give a history. Giving a history is essentially telling a story, a skill not possessed by everyone. Given your GP appointment is most likely ten minutes or less, you will need to develop a system to narrate your symptoms in an orderly fashion to help your GP make the correct diagnosis in a set time frame.

Using a well-organised system also sets a good first impression. It shows you are knowledgeable and reduces the chances of being fobbed off with phrases like, "It just happens," "It's just old age," my favourite, "If it doesn't get any better come back." (Despite having the problem for months or even years)

A good doctor will first of all let you describe your symptoms then start asking *open-ended questions* to get some more answers. To finalize they might then ask for focused or closed-ended questions to get answers to specific questions.

Listening to your account of the symptoms you may have is called *taking a history.*

Before we get into the system, I must mention two things: The first one is the concept of *the hidden agenda* and the second one is the power of your smartphone.

The *hidden agenda* is usually the true reason some patients present to their doctor. However, due to anxieties or apprehension, they typically start off the consultation with what I term a *filler*—something quite safe. For example, a 14-year-old boy might have found a lump on his testicle but mention a sore throat instead.

Throughout the consultation, they might drop verbal or non-verbal cues in the hope the doctor catches on and explores the real reason they have booked. In some cases, they might make a throwaway statement at the ninth minute.

"Could a virus that causes a sore throat also cause pain to my testes?"

Although GPs are taught consultation models and skills, picking up on the hidden agenda is not always straightforward. If you mention the true reason for your presentation at the ninth minute, you risk being told to rebook another appointment! To avoid this scenario, I recommend a direct approach as time is of the essence. In other words, depend on yourself and don't bank on a doctor picking up on your hidden agenda.

Now let's discuss the power of your smartphone. I see this countless times when a patient comes in with a rash which was present but now gone. They try to describe it, but the possibilities are endless. I always remind the younger patients that smartphones are not only for *selfies.* If you are a parent and your child makes any funny noises or acts strangely, if possible record them ready for the consultation.

With these two factors out of the way, let's delve into the system.

The best system I have found to give a history is SOCRATES, a mnemonic not formulated by me that has been used for years by medical students to take a history. Let's go through it briefly:

Site (S)
Where is the problem? Head? Leg? Nose? Etc.

Onset (O)
When did it start? Three months, two days, one week?

Being specific with times is paramount, for example using days, weeks or months to describe the length of time you have had a particular symptom, rather than phrases like *a bit*, *a while*, *quite some time* and so on.

Character (C)
This is a description of what the symptom is like.

Using pain as an example—is it sharp, dull, does it come in waves, is it griping in nature? It is worth mentioning the word sharp here relates to the character and not intensity. Let me explain: While your chest pain might be described as sharp (like a needle) some might use this word to describe its severity, a word that relates to how bad the pain is (See S below)

Radiation (R)
Mainly attributable to pain, which can stay in one area or project/radiate to other areas due to nerve distribution. Back pain sometimes goes (radiates) to the lower leg, commonly known as sciatica. Gallstone pain occasionally radiates to the shoulder or upper back, between the shoulder blades.

Associated symptoms (A)
This is a mention of other symptoms related with the main symptom if you like.

Is your vomiting accompanied by diarrhoea? Does the burning sensation in your legs appear only when you get a rash?

Timing (T)

When does it come on? Is it all the time or only when you run to the ice cream van to get some ice cream for the kids? Do your symptoms come on only in the spring?

Exacerbating features (E)

Here we describe factors that make your symptoms worse. We can also describe factors that make your symptoms better here too.

Does your breathing get worse when you lie flat? Does it get better when you sit up?

Is your stomach pain worse with food or does it get better?

Severity (S)

Heere we attempt to grade how bad a symptoms is.

You can use a scale of 1–10 to make things measurable and clearer if pain is the main symptom. For women, rating childbirth as a 10 gives some perspective to the scale.

As you can see, this mnemonic is a fantastic tool that attempts to cover all angles with the aim of delivering as much information as you can.

Once you have presented your symptoms nicely in this manner, all your GP has left to do is ask a few additional questions, which might help narrow down a diagnosis.

Given we live in the internet age, you will most likely have diagnosed yourself before your visit.

If you do come in armed with information from Google and think you already know your diagnosis, instead of mentioning it outright it is best to still start with your symptoms (history). You can then conclude by stating what you think the diagnosis is.

So, instead of, "Doctor, I have a urinary tract infection (UTI)," start with, "I have burning when I pass urine and think it is a UTI."

If you come in already stating your diagnosis, you risk two things: Firstly, some doctors might be put off and wonder why you bothered coming to see them in the first place. Secondly, by mentioning a diagnosis at the outset, the doctor's differential diagnosis might be clouded, and they may now focus on trying to refute your presumed diagnosis rather than focusing on trying to get one.

A&E doctors inadvertently fall into this trap with chest pain cases. Because they assume the patient must be worried about their heart, they focus on *ruling out* cardiac disease and in the process ignore all other potentially significant causes.

Another frequent mistake I see is when patients spend time explaining diagnoses made by clinicians they have previously seen instead of mentioning their symptoms.

Here is an example: "I have been coming here for months and each time I get told something else. I came three weeks ago to see the nurse and she thought I had a grumbling appendix. I then came to see the GP last week and he thought it was diverticulitis. The pain got worse and I went to the emergency department, and the doctor there told me it definitely wasn't appendicitis."

While the information above is relevant, it is important to first mention your symptoms to whoever you are seeing; this avoids using up valuable consultation time without providing information of diagnostic relevance—remember time is of the essence.

So, putting all the above together and more, here is how to sound like a pro:

Start with your past medical history, and medication list if short, before delving into your present symptoms.

Here is an example:

Dear Dr Hunt,

I have a history of heart problems, diabetes and rheumatoid arthritis. I take many tablets as you can see, including Azathioprine.

Over the last five days, I have had some pain in my tummy, which seemed to start in the centre. Two days later, the pain moved more to my right side.

I would liken the pain to a persistent ache, with a score of about six out of ten. I also feel a little sick, but I haven't vomited. The pain seems worse with brisk walking or jumping.

At this point, all your doctor has to do is ask a few more questions before making a diagnosis.

If English is your second language, try as much as possible to rehearse your symptoms using the right vocabulary. Failing this, some doctors might unfairly equate your poor grasp of the language with lack of knowledge. This can potentially influence the diagnosis made.

CHAPTER 37

SELF-DIAGNOSIS, TIPS AND PITFALLS

Yes We Can!

-Barack Obama

Let's face it; most people who come to see a doctor have already researched their condition to some degree on the internet. In my opinion, this is a step in the right direction if done appropriately.

Like everything in life, preparation is the key. It is good practice to have an idea of what is wrong with you but not necessarily a diagnosis.

To do this, you'll need some basic knowledge, and this is where this book comes into use. Ringing an advice line or booking an appointment to see a doctor as soon as you develop any symptoms without any thought is selling yourself short. This habit simply makes you entirely dependent on another person, which in my opinion is not a good idea.

A crucial step towards self-diagnosis is *listening to your body*, developing an attitude of curiosity and willingness to learn.

There are potential pitfalls involved with dwelling on the internet as you might have realised. More often than not everything you read sounds exactly like what you have. This is no coincidence as many pathologies share similar symptoms. Mastering the skill of how to research your symptoms is therefore extremely important to make sense of it all.

Looking up a symptom in isolation without any prior knowledge whatsoever in basic physiology is the root of most anxiety when you search blindly on the internet. A symptom only really makes sense when you have an idea of how everything fits or works together.

Google Your Symptoms

Googling your symptoms is probably the commonest approach. Essentially, you type your symptoms into the search bar and *Google* returns a list of possibilities.

Internet search engines like *Google* work by trolling the entire world wide web and pulling up relevant results based on information fed into it. (A symptom checker website does this for you already)

To get more refined results, it is therefore imperative you input all of your symptoms and not just a few of them. The more symptoms you add, the more accurate the result you get.

If you were to type *chest pain, chest pain and nausea, chest pain and left arm pain, chest pain and clammy,* you would get different pages each time.

Another technique is to use the word *common. Common causes of headache and visual loss, common causes of headache, rash and vomiting* and so on.

Once you get a list of possibilities, the next step is to read up on the common conditions that come up. There is a plethora of websites with endless amounts of information on any pathology you can think of. Each site has a different layout, tone, and style like a book with some more user friendly than others.

The secret here is to have two or three websites that suit you and keep things simple, rather than overwhelming you with detail.

Symptom Checker Websites

There are numerous fantastic symptom checker type websites you can visit, which would help you to reach a diagnosis in a few easy steps. Symptom checkers use a built-in medical algorithm to formulate a list of probable diagnoses based on the symptoms you feed into it. Medical algorithms do essentially what your doctor does on a daily basis, *qualifying* the symptoms you have and grouping them together to form a probable diagnosis based on your age, sex and underlying medical conditions. I recommend you use at least two or three sites and compare the list of the *common* conditions you find.

I once saw a lady over many weeks with a headache but was unable to make a diagnosis. She had seen three other doctors and had been diagnosed with sinusitis and cluster headache. Her daughter eventually used a symptom checker website, which diagnosed polymyalgia rheumatic (PMR)—the right diagnosis! In retrospect, the symptoms inputted into the website weren't exactly what she had said over the weeks she had been seen. This shows how important an accurate history is.

Once you get a differential diagnosis from a symptom checker website, the next thing to do is read up on the common conditions it brings up. You will quickly discount some of the diagnoses after a few minutes of reading.

Visit Forums

Forums are a fantastic place to visit as most people on there are highly knowledgeable and have actually experienced every bit of a pathology they write about. In a way, this is actually probably better than reading medical literature, but the difficulty lies in knowing who is credible. Personal stories always carry an emotional touch, something which can sway your judgement.

Again, this is the reason why it is best to go on forums with some prior knowledge and objectivity.

I do not recommend going onto forums without first getting an idea of what you have or you will be convinced by any story you read. You might hear things like it could still be chest pain without actually getting any pain; your tiredness might be lymphoma and so on. While all reasonable and possible, the forum in effect only widens your differential diagnosis and makes things even more complicated for you.

Visit YouTube

Similar to *Google*, *YouTube* has a search bar in which you can simply input your symptoms. Various combinations of symptoms also bring up videos that you can click on. I recommend short videos by posters with some medical background.

Once you spend some time on YouTube, you will soon familiarise yourself with your favourite posters. I recommend going a step further by creating an account and subscribing to your favourite doctor/clinician. To get updates whenever they download a new video, click on the *bell*. In a few months, I guarantee you could potentially become extremely knowledgeable in an area of health just by watching YouTube videos.

This method is best for those whose learning style is more visual, especially if there is additional use of sketches to help explain concepts.

Talking to Friends and Family

I remember seeing a man who had some pain in his thumb and wrist area.

After examination, I told him he had a type of tendonitis called De Quervain's. He looked a little surprised and relieved at the same time. "So, it is not carpal tunnel then?"

I replied that it wasn't and asked him why he thought so.

He then mentioned he was an ex-miner and knew many of his fellow miners who had been diagnosed with carpal tunnel syndrome. With this in mind, he had started off first by *googling* the diagnosis of carpal tunnel syndrome and then matching his symptoms. Some of the symptoms seemed similar to what he was experiencing, and his diagnosis was made.

Talking to family and friends is another approach worth considering. If any of your family and friends has a medical background, you are in luck.

The mind is a powerful tool, and it is human nature to form associations. In trying to help, people tend to relate something similar to what they hear. So you might tell them you have abdominal pain, and the first thing they would say is to make sure it is not X or Y as they or someone they know had it.

If you then get swayed by this, you risk being biased in your own analysis. You might then resort to using the internet to confirm your preconceived diagnosis, rather than trying to find one.

With all the information available to you these days, you shouldn't limit yourself to getting a diagnosis only. Browsing through the health section of popular magazines or watching medical dramas are fantastic ways of improving your knowledge.

I once saw a lady in her early twenties who had an incredible amount of knowledge on cardiac (heart) conditions including medication. I was mesmerised, and to my surprise she had gained all her knowledge from watching endless episodes of her favourite medical drama.

In your spare time, browse the internet to find out about common conditions you have heard about or seen. Again, I would advise you to have two or three favourite sites to go to that suit your needs.

With time and experience you will learn to read your body, diagnose common conditions with confidence, and self-medicate appropriately. However, if you are ever unsure, please seek further assistance or call 999 if you think your case is an emergency.

Notice that so far we have attempted to self-diagnose by the history only. Part of the diagnostic process is the *examination*, which helps refine your diagnosis.

We will take a brief look at the basic clinical examination in the next section, and the beauty of it is you can practise some of it yourself at home.

CHAPTER 38

UNDERSTANDING THE BASIC CLINICAL EXAMINATION

The greatest education in the world is watching the masters at work.

-Michael Jackson

Introduction

Have you ever wondered what your doctos is doing when they examine you?

It might seem complicated, but it really is quite easy using simple fundamental principles of physics.

There are four basic steps involved in examination of the human body, which include inspection, palpation, percussion and auscultation.

Inspection

Inspection simply means observation. The relevant part is observed for any changes to colour, scars, rashes, symmetry and so on.

We all inspect each other on a daily basis. If you have ever called the doctor out after seeing a relative or friend who has been *off colour*, you have practised inspection.

Palpation

Palpation means feeling. This is generally done with the flat of the hand while exploring the area of interest. Any lumps, bumps or general swelling are noted with prior knowledge of what constitutes *normal*. This is where a doctor has a distinct advantage over you as they have knowledge of the body's anatomy. A woman who feels a breast lump or a man who feels a lump in their scrotum has palpated the various organs respectively.

Percussion

Percussion means tapping. The middle finger of one hand taps sharply and firmly on the middle finger of the other hand, placed flat against the relevant part.

The principle underlying percussion is similar to one used in musical instruments; sound waves emitted from materials of different types and densities are varied. The sound emitted from tapping on a table is different to the sound emitted from tapping on a drum, based on their characteristics. As air and fluids have different densities, the sound emitted by tapping on any organ changes depending on what they contain.

Auscultation

Auscultation is simply listening and is done with the aid of a stethoscope. A stethoscope amplifies the sound from its diaphragm through to the earpiece.

The character of the sounds heard from various organs are used to deduce the underlying pathology.

A wheeze, for example, is a classic whistling-like sound heard in the lungs when the airways narrow in conditions like asthma or emphysema. Another sound heard in the lungs with the aid of a stethoscope is *crackles* or *crepitations.*

Crackles are thought to occur when the small airways narrowed by fluid suddenly open up or close, creating a non-musical sound. This sound is traditionally described as a *popping sound*, although a Velcro sound is more apt.

Common pathologies that produce crackles are pneumonia and pulmonary oedema. In both conditions, there is fluid build-up in the lungs. Pulmonary oedema is mostly caused by heart failure.

CHAPTER 39

UNDERSTANDING THE GASTROINTESTINAL EXAMINATION

How many weeks are you?
I am NOT pregnant!

-Consultation

Now that we have described the basis of the clinical examination, let's use the digestive system to explore these concepts a bit more.

To help understand the abdominal examination, think of the abdomen like a wine barrel.

Then imagine an imaginary line from top middle to bottom and from mid side to side. We now have four areas, also known as quadrants, namely right upper quadrant (RUQ), right lower quadrant (RLQ), left upper quadrant (LUQ) and finally the left lower quadrant (LLQ)

Prior knowledge of organs in each quadrant, as well as the structures and organs around them (*anatomical borders*), is vital to make sense of your examination. Once you know this then everything else falls into place easily.

Below are the main organs in each abdominal quadrant:

The right upper quadrant houses the liver and gallbladder while the right lower quadrant houses the appendix.

The left upper quadrant houses the spleen while the left lower quadrant houses the descending colon.

Another important area just below the breast bone is the epigastrium, where we can stick the stomach in, using the above division. The epigastrium is a frequent area of pain from indigestion or reflux disease.

Inspection

Inspection of the abdomen might reveal its general shape or reveal clues like previous scars from operations, characteristic rashes or lumps. A relatively common lump in the midline of the abdomen of newborns, pregnant women or obese men is called diastasis recti. In the case of a newborn, it is simply due to laxity of the abdominal muscles, which have not yet fully developed, while in pregnant women and the obese it is due to increased intrabdominal pressure.

Although it is a frequent cause of worry, it is generally harmless.

Palpation

Palpation is a vital technique used in abdominal examination by clinicians. With knowledge of location, border and the *landmarks* of each organ, the examination is performed to pick up any abnormalities.

An organ's landmark is a structure the examiner can see or feel on the surface of the body that corresponds to its location deep inside the abdomen.

Here are two examples to illustrate what might seem complicated at first. The upper limit of a normal liver, for example, lies just below a line joining both nipples, while the lower limit is just around the lower right rib edge.

Two thirds along the way of an imaginary line drawn from the belly button (umbilicus) to a bulge on a part of the bony pelvis (anterior superior iliac spine) is located McBurney's point. This area is where the appendix is *normally* located, which is tender during appendicitis and serves as a guide for the surgeon to do an appendicectomy. (Removal of the appendix) Note I have stressed the word *normally* as the appendix can be located in slightly different positions in the abdomen. This so-called *anatomical variation* is one of the reasons why appendicitis can present in different ways, making it quite tricky to diagnose, especially during its early stages.

Knowledge of landmarks is not only important for clinical examination but also for diagnostic procedures and surgery.

As mentioned above, a prior knowledge of each organ's position and its borders is vital to make sense of your findings. During palpation, the examiner uses the flat of their hand to first lightly examine all four quadrants of the abdomen in a systematic manner, followed by a deeper feel of the quadrants.

Palpation is used to check for pain or enlarged organs (organomegaly) in the various quadrants described above. Palpation is done with the history and differential diagnosis in mind.

Pain in the right upper quadrant on palpation on a 45-year-old obese lady who complains of abdominal pain made worse by eating her favourite tiramisu is most likely gallbladder disease. There is a common medical mnemonic called the 4Fs of gallbladder disease: Female, Forty, Fertile and Fat.

A 15-year-old boy who falls off his mountain bike and is in excruciating pain in the left upper quadrant on palpation might have a ruptured spleen.

Percussion

Percussion of the abdomen is also an important technique used to diagnose pathology, with all four quadrants percussed in a systematic manner. During percussion, the flat palm of one hand is placed against the abdomen with the middle finger of the other hand tapping firmly but steadily against the middle finger of the other. This action is similar to the repetitive strike by some mechanical watches or clock *movements*.

A barrel full of gas sounds different from the same barrel full of varying amounts of water. Similarly, an abdomen full of gas will produce a sound at a higher pitch, also called hyper resonance, while an abdomen full of liquid (ascites) will produce a dull sound.

Different organs have different notes on percussion with varying constituency.

An enlarged liver from cancer, for example, would sound *stony dull* compared to a healthy liver.

Percussion is skill that is perfected with practice and a trained ear.

Auscultation

The normal transit or movement of food, liquids and gas produces so-called b*owel sounds* under normal circumstances. Reduced or absent bowel sounds are most often caused by constipation, while high-pitched or hyper resonant sounds occur in intestinal obstruction, heard with a lightly placed stethoscope on the abdominal wall.

Audible bowel sounds – or *grumbling stomach* – caused by the movement of gas are slightly different to b*owel sounds* that are heard only with a stethoscope. The medical term for the sound of a grumbling stomach is b*orborygmi.*

CHAPTER 40

UNDERSTANDING COMMON LABORATORY TESTS

Simplicity is the ultimate sophistication.

-Leonardo da Vinci

Introduction

When the history you provide points towards a particular diagnosis, a blood test may be requested to confirm it. Sometimes a blood test is used as an exclusion criterion for a particular condition. In other words, a negative test strengthens the probability of the disease not being part of our differential diagnosis. The phrase to *rule out* is usually used in the above situation by clinicians. Always remember, however, that the history makes up about 85% of the diagnostic process and is therefore paramount.

Blood tests are sometimes also requested in the absence of pathology as part of so-called *health checks.* This is because some subtle abnormalities in the blood might sometimes precede clinical symptoms. As a general rule, blood test abnormalities get worse with time, but occasionally, on repeating blood tests following infections or other factors, the blood picture might improve and revert to normal levels.

Before we discuss common blood tests, there are a few important concepts to grasp. These include sensitivity and specificity of a test, *range of normality*, ethnicity, variation in lab reference ranges and interpretation alongside clinical history.

Sensitivity

The term sensitivity of a test simply describes how good a test is at picking up patients who have a particular disease. A test with a sensitivity of 100% means it would pick up all patients who have the disease every time it is performed. It follows that a test with a sensitivity of less than 100% would sometimes miss patients who actually do have the disease.

Specificity

The term specificity of a test describes how good a test is at not picking up patients without a particular disease. In other words, a test with 100% specificity means it would not pick up healthy people—healthy people here means anyone without the disease we are testing for. These terms might seem confusing at first, but I'll use a neat analogy to hopefully make these concepts clearer.

A shop or supermarket security alarm that bleeps on every occasion a shoplifter tries to smuggle items out of the premises has 100% sensitivity. The test (security alarm) picks up a shoplifter (disease) accurately each time.

An alarm system that goes off while innocent customers (non-shoplifters) go through the gates has specificity lower than 100%. The test (alarm system) falsely classes non-shoplifters (disease-free) as having the disease. An ideal test would therefore have 100% sensitivity and 100% specificity, but in practice all tests have a trade-off.

Range of Normality

The second concept is to do with ranges of normality. We are all individual and thus might have slightly different ranges that are normal for us.

Ethnicity

There are some subtle differences within the races with regards to certain blood tests. Black patients usually have lower levels of white blood cells (neutrophils), for example. The formula used to calculate a patient's kidney function (estimated glomerular filtration rate (eGFR)) is also different in black and non-black patients.

Lab reference range variation

Reference ranges vary from one lab to another and from one country to another. This is the reason why your GP might want to repeat any tests done from a private lab or another country for consistency.

Interpretation alongside clinical history

Last but not least, always remember a blood test is best interpreted alongside the full clinical picture and not in isolation. This is an important concept that can save you lots of worry and unnecessary angst.

With this out of the way, let's delve into the commonly requested blood tests.

Full Blood Count (FBC)

The FBC test shows the quantity of blood cells you have as well as their shape and size. As a reminder, the different blood cells in the body are red blood cells, white blood cells, comprising neutrophils, lymphocytes, basophils and eosinophils, and platelets. Each of these cell types has general specific reference ranges, which serve as a guide for interpretation.

The red blood cells carry oxygen in the blood with the aid of a structure called haemoglobin, (Hb) a protein structure with iron (Fe) in its centre. A reduced number of red blood cells in the blood or lower than normal haemoglobin levels is called anaemia. You can now see why iron tablets (Ferrous Sulfate or Ferrous Fumarate) are sometimes prescribed to people who have low haemoglobin levels. The normal Hb range for Men is between 13 and 18g/dL and for women11.5–16.5 g/dL.

An FBC is commonly requested for a wide array of presenting complaints, notably tiredness, blood loss from the urinary tract (haematuria), gastrointestinal tract (PR bleeding), reproductive system (menorrhagia) infection, to name a few.

A low Hb is the usual picture with blood loss of any kind, but this is only half the story. Iron is also stored in the body tissues in a form called ferritin and gets released into the blood in small amounts each time the Hb gets low. This means in a severe form of anaemia both the Hb and the ferritin become low. A routine FBC request, however, does not include a ferritin level and has to be requested as an extra if needed.

A brilliant way of explaining the concept of Hb and ferritin is using the analogy of your current and savings bank account. The Hb could be seen as your current account while the ferritin your savings account. As you spend money and eventually start to run out (anaemia from low Hb) you might need to start dipping into your savings (ferritin). Supplementing your spending with your savings might hold you over for short period before that also runs out.

Interestingly, your Hb might read higher than normal. This is called polycythaemia and can be caused by smoking, living at high altitudes, respiratory diseases or some blood cancers.

Lastly, information about the RBC size is also shown in the FBC and is called the mean cell volume (MCV). Some types of anaemia and blood disorders like sickle cell disease and thalassaemia cause small red cells (low MCVs). High alcohol intake, low vitamin B12 among others cause large red cells (high MCV). Normal MCV ranges for men and women are 84-102X109.

I once went to visit an 89-year-old lady whose blood test results had been rung through directly from the labs. This is common practice when there is an unexpected result. Her Hb was 3.7g/dL (normal range for females is 11.5–16).

This was clearly extremely low so I sped off to see what her clinical condition was before admitting her for a likely blood transfusion. Surprisingly, I was greeted with a smile by a stoic little old lady still in her nightgown just over midday. She had been breathless for a long time but was keen to point out this was nothing compared to the hardship she had endured during the war.

"Your blood level is very low, Mrs X, I think you will need a blood transfusion."

"I knew it. She refuses to take her antidepressant, doctor," her husband said dryly, sitting in his seat dangerously close to an extremely loud television.

I have since still been looking for a better way to explain anaemia…

Wondering how anyone could survive on such a low Hb level? The answer lies in the human body's resilience in compensating for changes that happen slowly over time. In this case, blood loss slowly occurring over a prolonged period of time.

Bleeding occurring suddenly over a very short space of time, say in an accident or from profuse rectal bleeding or other, is another matter. The body does not have adequate time to compensate, which means a potentially fatal outcome.

As a reminder, the white blood cells are made up of the neutrophils, lymphocytes, basophils and eosinophils. These cells fight infections, and their levels increase in the process. The *total white cell count* gives information regarding all the white cells, while the *differential white cell count* gives information on each white cell subtype—simple.

The differential white cell count is important as it can give clues as to potential causes. The neutrophils, the commonest of the white blood cells, predominantly increase with bacterial infections, while the lymphocytes predominantly increase with viral infections. An increase in eosinophils is usually due to parasites like worms.

Normal ranges for all four subtypes for Men and Women are as follows: Neutrophils: 2-7.5X109, Lymphocytes: 1-4X 109, Monocytes: 0.1-1.5X 109 -Eosinophils-0.04-0.4X109.

A slight increase in the platelet count is generally nothing to worry about.

Common causes include infection, blood loss and anaemia. Smoking and living at high altitude also occasionally increase the platelet count. Very rarely, a high platelet count is due to a blood cancer.

Normal ranges for platelets in men and women are 150-450X10^9/L.

In summary, the FBC shows the number, size and shapes of the red blood cells, white blood cells and platelets.

Kidney Function Tests

The main role of the kidneys is elimination of the by-products of metabolism, called urea and creatinine. The kidneys also control the body's electrolyte (Na+ and K+) levels and maintain its *acid base balance.*

Kidney function tests measure how well your kidneys are functioning and comprise: Urea and electrolytes (U&Es), creatinine levels, and the estimated glomerular filtration rate (eGFR).

Kidney dysfunction thus results in accumulation of urea and creatinine, varying changes in electrolyte levels in the blood, and a shift in the acid base balance of the body.

U&Es

The U&E test comprises levels of urea, salts or electrolytes (potassium (K+), sodium (Na+)) and creatinine. Normal U&E values are as follows: Urea-2.9-7.7mmol/L, Na-134-145mmol/L, K-3.5-5.3mmol/L and creatinine-45-84umol/L.

Electrolyte imbalances are common reasons for phone calls requesting repeat blood tests. In my experience, high K+ comes at the top of the list. In many cases, a high K+ results from the blood sample clotting after being drawn or simple dehydration. Another relatively common reason for a high K is the class of blood pressure tablets called ACE inhibitors like Ramipril, lisinopril and more.

A low Na+ can result from alcohol abuse and from a class of blood pressure tablets called diuretics like Bendrofluazide, Furosemide and similar.

Relatively high Na+, K+, urea and creatinine signify a more serious kidney disorder.

eFGR

The estimated glomerular filtration rate (eGFR), as the name implies, measures the rate at which the kidneys filter blood passing through the glomerulus—part of the kidney's filtration apparatus.

There are five stages of kidney dysfunction, based on eGFR values, classed as normal, mild, moderate, severe and kidney failure. Stage1 (eGFR>90) stage (eGFR 89-60) Stage 3a (59-45) stage 3b (44-30), stage 4 (15-29) and stage 5 (<15).

An GFR of 90 or more is classed as optimal and by definition involves minimal kidney damage with a normal kidney function.

It is always worth repeating your kidney function as values could change with hydration levels or diets rich in meat. This explains why you might sometimes get a call from a receptionist asking you to book a repeat kidney function test after drinking lots of water.

An eGFR of <15 is defined as end-stage kidney failure, requiring dialysis or a kidney transplant.

Liver Function Tests (LFTs)

The liver has a pivotal role in digestion, metabolism and detoxification of the body. A liver function test, commonly known as LFT, measures how well the liver is working. A complete LFT panel comprises liver enzymes, albumin (protein) and bilirubin levels. Raised levels of any of these signify varying degrees of liver damage.

Four of the liver enzymes included are aspartate amino transferase (AST), alanine aminotransferase (ALT), gamma-glutamyl transferase (GGT) and alkaline phosphatase (ALP). These enzymes normally reside in the liver cells (hepatocytes) and bile duct cells. With liver damage of any sort, these enzymes seep from the cells into the bloodstream, causing raised levels, which are detected. Normal LFT levels are: AST (0-30iu/L), ALT (0-35iu/L), ALP (40-130iu/L).

Raised AST and ALT levels might occur from fatty liver, toxins, and drugs.

A rise in liver enzymes in the thousands is more often than not due to viral hepatitis like Hepatitis B and C. Raised GGT levels are particularly sensitive to alcohol.

Although ALP is present in the liver cells, it mainly lines the bile duct and in addition is also found in other tissues like bone. An ALP Isoenzyme test can help distinguish the origin of a raised ALP and thus help diagnosis.

I remember a story told to me many years ago by a friend who recounted with excitement his first few months at university. He had no culinary experience whatsoever and resorted to vodka and Red Bull for breakfast. After pouring his first vodka and Red Bull, he quickly made an acute observation—the fully emptied Red Bull just reached the level of the pint glass bulge. He then carefully topped the rest of the glass off with vodka like a laboratory scientist. He would continue this perfect measuring exercise for many weeks like a ritual.

After about a month, he was out on campus about noon when a friend called out, "Pete, you are yellow."

He really didn't take any notice of the comment at the time, till the next day when he looked at himself in the mirror. "Gosh, I am yellow," he said, slightly perplexed, gazing into the mirror through his yellow sclerae, clutching a full pint.

What's even more hilarious is the fact that to this day Pete still doesn't think the amount of vodka he consumed was significant. "It was just this much," he will say, demonstrating the amount of vodka with his index finger and thumb parallel to each other.

I am sure you have guessed by now that Pete had alcohol-related liver damage, resulting in jaundice. Had he paid a visit to his doctor for a liver test, his LFTs would have likely have been deranged.

In fact, the yellow in jaundice colour is due to deposition of bilirubin in the tissues. Occasionally, a routine LFT will show a slightly raised bilirubin level, with all the other enzymes in the normal range. This condition is called Gilbert's disease, named after French gastroenterologist Augustin Gilbert in 1901. The word disease used in conjunction with Gilbert's is a misnomer as this is not a disease per say, although individuals with Gilbert's sometimes become mildly jaundiced.

Fasting Blood Glucose

For the sake of blood tests, the term fasting generally applies to a period of 8–10 hrs without any food or drink, excluding water.

A *fasting blood glucose* is thus a glucose reading taken after a period of fasting.

The world health organization (WHO) criteria for diagnosing diabetes is a fasting blood glucose of 7mmol/L or more.

Random Blood Glucose

A random blood glucose test is a glucose reading test taken without having fasted.

The world health organization (WHO) criteria for diagnosing diabetes is 11.1mmol/L or more.

If you are found to have raised fasting or random plasma glucose readings on a routine test, it is worth repeating after two weeks or so for confirmation. There is no need to repeat this with extremely high levels.

Impaired Fasting Glucose

A fasting glucose of 6.1-6.9mmol/L is termed impaired fasting glucose, commonly known as prediabetes.

If you are diagnosed with prediabetes, a lifestyle change involving diet and exercise can make a dramatic change in a few months with willpower and dedication. Please see Part 4 of this book dedicated to prevention and healthy eating.

HBA1C (A1C)

HBA1C, also known as A1C or glycated haemoglobin, is the structure formed when glucose (sugar) attaches to haemoglobin, the oxygen carrier found in the red blood cells.

The higher the glucose levels in the blood, the higher the HBA1C, thus HBA1C is used as both a diagnostic test as well as monitoring treatment.

However, the average lifespan of a red blood cell is three months, meaning the HBA1C provides information on glucose control over a two to three-month period at most.

The HBA1C test is now considered the gold standard for diagnosing diabetes, the world health organization (WHO) diagnostic criteria being 48mmol/L (6.5%) and above.

HBA1C values of between 42 and 47 mmol/mol (6.0-6.4%) are classed as prediabetic while HBA1C levels of below 42mmol/mol (6.0%) are non-diabetic.

If you are in the prediabetic range, a lifestyle change involving diet and exercise can make a dramatic change in a few months with willpower and dedication.

As HBA1C readings depend on haemoglobin in the red blood cells, any condition that alters either the lifespan or form of the red blood cells limit its use. A few such conditions include blood disorders (haemoglobinopathies) like sickle cell anaemias in black patients and thalassaemia in people of Asian and Mediterranean ancestry.

Due to changes in pregnancy, the role of HBA1C is also limited. The best test for diagnosing diabetes in pregnancy is the oral glucose tolerance test (OGTT).

Thyroid Function Tests (TFTs)

In my experience, TFTs are one of the most misunderstood tests among patients and doctors alike. This is partly because the usual tests historically requested by conventional medicine are only part of the picture at best.

Interpretation is therefore potentially erroneous based on this basic premise.

A comprehensive interpretation of TFTs is beyond the scope of this book and I'll try my best here to cover the absolute basics.

Starting from the top, the brain signals the master gland, the pituitary, to produce a hormone called thyroid stimulating hormone (TSH). The pituitary gland is known as the master gland as it signals many other glands to synthesize hormones.

TSH produced by the pituitary in turn tells the thyroid to produce two hormones by combining iodine (I), which we get from our diet, and a molecule called tyrosine. These two hormones are tetra-iodothyronine, known as T4, and a small amount of Tri-iodothyronine or T3. An enzyme called thyroid peroxidase (TPO) facilitates this combining process. For purists, T4 has four iodine molecules attached to tyrosine while T3 has three iodine molecules attached.

Now, T4 is mainly inactive and is converted to the active form T3. This is achieved by an enzyme present in different tissues of the body, which removes one iodine molecule in the process.

Production of thyroid hormones by the pituitary gland is under negative feedback control. In other words, high T4 levels signal the pituitary to make less TSH while low T4 levels signals the pituitary to make more TSH. However, this feedback loop is dependent on T4 levels, and not T3, even though T3 is the active form of the hormone.

The active form T3 are responsible for the familiar symptoms we know of like tiredness, weight gain, palpitations, anxiety and so on.

So, what tests are commonly requested?

It is quite common for some doctors to request a TSH level only. This simply does not provide enough information whatsoever on the functioning of the thyroid. The bare minimum, in my opinion, is a TSH, T4, T3 and thyroid autoantibodies.

Keeping things simple, we have the following patterns:

Low T4, high TSH signifying hypothyroidism.

High T4 and low TSH signifying hyperthyroidism.

Now, could you have thyroid symptoms and have a normal T4 and TSH? The answer is a resounding *Yes*. Remember, the active form of thyroid hormone is T3 and not T4. You could therefore have a conversion problem. In other words, T4 not converting to T3 in the tissues. Your T4 levels in such cases may be normal and consequently TSH through the negative feedback loop.

I was once victim of this years ago. A patient I saw was adamant she was hypothyroid and made her case by showing me peer-reviewed articles, including one from the queen's endocrinologist, she told me.

A proportion of hypothyroidism and hyperthyroidism are caused by autoimmune disease, thus autoimmune antibody levels are worth checking all the time.

Hypothyroidism generally gets treated with Levothyroxine tablets. A blood test is usually booked in about eight weeks to check hormone levels and the Levothyroxine dose either increased or decreased depending on response.

Hyperthyroidism is usually treated with a drug called Carbimazole, usually initially prescribed by an endocrinologist. Many patients become hypothyroid, eventually needing thyroxine to support the thyroid gland.

A point worth stressing here is that abnormal thyroid function tests aren't always as a result of the thyroid gland itself. In fact, the majority of abnormal thyroid function tests happen as a result of problems in other organs or systems. This is because all the body systems are interconnected, and looking at the thyroid in isolation is only part of the big picture.

As mentioned at the start, the thyroid can be complicated, and I have only just touched the surface here. There are lots of thyroid patterns and further tests that could be done as there is potential for dysfunction at every step of the process described above. At the time of writing, the tests available on the National Health Service are limited; until then, your only chance of getting further testing is via private labs.

Cholesterol

If there is one test that patients are most keen to improve it is their cholesterol level. This is because over the years cholesterol has been vilified due to its proposed link with cardiovascular disease.

To start with, it is worth pointing out that cholesterol is an essential part of the body's cell membranes, bile acids, sex hormones (oestrogen, testosterone, progesterone), adrenal hormones and fat-soluble vitamins (A, D, E and K).

Cholesterol is a complicated topic, which has evolved a lot over the years. To get a head start, let's start with the basic physiology.

First of all, cholesterol is a kind of fat, and you might be surprised to learn that you get only about 20% of it from diet, with the remaining 80% made by your liver.

To help cholesterol dissolve in the blood, it is encased in a protein shell or matrix called a *lipoprotein.* It is in this form that it is transported in the blood around the body.

There are two main forms of cholesterol, namely low-density lipoproteins (LDL) and high-density lipoproteins (HDL).

Low-density lipoproteins (LDL) transport cholesterol from the liver to the cells.

Excess LDL is thought to accumulate in the arteries causing plaque (atherosclerosis). As such, LDL is also called *bad cholesterol.*

High-density lipoproteins (HDL) transport cholesterol from the blood back into the liver, where it is metabolised and excreted in the bile. As such, HDL is called *good cholesterol.*

Now, if you wanted to know your cholesterol level, your doctor would tick the box with the word *lipids* on paper or computer. Another word for lipids is *fats,* and cholesterol is only one type. Other examples of lipids are triglycerides, which are also measured.

A full lipid profile includes: Total cholesterol, LDL, HDL, cholesterol ratio and triglycerides.

Total cholesterol, as the name implies, is the total amount of cholesterol in the body and includes LDL and HDL.

LDL – Low-density lipoprotein or bad cholesterol. It is hypothesised that the higher the LDL, the higher the risk of cardiovascular outcomes.

HDL – High-density lipoprotein or good cholesterol. It is hypothesised that the higher the HDL the lower your risk of cardiovascular outcomes.

Cholesterol ratio – This is the number you get by dividing your total cholesterol by your HDL. Following this, two people with the same total cholesterol level could have a different cholesterol ratio, depending on their HDL value.

Triglycerides – Although triglycerides are not commonly known or talked about by patients, they are the most abundant kind of fat (lipid) in the body. Triglycerides are not cholesterol but raised levels are thought to increase the risk of cardiovascular disease.

So, what do all these numbers mean for you, and what exactly is your risk of developing a cardiovascular event? The answer is it is complicated. I remember a time when the wisdom for cholesterol management was *the lower the better,* followed by various acceptable ranges that kept changing over time.

There also seems to be some debate about the use of LDL and total cholesterol as a predictor of cardiovascular risk, given other LDL subtypes and sizes have been individualised as being more accurate in this respect.

In addition, the varying theories seeking to explain plaque formation in the arteries differ. Some say it isn't LDL that's the problem but damage to the arterial wall by free radicals (e.g. smoking), which cause an oxidised form of LDL to deposit in the arterial wall forming plaques. According to this theory, LDL is just a bystander in some respects.

Moreover, some new research is looking beyond the amount of HDL, focusing on its ability to *mop up* cholesterol. In other words, it's not just a *numbers game.*

However, one thing is clear—your overall risk of a cardiovascular event is not based solely on your cholesterol or triglyceride numbers alone.

To get your overall risk, a group of UK researchers came up with the QRISK2 score. This is an algorithm used to work out the risk of healthy individuals having a cardiovascular event over a 10-year period.

The QRISK 2 algorithm takes into account the following: Age, sex, ethnicity, postcode, smoking status, diabetes, angina or heart attack in a first-degree relative< 60 years, chronic kidney disease (stage 4 or 5), atrial fibrillation, on blood pressure treatment, rheumatoid arthritis, body mass index (weight and height), systolic blood pressure, and finally cholesterol/HDL ratio. You can *google* QRISK2 score anytime and calculate your risk. Statins are recommended for individuals with a QRISK2 score of >10 %.

As you can see, the QRISK2 score takes into account many parameters including cholesterol. Moreover, there is now a QRISK3 score developed with additional parameters to help predict risk.

The story doesn't end here, as there are other cutting-edge scoring systems or algorithms that include even more parameters like stress levels, nutrition, state of the microbiome and many more parameters that are also thought to be important in the development of cardiovascular risk.

Theories aside, the question you should be asking is what *you* can do to reduce your risk of cardiovascular disease. The answer is of course diet and exercise, which is also where it gets complicated due to the varying diets suggested.

Please have a look at the section on *weight loss mistakes and secrets* for what I recommend.

As we will see in the next section, diet and exercise potentially improve sugar control, reduce BP readings and optimise your lipid profile. If we agree this to be the case, then your QRISK2 score is automatically lowered provided any of the above parameters improve.

If your LDL level is markedly raised, you might have a genetic disease called familial hypercholesterolaemia. The lifestyle changes above still apply, but you might get better protection with a statin.

Last but not least, probably the single most important thing you could do to reduce your risk is to stop smoking.

C Reactive Protein (CRP)

(Normal range: 0-10mg/L)

CRP is a protein produced by the liver, especially during the early stages of inflammation or infection. The higher the CRP, the greater the degree of infection or inflammation present.

CRP is a non-specific test as it only gives information on the degree on tissue infection or inflammation and not where the problem lies. A good history will hopefully point your doctor towards the probable cause of a raised CRP.

Erythrocyte Sedimentation Rate (ESR)

(Normal range: 1-20mm/hr)

ESR means the rate at which the erythrocytes (red blood cells) form sediment (fall to the bottom of a test tube). The higher the ESR, the greater degree of inflammation in the body there is. Some rheumatological conditions are known to produce a high ESR values, like polymyalgia rheumatica, (PMR) giant cell arteritis (GCA) and inflammatory joint diseases.

Like CRP, ESR is also a non-specific marker for disease and only gives information on the presence and degree of inflammation but not on the cause of it. Again, like CRP, a good history will hopefully point your doctor towards the cause of a raised ESR.

Rheumatoid Factor

(Normal range: 0-12iu/mL)

Rheumatoid factor is an antibody that is produced against the body's own cells.

It is thus defined as an autoantibody, and its levels are raised in autoimmune disorders like rheumatoid arthritis, SLE (systemic lupus erythematosus), just to name a few. The commonest reason for an RH factor test being requested is when your joint pain and/or stiffness is thought to be due to rheumatoid arthritis.

Anti-Citrulline antibodies test. (anti-CCP)

(Ranges: < 7 U/mL, negative, 7-10 U/mL equivocal, >10 U/mL positive)

The CCP test is requested when rheumatoid factor is suspected. This test is based on the hypothesis that the amino acid arginine is converted to citrulline, which lines the joints. In rheumatoid arthritis, antibodies then attack the citrulline in the joint lining causing pain, swelling and stiffness seen in the disease.

Vitamin D (Cholecalciferol)

Vitamin D has gained tremendous popularity over the last few years. This is most probably largely due to work by Dr Michael Holick, an endocrinologist from Boston University.

The name vitamin D is a misnomer as it is a hormone. Vitamin D is made in the skin from cholesterol, aided by ultraviolet light from the sun. This form of vitamin D is called cholecalciferol, and the liver converts it to calcidiol (25-hydroxycholecalciferol). The kidneys then convert calcidiol to calcitriol (1,25 hydroxycholecalciferol), the active form of the hormone.

Vitamin D has traditionally been known for increasing absorption of calcium from the intestines, which is used to build bone tissue. This explains why a deficiency of vitamin D causes a form of rickets.

Over the last few years, vitamin D's role in the body has been studied and found to impact multiple body systems. It has been found to have a role in immunity, obesity and even mental health diseases like depression.

Most laboratories test the calcidiol form of vitamin D, but the normal range is not universally accepted. Most NHS trusts use a range of 24–167 nmol/L.

If you are vitamin D deficient, the recommended treatment regime is to take one 20,000IU tablet of vitamin D twice a week for seven weeks. This is called a *loading dose* and is important, especially if your levels are very low. After a loading dose, you can start taking a much lower dose on a daily basis. Make sure you check how many IU of vitamin D you buy in your local health shop or trusted online shop. Don't just get the *strongest vitamin D we have* or you risk an overdose. I personally take 1000IU per day in the autumn and winter months.

Coeliac Antibodies

Coeliac disease is an autoimmune disease resulting from ingestion of gluten, a family of proteins mainly found in wheat, rye and barley.

Traditionally, the main symptoms of gluten intolerance described are gastrointestinal symptoms, including bloating, diarrhoea, constipation and abdominal pain. However, the effects of gluten in coeliac disease are far reaching, involving every organ system in the human body. As such, coeliac disease is best described as a multi-system disease.

In susceptible individuals, ingestion of gluten triggers production of antibodies.

These antibodies then attack the small intestinal tissue, destroying the finger-like projections of the small intestinal tissue (villi), which eventually get flattened. As mentioned, other healthy tissues in the body are also targeted and destroyed.

The two tests commonly requested to check for coeliac disease are anti-tissue transglutaminase (tTG) antibodies and endomysial antibodies (EMA). It is preferable to request both tests, and to increase their sensitivity patients are sometimes advised to eat a gluten-rich diet for four weeks prior. If you have definitely experienced worsening symptoms when you have eaten gluten, then there is no need to bother with the test.

The traditional gold standard for diagnosing coeliac disease is a small intestinal biopsy.

Coeliac disease is a complicated topic beyond the scope of this book. However, here are a few points worth mentioning at this point.

Gluten is a protein composed of two parts, namely glutenins and gliadins.

Each of these parts is in turn made up of hundreds of amino acids, linked together called peptides. The gliadin part of gluten is itself made up of 12 sub-fragments. Traditional testing only looks for antibodies towards one of the 12 sub-fragments called alpha gliadin. This means you could have coeliac disease but your blood test comes back normal.

Most importantly, there is another entity to be distinguished from coeliac disease called non-coeliac wheat sensitivity (NSGS), also known as non-coeliac wheat sensitivity (NCWS). In this condition, the body's non-specific immune system (innate immunity) reacts to components of wheat other than gluten.

This potentially causes increased gut permeability (leaky gut), leading to a myriad of symptoms from digestive disorders to brain fog and fatigue. [1]

Some patients with NSGS eventually develop coeliac disease, but those who don't suffer for years on end as their tests keep showing up normal all the time.

If you suspect you might have coeliac disease or NCGS, I recommend an *elimination diet* to see if your symptoms improve.

Apart from the grains previously mentioned, gluten is also found hidden in a vast array of other food types. If you are unsure, I recommend reading food labels meticulously.

Faecal Calprotectin

Calprotectin is a protein present in the faeces due to gut inflammation.

The faecal calprotectin test is primarily requested to distinguish irritable bowel syndrome (IBS) from inflammatory bowel diseases (Crohn's and ulcerative colitis), given the overlap of symptoms.

This test is particularly useful as it avoids the need for endoscopies, traditionally used to diagnose inflammatory bowel disease.

PSA (Prostate Specific Antigen)

A PSA is a protein produced by cells of the prostate gland and considered a marker for prostate cancer.

A raised PSA does not necessarily signify prostate cancer as other factors like ejaculation within 24 hours, urinary tract infections, (UTI) inflammation of the prostate (prostatitis), and benign prostatic hyperplasia (BPH) are potential causes.

A normal PSA level does not exist as such, and results are adjusted for age in an attempt to provide a more accurate interpretation.

Despite the above, PSA interpretation remains a tricky business, especially as some prostate cancers do not raise the PSA level at all.

A strategy used by some GPs and hospital consultants is monitoring serial PSA readings over a defined period of time.

A close eye is kept on PSA trends, with swift intervention following any sharp rises.

An MRI scan of your prostate or biopsy ultimately confirms the presence or absence of cancer.

Brain Natriuretic Peptide (BNP)

Normal levels-

Brain natriuretic peptide (BNP) is a protein molecule released when the heart ventricle is *stressed*. It reduces the circulating volume of blood, as well as reducing pressure in the blood vessels, by its diuretic effect. Conditions that increase the stress of the ventricular wall, like heart failure, therefore increase the levels of BNP.

Helicobacter Pylori (H Pylori)

The story of H Pylori is an interesting one. For years, the mainstream medical establishment believed ulcers were caused by lifestyle and stress—a rare case of mainstream medicine asserting the role of lifestyle in pathology. However, two Australian researchers, Barry Marshall and Robin Warren, went against the establishment.

They proposed the idea that gastritis (inflammation of the stomach) and ulcers were caused by a species of bacteria called Helicobacter Pylori (H Pylori) that lived in the stomach. To prove the point, Barry Marshall gave himself an ulcer by drinking a culture of H Pylori! He then biopsied his stomach to show the bacteria. Twenty-one years later, both Barry Marshall and Robin Warren were awarded the Nobel Prize in physiology.

There are four ways to test for H Pylori: A breath test, a stool test, a blood test and a biopsy of the stomach.

The H Pylori breath test detects urea, a waste product formed by H Pylori's activity. It is important to stop any antacids, especially proton pump inhibitors like omeprazole, lansoprazole and similar drugs, two weeks before the test to avoid false negative results.

The H Pylori stool test checks for antigens produced by the bacteria. It is therefore also called the H pylori stool antigen test. Similar to the breath test, it is imperative to stop any proton pump inhibitors at least two weeks before the test. Failing this, you might get a false negative result.

Finally, the blood test detects antibodies to H pylori while a biopsy shows H Pylori.

Urine Dip

A urine dip test is a *bedside test* that enables doctors to quickly analyse your urine. The test involves dipping a thin colour-coded strip of paper in and out of a urine sample bottle. After a few seconds, any colour changes reflective of the *metabolites* in the urine are noted.

A urine dip that shows infection might be positive for either leucocytes (white blood cells), nitrites (breakdown products of nitrates) or erythrocytes (Red blood cells). The presence of protein and/or blood might signify kidney or bladder disease. A positive glucose on a urine dip more often than not means diabetes.

It is worth noting a negative dipstick test does not preclude infection or any other diagnosis due to varying sensitivity and specificity of the test.

Due to the high incidence of UTIs in the elderly, some care homes stock their own urine testing strips.

If you get recurrent UTIs, especially if female, they are available online or at your local chemist.

It is important to always report the results to your GP as recurrent UTIs could signify underlying diabetes in some cases or, rarely, more sinister pathology.

MSU (Mid-Stream Urine)

MSU stands for mid-stream urine and is a laboratory test performed on a urine sample to identify bacteria present. An MSU takes two to three days to process, in comparison to a urine dip, which takes seconds. More importantly, not only does an MSU state the bugs present, it also lists the antibiotics the bugs are sensitive to—this makes an MSU relatively precise.

A common strategy used by clinicians is to prescribe an initial course of antibiotics (empirical antibiotics) while awaiting an MSU result. In practice, this might mean swapping empirical antibiotics already prescribed halfway into treatment for the appropriate one identified by the MSU. This is the reason you might have got a phone call from a receptionist telling you to pick up a new prescription after having started a course of antibiotics.

Similar to a urine dip test, it is worth noting a negative MSU test does not preclude infection.

This is because the MSU test reads as positive based on a certain quantity of bacteria present in the urine.

So, you could still have a UTI if the quantity of bacteria is just under this amount.

As some clinicians do not appreciate this fact, it is a frequent area of frustration among patients who do have classic symptoms of a urine infection, but are repeatedly told their test is negative.

MC&S (Microscopy, Culture and Sensitivity)

This is a test to identify microbes and effective treatment on various bodily fluids like mucous, stool, wounds, ear discharge and so on. This test is usually requested when an infection that would normally respond to known antibiotics or antifungals (empirical treatment) does not resolve. Let's say a cough you had for eight weeks has not responded to three different courses of antibiotics, your doctor might request an MC&S of your sputum (phlegm).

Always remember to label the bottle with your name and date of birth as labs are notorious for rejecting partially labelled samples. A rejected sample is a potential headache, especially if you were prescribed an empirical course of antibiotics in the meantime. This is because the results of an MC&S are inaccurate in the presence of antibiotics.

Although not available on the NHS, there are many cutting-edge lab tests that detect disease and non-disease-causing microbes using advanced DNA technology. In fact, some of these tests map out your entire gut microbiome.

Female Hormones-Oestrogen, Progesterone, Testosterone, Follicle Stimulating Hormone (FSH), Luteinising Hormone (LH)

Interpretation of female hormonal profiles can be complicated and beyond the scope of this book. As with any test, interpreting the results alongside the clinical picture is recommended.

In general practice, the female hormones are commonly requested for polycystic ovarian syndrome (PCOS) or to *confirm* menopause. Normally, the ratio of FSH to LH is equal or FSH being slightly higher than LH. In PCOS, this ratio is inverted, with LH being higher than FSH up to 3:1.

Although many women request a blood test to *confirm* menopause, the results are not as straightforward as they think.

The hormone usually requested to diagnose the menopause is follicle stimulating hormone (FSH). However, FSH levels fluctuate during the period around the menopause (perimenopause). In other words, the levels could be normal, high or low. Thus, if a woman's periods become erratic (too heavy or too light), there is no point testing at that point.

FSH levels greater than 30iu/L with absence of periods for more than a year is by definition considered menopause.

In some cases, serial FSH levels are requested to monitor the trends to help establish a clearer picture.

Cancer Test

Once in a while I get requests for a *cancer test.* This usually happens after a patient's close relative has been diagnosed with some form of cancer or they have recently watched a TV program with a cancer theme. If you have got this far, you will realise that a universal cancer test does not exist. As cancers occur in different organs and tissues, each test is unique to the type of cancer tested for.

---

1) Antonio Di Sabatino et al., "Small amounts of Gluten in Subjects with Suspected Noncoeliac Gluten Sensitivity: A randomized Double-Blind, Placebo-Controlled, Crossover Trial," *Clinical Gastroenterology and Hepatology* 13,no.9 (2015): 1604-12,doi:10.1016/j.cgh.2015.01.029

CHAPTER 41

UNDERSTANDING COMMON DIAGNOSTIC TESTS

Belief gets in the way of learning.

-Robert Heinlein

Introduction

The decision to request a diagnostic test is usually made to confirm a diagnosis based on the patient's history. In some cases, a diagnostic test is requested to prove the absence of pathology.

The choice of diagnostic test is of paramount importance as different tests are best suited to picking up different pathologies.

Radiology departments are now sending back scan requests that *do not meet referral criteria.*

In practice, your GP either fills in a paper request or accesses a system called ICE on which the request is made. You then get a call from the relevant department to come for the test requested.

There are a few concepts worth mentioning at this stage, which are sensitivity and specificity as well as operator dependency of tests.

Sensitivity

The term Sensitivity of a test simply describes how good a test is at picking up patients who have a particular disease. A test with a sensitivity of 100% means it will pick up all patients who have the disease every time it is performed. It follows that a test with a sensitivity of less than 100% will sometimes miss patients who actually do have the disease.

Specificity

The term Specificity of a test describes how good a test is at not picking up patients without a particular disease. In other words, a test with 100% specificity means it will not pick up anyone without the disease (healthy people).

In other words, a test with a 100% specificity means it will not pick up healthy people—healthy people here means anyone without the disease we are testing for.

These terms might seem confusing at first, but I'll use a neat analogy to hopefully make these concepts clearer.

A shop or supermarket security alarm that bleeps on every occasion a shoplifter tries to smuggle items out of the premises has 100% sensitivity. The test (security alarm) picks up a shoplifter (disease) each time accurately.

An alarm system that goes off while innocent customers (non-shoplifters) go through the gates has specificity lower than 100%. The test (alarm system) falsely classes non-shoplifters (disease-free) as having the disease.

An ideal test would therefore have 100% sensitivity and 100% specificity, but in practice all tests have a trade-off.

Operator dependency

Finally, all diagnostic tests are *operator dependent,* meaning a more experienced and skilled operator might potentially be able to pick things up better. I suspect this is not a common issue as most operators are generally well trained.

With this out of the way, lets delve into the commonly requested investigative tests.

X-ray (Radiograph)

In 1895, Wilhelm Roentgen, a German professor of physics, discovered X-rays.

It was the first time in medicine the inside of the body could be visualised without having to cut it open. Prior to this, doctors just used their clinical judgement and a bit of guesswork to diagnose.

X-ray requests are probably the commonest diagnostic tests requested by both patient and GP. Although GPs don't get the actual X-ray film, they do get the written report by the radiologist a few days or weeks later.

The commonest X-ray requests by GPs are for bones, to *rule out* fractures, and for the chest. Fractures can occasionally be missed in the presence of tissue swelling, so a repeat X-ray after the swelling has subsided is worth considering.

Although X-rays are commonly requested to confirm arthritis, it is worth noting that X-ray results can be normal despite advanced arthritis and abnormal with no pain. Your X-ray could thus state severe arthritis of the right hip, for example, while you presented with pain in the left one.

A chest X-ray can show pneumonia, lung cancer or cancer spread (metastasis) from other cancers, among other pathologies. A chest X-ray also gives information on heart size.

A common mistake seen in general practice is X-ray requests for shoulder problems. While X-rays are good at picking up bone abnormalities, they aren't so good with soft tissue like ligaments and tendons. Unless your GP suspects arthritis of the acromioclavicular joint, an ultrasound scan is the preferred choice.

The drawback of X-rays is radiation and one of the reasons to avoid repeating them if not clinically needed.

Computer Tomography (CT)

A CT scan uses X-rays oriented at different angles to produce computer-generated three-dimensional images of the body. It is superior to X-rays in diagnostic capability and mostly requested by hospitals.

CT scans are used to diagnose a variety of pathologies including cancer and hidden masses. They are also heavy on radiation and thus not commonly performed unless absolutely necessary. To put things into perspective, the dose of radiation is easily up to 200 times the radiation from a chest X-ray.

Ultrasound Scans (USS)

As the name suggests, a USS uses high-frequency (ultra) sound waves to create images of organs in the body. During the test, gel is applied to the skin and a probe is moved around the area concerned.

Ultrasound scans are great for looking at *soft tissue* in the body. These include an organ's shape and size, lumps within or outside them, tendons, ligaments and more. A USS is thus ideal for suspected masses in the abdomen or pelvis, lumps felt in the skin and pathologies of the shoulder.

Echocardiogram (Echo)

An echocardiogram is essentially an ultrasound scan of the heart, which uses sound waves to reconstruct a three-dimensional picture of the heart. An echo gives vital information on the heart size, wall thickness and valves. It also calculates how well the heart contracts. An echo is usually requested in cases where heart failure or diseases of the valves are suspected.

Magnetic Resonance Imaging (MRI)

An MRI scan uses a combination of magnetic and radio waves to generate images of the body.

Although MRI scans can be used for almost every part of the body, in most parts of the country, GPs can only request MRI scans of the musculoskeletal system.

MRI scans are great at detecting slipped discs in the back as well as knee ligaments and menisci.

Electrocardiogram (ECG)

An electrocardiogram or ECG is a heart *trace*, which is obtained from a machine with numerous "leads" attached to the chest, arms and legs in set configurations.

The recurring pattern seen in each trace results from the electrical activity within the heart and looks grossly similar in all non-diseased hearts.

The patterns within each trace change in characteristic ways, depending on the area of muscle damage, structural change or abnormality present in the heart.

An ECG also shows patterns that correspond to a thickened heart muscle wall (hypertrophy) as well as narrowed or leaky valves.

For purists, the wave pattern produced by an ECG is called the PQRST waves.

The P wave is generated by the atria and the QRS wave by the ventricles.

Any change in the pattern of either part of the wave gives an indication on the abnormality present.

A common pattern change on the ECG is *ST elevation*, which is normally present after a myocardial infarction(heart attack.)

Duplex Ultrasound (Doppler)

A doppler is an ultrasound scan that measures blood flow in the blood vessels (arteries and veins). A doppler is usually used to diagnose pathologies in the veins, called a deep venous thrombosis (DVT), or diseases in the arteries, called peripheral vascular disease (PVD) in the legs or carotid artery stenosis in the neck.

Upper Gastrointestinal Endoscopy /Oesophago-Gastro-Duodenoscopy (OGD)

An OGD is a test that involves a thin flexible tube called an endoscope to be inserted from the mouth through to the oesophagus, stomach and duodenum. An endoscope relays images to a monitor with the aid of a light source and camera. GPs mostly request OGDs when they suspect ulcers or stomach cancer.

During the test, a biopsy for Helicobacter Pylori (H Pylori) is usually made.

Sigmoidoscopy

A sigmoidoscopy involves insertion of a flexible tube into the lower S-shaped section between the descending colon and rectum, called the sigmoid colon. A sigmoidoscopy relays images to a monitor with the aid of a light source and camera.

A sigmoidoscopy is usually requested in cases of suspected inflammatory bowel disease (Crohn's and ulcerative colitis) or cancer. It is worth emphasising that a sigmoidoscopy only visualises the left lower end of the colon.This means a potential mass present in the right side of the colon cannot be seen.

Colonoscopy

A colonoscopy involves insertion of a thin flexible tube into the whole of the colon. A colonoscopy relays images to a monitor with the aid of a light source and camera.

A sigmoidoscopy is usually requested in cases of suspected inflammatory bowel disease (Crohn's and ulcerative colitis) or cancer. In comparison to a sigmoidoscopy, a colonoscopy is more thorough as it visualizes the entire colon.

CHAPTER 42

MAKING THE MOST OF YOUR MEDICINE REVIEW

Forget sex and money, tablets are what's causing problems in our household.

-Patient

If you have a chronic condition requiring medication on a long-term basis, your doctor, pharmacist or nurse prescriber will add them to your *repeat medication list* by ticking a box.

Once a drug is on your *repeat medication list*, you will see it on the right (white) side of the prescription. You can now either order it online, call the surgery to order items or nominate a pharmacy to do it on your behalf.

However, every drug on a repeat medication list has a set time limit or review date, after which you will be required to book an appointment to *review your medication*. The average time limit set for most repeat medications is 12 months, although any interval period from three to 12 months is possible depending on the drug and condition. After an appointment for a medication review, your medication is *re-authorised*, and the time limit refreshed.

Before you get your medication *re-authorised*, it is important to do the following:

Crosscheck and Tidy

The first thing to do before a medication review is to write down the medications you actually take on a daily basis. This simple exercise automatically allows your doctor to take off any medications on your repeat list as they read them out.

It is relatively common for some patients, usually the elderly, to keep requesting medication they don't need. In some instances, the local chemist keeps requesting their medication on their behalf. These stacks of medication are usually eventually discovered, piled up in a cupboard or room, by a GP on a home visit.

In some cases, you might find some drugs you have been taking for months are surprisingly not on your medication list. This can occur when the drug originally prescribed was not added to your repeat list in the first place. You might have then phoned the practice a month after the initial prescription, and a receptionist just reprinted the original prescription. This is the time to have it added to your repeat medication list.

Stop Medications if Possible

Once your repeat list is tidied, ask yourself if you really need all of these drugs.

In the elderly especially, the use of numerous medications, known as *polypharmacy*, is common. This often leads to drug interactions and unpleasant side effects. Thus, in many such cases, less is more.

Explore the idea of actually coming off some of the medication where appropriate. Long-term antibiotics for acne, years of antidepressants for anxiety or depression, and cocktails of painkillers are common ones.

Coming off medication is not for everyone and can be a challenge, requiring willpower, commitment and lifestyle change.

Many chronic conditions, like type II diabetes and some forms of hypertension, to name a few, can be reversed by weight loss through a change in diet and lifestyle.

Ask your GP, nurse or pharmacist what lifestyle modifications you can make and formulate a plan. If you feel you can't come off any of your tablets, make sure they are actually working for what they were prescribed for.

The Prince of Wales once remarked how dependent on drugs we are all becoming, adding how easily doctors prescribe them as a universal panacea.

I must say I agree with him—doctors and patients must change their approach to get better results, especially with regards to chronic disease.

I remember a nice man who came with his wife for a medication review. He looked extremely anxious, breathing heavily as sweat poured down his forehead. He was taking a total of 22 tablets and had every ailment you can think of. His ever-so-pleasant wife, who always accompanied him, pointed to his direction and said, "So, in a nutshell..." I almost missed the pun.

Trim

Medication compliance falls as the number of drugs increase [(1)]. This is particularly true with the elderly. A simple way of reducing the number of drugs is to opt for combination drugs. A commonly known combination drug is Co-codamol, made up of varying doses of codeine and a fixed dose of paracetamol.

Alternatively, you could be prescribed codeine phosphate and paracetamol separately, making two tablets.

There are many blood pressure combinations as well as oral antidiabetic drug combinations.

The drawback of drug combinations is less flexibility with dose increases.

Dosing

The number of times and tablets you take can be reduced by simply changing the dosing regimen. A twice-a-day formulation is better than a four-times-a-day one.

A common example of this is the antibiotic Nitrofurantoin prescribed for urinary tract infections (UTI), which comes in a 100mg modified release form (MR) or a 50mg form. The dosing regimens are one 100mg MR twice a day or one 50mg tablets four times a day.

I would prefer twice a twice-a-day formulation anytime.

Mention Side Effects

Surprisingly, some patients never mention side effects, allergies or intolerances they have while taking their medication. They thus keep taking their medication religiously, probably because they have been *prescribed by a doctor!* Generally speaking, there is always an alternative to a drug you are taking, and enduring endless suffering can therefore be avoided.

Establishing if a symptom you develop is a side effect or not can be a tricky business. Don't expect your GP therefore to be able to tell you with precision if your tablets are the culprit. Stopping your medication for a few days and monitoring your symptoms is sometimes the only way to establish *causation* and thus rule out coincidence. In essence, you are the best doctor in this circumstance to figure this out.

Some drugs have commonly known side effects, which I discuss in Chapter 44.

Consider a Drug Formulation Change

It is also important to realise there are differences between tablets and capsules. Tablets and capsules use different excipients, which themselves might cause intolerances.

An excipient, also known as a bulking agent or filler, is a substance added to the active ingredient of a particular medication. Excipients help increase a drug's effect by improving absorption, increasing stability and more.

In some cases, intolerance could be solved by simply switching from tablets to capsules or vice versa. Tablets tend to have additional colours, which sometimes cause intolerances.

An advantage capsules have is the inability to taste the medication, which in some cases is quite unpalatable. However, they cannot be scored if you need half the dose prescribed.

I once visited an elderly lady who had recently been discharged from hospital.

She had been prescribed a 20mg dose of Omeprazole, but the hospital pharmacy had dispensed 40mg. As I walked into her home, she had the capsules on the chopping board with powder everywhere and was holding a bread knife!

If you have problems swallowing tablets, you can crush them and mix them with water. Equally, you could open up the capsules and mix the powder with water or a liquid of your choice, but please check with your pharmacist first.

If tablets or capsules are simply not for you then a liquid formulation could do, but some are extremely expensive, costing in excess of £500 for a 50ml bottle.

The same argument above holds for branded and generic medications, which have similar active ingredients but generally different excipients. This explains why you might tolerate a branded drug but have side effects with a generic one.

However, your GP might swear they are identical and refute whatever you say.

I used to maintain this position myself many years ago!

Food-Drug Interactions

An area most often overlooked is food drug interactions.

Probably the most commonly known of these interactions is the blood thinner warfarin and leafy vegetables. These vegetables contain high levels of vitamin K, which reverse the blood-thinning effects of warfarin.

Grapefruit juice contains chemical compounds called furanocoumarins. These compounds interact with some statins, mainly simvastatin and atorvastatin, to increase their levels. As a result, the risk of side effects increases.

Tyramine foods and monoamine oxidase (MAO) inhibitors and Parkinson's drugs—aged and fermented foods like cheeses, red wine, processed meats, sauerkraut, miso, tempeh contain an amino acid called tyramine. Tyramine potentially interacts with MAO inhibitors, causing spuriously high blood pressures.

Beware of Alcohol

Many patients often ask if they can drink alcohol while taking their medication. This is not advisable, why? Alcohol increases the activity of an enzyme in the liver called cytochrome P450 (CYP 450), involved in the metabolism of drugs.

Increased levels of CYP450 can thus alter drug levels in the blood with potential consequences. Some anti-epileptics like phenytoin and carbamazepine increase the activity of CYP450, while some antibiotics like erythromycin and ciprofloxacin, antifungals like fluconazole, and antidepressants like fluoxetine inhibit it.

Double-Check

Once your prescription has been printed out, the first thing to do is double-check the medication and dose on the prescription. Don't be surprised if at some point down the line you notice a generic drug on your list. This is usually done to save money as some drugs are simply too expensive, thus increasing the practice's prescribing budget and consequently NHS spend. All in all, generic drugs are just as effective as the branded ones, although there are some differences that astute patients quickly pick up on.

Some drugs, however, are best prescribed in branded form and include some anti-epileptics and some long-acting blood pressure medications.

The Medication Label

I feel confident in saying that most GPs loathe the phone call or *task* about a patient querying a drug just prescribed after reading the prescription label.

It is good practice to read the label, but some of the exhaustive listed contraindications are probably just drug companies taking extra precautions (covering their backs).

If your GP were to follow everything written on the leaflet, they would only be able to safely prescribe ice or water. However, do seek advice from your GP if unsure ☺

---

1) Michael D Murray, Kurt Kroenke, "Polypharmacy and Medication Adherence Small Steps on a Long Road." *J Gen Intern Med.* 2001 Feb; 16(2): 137–139. doi: 10.1111/j.1525-1497.2001.01229.x

CHAPTER 43

WORKING EFFICIENTLY WITH THE PRACTICE AND PHARMACIST

It is easy to get a thousand prescriptions but hard to get one single remedy.

-Chinese proverb

Repeat prescriptions by your GP can either be issued as paper copies or as electronic prescriptions (EPS).

NHS paper prescriptions, also known as FP10s, are divided into two parts—a left side in green, where your requested medication is printed and signed, and a right side in white. The white side has all your repeat medications listed and is also where any private prescriptions are printed and signed.

As mentioned above, you can phone the surgery to request items from your repeat prescription list when you run out. Most surgeries allow a 48-hour turnover period for your prescription to be ready. This is a frequent area of frustration as patients expect everything to be ready instantly. However, please remember the GP working day is extremely busy, and most GPs need to check any prescriptions they sign to avoid any errors.

Medications on your repeat list are dispensed by the chemist, who tears the green side off for use and hands you the right side. If they are your *nominated pharmacy* they get to keep the white side with which they can request further prescriptions from your GP on your behalf.

However, every drug on a repeat medication list has a time limit, after which you will be required to book an appointment to *review your medication*. The time limit set for most repeat medications on average is 12 months, although any interval period from two to 12 months is possible.

You will normally get a message from your GP surgery advising you to book a medication review or from your pharmacy if they request medications on your behalf.

With regards to electronic prescriptions (EPS), the process is slightly different.

Your GP generates an EPS, which gets sent to a digital hub or platform called *spine*.

Spine is a digital healthcare platform that was built by British Telecom (BT).

From the *spine* the prescription then gets relayed to your *nominated* pharmacy.

The process should take no more than a few minutes, but occasionally IT glitches might delay the transfer—*the computer says no!*

Once the transfer is made, the chemist can now *download* your prescription and dispense the relevant medication.

In the event the medication you need is not in stock please ask them to issue a *token* for you take to an alternate pharmacy. A *token* contains a barcode that can be scanned in seconds, revealing your required medication.

Failing this, you will need to provide three forms of ID to get your medication at another chemist. A *token* thus saves time for you, the chemist and anyone else waiting.

CHAPTER 44

COMMONLY PRESCRIBED DRUGS & THEIR SIDE EFFECTS

I counted everything. I counted the steps to the road, the steps to church, the number of dishes and silverware I washed... Anything that could be counted, I did.

-Katherine Johnson

Non-Steroidal Anti-Inflammatories (NSAIDs)

To understand these drugs, it is best to start with the inflammatory process.

Inflammation is a complex process that serves as the body's defence, involving blood cells, blood vessels and powerful chemicals called prostaglandins.

Prostaglandins are involved in varied processes in the body, namely the sensation of pain, narrowing or widening of blood vessels, platelet clumping (aggregation) and temperature control regulation, to name a few.

NSAIDs block the production of prostaglandins, thus interfering with pain sensation, temperature regulation and platelet aggregation, among other functions. All NSAIDs therefore provide pain relief, reduce inflammation and reduce temperature, although to different degrees.

Aspirin and Ibuprofen are probably the commonest NSAIDS prescribed.

Aspirin's strength lies in its antiplatelet activity, and it has a weak pain reduction property at low doses, while Ibuprofen is used more for its anti-inflammatory action, great for musculoskeletal (joint) pain.

Other commonly prescribed NSAIDs are Naproxen and Diclofenac, with Naproxen having the lowest cardiovascular risk profile of the two.

Indomethacin is sometimes prescribed to treat gout but tends to have higher side effects.

Common side effects of NSAID are stomach pain and occasionally bleeding. This is because the prostaglandins are involved in the production of mucous, which lines the stomach. As the NSAIDs block prostaglandin production, the stomach is not protected, leading to gastric symptoms from irritation.

Painkillers (Analgesics)

Paracetamol

Paracetamol is probably the most popular drug known to all. It is mainly used to treat fever and pain and is available as a syrup, tablets, capsules, suppositories and in intravenous form. It is also available in combination with codeine (cocodamol), tramadol (tramacet) or many over-the-counter cold and cough remedies.

The normal adult dose of paracetamol is 1g (two tablets) four times a day.

Paracetamol is highly toxic to the liver cells at high doses and thus a preferred drug used in overdoses in suicidal patients.

In an attempt to reduce suicide risk, the over-the-counter sale of paracetamol has been limited to two boxes of 16 paracetamols per pack per transaction.

Opiate-Based Drugs

These are a commonly prescribed category of painkillers that are generally speaking quite potent and thus good for pain control. The only problem with them is the high risk of dependence, and thus they are frequently abused.

They are also notorious for causing constipation, therefore having a laxative on standby is a good idea.

Examples include Codeine Phosphate, Cocodamol and Dihydrocodeine.

Both Cocodamol and Dihydrocodeine come in 15mg, 30mg or 60mg doses.

Cocodamol comprises a fixed 500mg dose of paracetamol with varying doses of 8mg, 15mg and 30mg doses of codeine.

Tramadol is another commonly prescribed opioid, which promises less constipation but occasionally causes drowsiness and even hallucinations.

Morphine is commonly prescribed in various forms but all generally quite potent and for severe pain. It comes in tablets, capsules, liquids or patches, and the side effects of constipation and drowsiness equally apply.

Buprenorphine (Butrans) are opioid-based pain patches, ideal for either those who can't swallow or those who require a steady constant dose of pain control over time. They come in three doses and last a week before a new patch is applied. Pain patches are ideal in the nursing or care home setting.

Methotrexate

Methotrexate is a drug mainly used to suppress the immune system (immune suppressant) and for chemotherapy of some types of cancers.

Methotrexate works by blocking dihydrofolate reductase, an enzyme necessary in the formation of DNA. It is most commonly prescribed to treat rheumatoid arthritis and belongs to the group of drugs called disease modifying anti rheumatic drugs (DMARDs).

Methotrexate is a potent drug, potentially causing bone marrow suppression, liver and kidney toxicity among other effects. Frequent monitoring in the way of blood tests is therefore needed, including FBCs, U&Es, and LFTs.

Methotrexate is not tolerated by all, and if you are struggling, your consultant might swap your treatment for the newer *biologic agents.*

Due to its enzyme-blocking activity, it is recommended to take folic acid tablets while taking methotrexate.

Prednisolone

Prednisolone is a steroid mainly prescribed for acute attacks of asthma or chronic obstructive pulmonary disease (COPD). It is also used for gout, polymyalgia rheumatica, rheumatoid arthritis and many other autoimmune conditions.

Depending on length of time taken, weaning off the dose gradually before stopping is advised. It is not recommended to stay on high-dose steroids for prolonged periods of time as this can potentially lead to diabetes and Cushing's syndrome. My recommendation is always to opt for the lowest dose possible.

Proton Pump Inhibitors (PPIs)

The stomach lining is made up of special cells called parietal cells. Parietal cells secrete hydrochloric acid (HCL) and intrinsic factor, a protein necessary for the absorption of vitamin B12.

PPIs like Lanzoprazole, Omeprazole, Esomeprazole and so on block the production of HCL. The rationale for their use is that High HCL causes reflux symptoms and *indigestion.*

PPIs generally work quite fast and are great for healing ulcers.

However, taking them long term can lead to chronic low acid (achlorhydria), potentially resulting in mineral deficiencies, especially B12, dysbiosis and small intestinal overgrowth (SIBO) [(1)].

I remember a nice Polish lady who wanted a PPI prescribed and asked if she could get "a tablet for security of my stomach." What a creative mind!

Inhalers

Inhalers are handheld devices that deliver various types of medications via the lungs. They are commonly called *pumps* or *puffers*, due to their mode of operation. There are huge arrays of inhalers available and they are commonly prescribed for the treatment of asthma and emphysema/chronic obstructive pulmonary disease (COPD).

Asthma Inhalers and Medication

There are two basic classes of drugs used in asthma treatment, namely bronchodilators and anti-inflammatory drugs. Bronchodilators increase the size of the airways (bronchi) while anti-inflammatory drugs reduce the inflammation present in them.

There are two main types of bronchodilators commonly prescribed and they're named according to the receptors they act on. One type of bronchodilator is further divided into short-acting and long-acting based on the duration of effect on the airways.

Short-acting bronchodilators are also called *relievers* and are taken as and when, depending on symptoms. The commonest example prescribed is Salbutamol/Ventolin/Blue inhaler. Salbutamol increases airway size by activating the beta 2 receptors. This explains why some *beta blockers* sometimes worsen breathing.

An example of a long-acting bronchodilator is Salmeterol.

The second class of drugs for asthma treatment are anti-inflammatory drugs.

There are two main types in this category, namely leukotriene receptor antagonists (LTRAs) and corticosteroids.

Leukotrienes are mediators of inflammation, thus LRTAs block their action, and they therefore reduce airway inflammation. They are a handy treatment option for children as they come in granules. A common example is Montelukast.

Corticosteroids reduce airway inflammation and come in two forms, namely inhalers or oral tablets. The commonest inhaled steroid or *preventer* is Beclomethasone (QVAR). It is commonly known as the brown inhaler due to its colour. Preventers are taken daily irrespective of symptoms, usually twice a day.

The commonest oral corticosteroid prescribed is prednisolone, already discussed above.

COPD Inhalers and Medication

There are generally two types of treatment, namely bronchodilators, which are mainly inhalers, and mucolytics, taken orally. Bronchodilators increase the size of the airways (bronchi) and are further divided into short-acting and long-acting.

First, we have the short-acting bronchodilators so named because of their short onset of action. Examples of short acting bronchodilator include Salbutamol (Blue inhaler/Ventolin) and Ipratropium (Atrovent).

A combination of Salbutamol and Atrovent is sold under the name Combivent.

Next, we have the **long-acting bronchodilators**, which have a longer action.

Common ones include Salmeterol (Serevent) and Tiotropium bromide (Spiriva/green inhaler).

Mucolytics are often prescribed to COPD sufferers who struggle to bring up phlegm, especially as the pathology progresses. They work by loosening up thick phlegm, making it easier to cough up. Carbocysteine is an example of a common mucolytic.

Vitamin D

Vitamin D has gained tremendous popularity over the last few years. This is most probably largely due to work by Dr Michael Holick, an endocrinologist from Boston University.

Vitamin D has been traditionally been known for increasing absorption of calcium from the intestines, which is used to build bone tissue. This explains why a deficiency of vitamin D causes a form of rickets.

Over the last few years, vitamin D's role in the body has been studied and found to impact multiple body systems. It has been found to possibly have a role in immunity, obesity and even mental health diseases like depression.

If you are vitamin D deficient, the recommended treatment regime is to take one 20,000IU tablet of vitamin D twice a week for seven weeks. This is called a loading dose and is important, especially if your levels are very low. After a loading dose, you can start taking a much lower dose on a daily basis.

Make sure you check how many IU of vitamin D you buy in your local health shop or trusted online shop. Don't just get the *strongest vitamin D we have* or you risk an overdose!

Antibiotics

Antibiotics are chemical substances that inhibit or kill the growth of bacteria.

The first ever antibiotic, penicillin G, was discovered by Sir Alexander Fleming, a Scottish physician and microbiologist, in 1928.

The discovery of antibiotics changed the course of medicine, before which millions of people died of infectious diseases. Today, however, overuse has led to resistant species of bacteria (superbugs) like Clostridium difficile (C diff) and Methicillin Resistant Staphylococcus Aureus (MRSA).

Antibiotics belong to different classes based on how they work, with some destroying the cell membranes, ribosomes or blocking specific proteins in the bacterial cell.

Many antibiotics cause thrush, but, more importantly, they can decimate your healthy gut flora (microbiome). This can result in dysbiosis [(2)], potentially having lasting implications with regards to your overall health and vitality.

There is more on this in Part 4 of this book.

Antihypertensives (Blood Pressure Tablets)

These are drugs used to treat high blood pressure and work in different ways.

A handy algorithm used as a guide by clinicians for initiation of BP medication is the **ACD** rule (previously **ABCD rule**), which stands for:

A-Angiotensin converting enzyme (**A**CE) Inhibitors
Most drugs in this category all end in *pril*. Eg Ramipril, Enalapril, Lisinopril, etc.
C-**C**alcium channel blockers, e.g. Amlodipine, Nifedipine
D-**D**iuretics e.g. Bendroflumethiazide, Indapamide, etc.
(The **B** in the ABCD rule stands for beta blockers, and mostly all end in olol. E.g. Propranolol, Labetolol, etc.)

Applying the ACD rule is easy, and here is how it works: Patients are classed into two groups based on age and race: Those aged <55 or non-Black in one group, while those aged>55 or Black in another.

In a newly diagnosed hypertensive age <55, or non-Black, the first choice/step antihypertensive is any drug from the **A** (ACE Inhibitor) category.

(Black patients don't respond well to ACE inhibitors, and are prone to an increased risk of angioedema (swelling of the lips and tongue)

Equally, in a newly diagnosed hypertensive age >55 or Black, the first choice/ step antihypertensive is taken from the C (calcium channel blocker) category.

The next (second) step in BP management in both groups is a drug from either category. In other words, both groups end up with an **A+C** or **C+A** picture, with the only difference being the order of initiation.

The third step in managing BP in both groups is addition of any drug from the **D** (Diuretic) category.

Here are two quick examples that will hopefully make things a little clearer.

You are 30-year-old Caucasian fit and well patient but have been diagnosed with high blood pressure.

The first choice antihypertensive would be from the **A** category (e.g. Ramipril). Assuming after a maximum dose of Ramipril your BP is still not controlled, the next choice would be from the **C** category (e.g. Amlodipine).

If after the maximum dose of Amlodipine your BP is still not controlled, it is now time to add a Diuretic (D, e.g. Bendrofluazide) to the mix.

In the second example, you are a 60-year-old Black fit and healthy man with recently diagnosed hypertension. Being more than 55 and Black the first choice is from the **C** category (Amlodipine 5mg). If, however, despite taking the maximum dose of Amlodipine your BP is still high, your GP will initiate a drug from the **A** category.

However, knowing you are Black and don't tolerate Ace Inhibitors like Ramipril, an option is a drug from the ARB (Angiotensin receptor Blocker) class like Losartan. If after a maximum dose of an ARB, your BP is still not controlled, similarly to the previous example, it is time to add a D to the mix. So, you would potentially end up with an **A** (ARB) **+C+D** combination to get adequate BP control.

If your GP has exhausted all the above drugs in the ACD algorithm, don't despair as there are still a few more drugs in their armoury. These drugs include beta blockers (Propranolol, Atenolol, etc.), alpha blockers (e.g. Doxazosin) and aldosterone antagonists (e.g. Spironolactone).

Please note these are guidelines only, which in application may vary depending on your medical history.

On a more practical note, once a drug is initiated, please double-check your GP has added them to your repeat medication list. If you don't tolerate a particular drug, also make sure this is added to your list of intolerances or allergies. Failing this, you might get muddled down the line, not knowing exactly what you are meant to be taking. Things get even more confusing if you see a different GP each time, who might struggle themselves to make sense of the whole situation.

Furosemide

Furosemide is a diuretic, commonly known as a *water tablet* due to its action on the kidneys by excreting excess water. It is mainly used to treat oedema (fluid overload) in the lower limbs of the elderly from poorly functioning veins and oedema in the lower limbs, abdomen and lung from congestive heart failure.

Furosemide is also used to treat hypertension.

Taking Furosemide in the evening isn't a good idea, unless you prefer to spend the night in the bathroom.

Antidepressants

Antidepressants are drugs used to treat patients suffering from moderate to severe depression.

In the 1950s, the biogenic amine theory was formulated, which explained depression as low levels of three neurotransmitters in the brain, namely norepinephrine, serotonin and dopamine. However, the mechanism of action of antidepressants is not fully understood.

Antidepressants are classified into various classes, with commonly prescribed ones belonging to the selective serotonin reuptake inhibitors (SSRIs), serotonin-norepinephrine reuptake inhibitors (SNRI), tricyclic antidepressants (TCAs) and atypical antidepressants.

Selective Serotonin Reuptake Inhibitors (SSRIs)

Commonly prescribed drugs under this class are Fluoxetine, Citalopram and Sertraline. They are generally used to treat anxiety as well as depression and can occasionally cause gastrointestinal side effects like nausea, bloating, diarrhoea or constipation.

Selective Noradrenaline Reuptake Inhibitors (SNRIs)

Venlafaxine is the commonest in this class.

Tricyclic Antidepressants (TCAs)

The TCAs block the uptake of serotonin and norepinephrine into the neuron.

They also block alpha adrenergic, histaminic and muscarinic receptors, whose normal functions are blocked, leading to potential side effects.

Amitriptyline is the commonest drug here and is used for depression as well as headaches, chronic neuropathic-type pain and back pain. It sometimes causes a dry mouth or drowsiness. With regards to drowsiness, taking the dose earlier in the evening might be all you need to do. A dry mouth is more difficult to resolve, and it might be worth swapping altogether.

Imipramine is used to treat bedwetting (enuresis).

TCAs commonly cause a dry mouth and are best avoided at high doses in the elderly as they also potentially cause markedly low blood pressure (hypotension) by blocking the muscarinic receptors. This is a relatively common cause of falls in the elderly.

Two commonly prescribed antidepressants are Trazodone and Mirtazapine, and they belong to the class of *atypical antidepressants.* These are the preferred choice of drug if insomnia is a symptom of depression.

The decision to start taking antidepressants should never be made lightly. It is quite common these days for doctors to prescribe them on a whim, partly due to expectations and pressure from patients.

Ideally you should try various lifestyle techniques like meditation, exercise, and dietary changes before contemplating medication. Any stressors at home or at work should be explored and a plan put in place to resolve them. There are many causes of a low mood, and throwing antidepressants at every case is never the answer.

It is worth pointing out that it takes on average two to three weeks for their effects to be felt. In some cases, you might feel worse, and the advice is usually to carry on for a few more weeks or so. This is easy to say by someone not going through the symptoms themselves. However, you might find swapping medication too early eventually leads to frustration and further exacerbation of symptoms as the right drug is never found.

If you still feel depressed despite being on a good dose of an antidepressant for a reasonable length of time, it might be worth revisiting the history. This is because you might actually have bipolar disorder, misdiagnosed as depression.

If we are definitely dealing with depression, an option would be to swap drugs in the same class or swap classes altogether.

Another option is to consider adding a drug from another class of antidepressant to the existing one. This method is called *augmentation* and involves a combination of various classes of antidepressants to achieve a good clinical effect.

It is also recommended to stay on any antidepressants for at least six months and then eventually taper off when ready, rather than stopping abruptly.

A simple tapering off regime could be taking a tablet on alternative days or halving your initial dose for a defined period.

Tranquilisers

These are drugs generally used to treat anxiety and agitation in the short term.

Common examples are Diazepam and Temazapam, which belong to the benzodiazepine drug class. These drugs are highly addictive and are best taken for short-term use only to prevent dependence.

Some patients either abuse these drugs or sell them on the black market.

Typically, they usually all turn up with familiar excuses like, "I forgot my tablets at my grandma's house," (poor grandma) or, "My girlfriend flushed my tablets down the toilet."

Many years ago, some law firms (Sue, Grabbit and Runne) had a field day suing GPs on the premise they had not told their patients tranquilisers were addictive!

Benzodiazepines are quite useful in the care home setting for agitation, restlessness and anxiety, from various reasons.

Sleeping Tablets

As the name suggests, sleeping tablets help with sleeplessness (insomnia).

Zoplicone is the commonest example and comes in 3.75 and 7mg tablets.

Similar to tranquilisers, it is recommended for short-term use only as dependence is common.

Gabapentin and Pregabalin

Gabapentin and Pregabalin are anticonvulsants (antiepileptics) but are also used for an array of conditions including restless leg syndrome, nerve pain, fibromyalgia and, anxiety. Both drugs are commonly abused with gabapentin and pregabalin commanding high prices on the black market and in prisons.

Statins

Statins are a group of drugs that inhibit cholesterol production by the liver by inhibiting the action of the enzyme HMG-CoA reductase.

Statins reduce a type of cholesterol called low-density lipoprotein (LDL) as well as the total cholesterol level. They also reduce to a lesser degree a type of fat called triglycerides, although a class of drug called fibrates do a better job of this.

A reduction in lipids or cholesterol is thought to translate to a reduction in cardiovascular risk. The lower the cholesterol level, the lower the cardiovascular risk one therefore has. It is, however, not that straightforward and a comprehensive risk profile can be calculated using a tool called the QRISK2.

(The Framingham risk score is used in America)

The QRISK2 score is simply an algorithm that predicts your risk of getting a cardiovascular event (stroke, TIA/mini stroke, angina, myocardial infarction/heart attack) within 10 years. To do this, it uses a combination of personal data (age, ethnicity, body mass index (BMI), blood pressure, cholesterol level) and medical history—hypertension, atrial fibrillation, history of cardiovascular disease, family history of cardiovascular diseases, smoking status, diabetes, rheumatoid arthritis and chronic kidney disease.

The commonest side effects of statins are muscle aches and pains, although there are many more reported from my clinical experience. Some patients just don't tolerate them even after switching from one drug to the other.

Rarely, they cause a condition called rhabdomyolysis, which means muscle damage. A quick blood test to check for an enzyme called creatinine phosphokinase (CPK) is recommended at this stage and preferably after initiation just in case.

Remember cell membranes are made of cholesterol, so beware of trying to reduce your cholesterol level to the lowest number. Taking statins long term can potentially reduce levels of co-enzyme Q10 (Co-Q10), a natural substance found in the body that acts as an antioxidant and energy regenerator in the cell.

This could potentially have implications with regards to overall cardiovascular health according to some studies. [(3)] I recommend supplementing with a high quality CoQ10 supplement.

Blood Thinners

Antiplatelets (Aspirin, Clopidogrel and Dipyridamole)
Platelets are the tiny cells that help your blood clot.

Aspirin

Aspirin usually comes as a 75mg tablet and works by preventing platelets clumping together, a term known as platelet aggregation. Aspirin is prescribed in patients to prevent strokes or heart attacks. It is also used for pain. Its commonest side effects are bleeding from the gastrointestinal tract.

Clopidogrel

This is another antiplatelet prescribed to prevent strokes or heart attacks.

It is sometimes prescribed in combination with aspirin

Dipyridamole

This prevents clot formation and also dilates blood vessels.

Anticoagulants (Warfarin, Heparin, NOAC)

All anticoagulants prevent the blood from clotting. A common side effect with all of them is bleeding to varying degrees.

Warfarin

The name warfarin is a composite of two words: WARF stands for Wisconstin Alumni Research Foundation, while ARIN stems from the word Coumarin.

Warfarin is an old drug, first used as rat poison in the 1950s and later in humans a few years later.

Warfarin is used to either thin the blood once a clot (thrombus) has formed or to prevent further ones from developing. It is used typically for clots in the leg, called deep venous thrombosis (DVT), or clots in the lung called pulmonary embolus (PE). It is also used in cases of an abnormal heart rhythm, called atrial fibrillation (AF).

Warfarin tablets come in different doses, which are constantly changed depending on how *thin* the blood is. An objective assessment of the blood *thinness* is measured by the internationalised normalised ratio (INR).

The INR is a blood test either measured by the lab or more commonly by an automated machine in surgery.

The best way to understand INR is to assume an INR of 1 as standard (without warfarin). Following this, an INR of 2 means it takes twice the amount of time for the blood to clot. An INR of 3 translates to three times the amount of time for the blood to clot, and so on.

Different pathologies have different *target INRs*, but most have a target of between 2 and 3. Pulmonary embolus (PE), deep vein thrombosis (DVT) and atrial fibrillation (AF) all have target INRs of 2.5. In practice, any reading between 2 and 3 is acceptable. If you have a metallic heart valve, the target INR is usually 3–3.5.

So, the higher the INR, the *thinner* your blood becomes, and consequently the longer it takes to clot. With this in mind, it follows the thinner the blood, the less warfarin you need.

All patients taking warfarin should have a *Yellow Book*, which states clearly at the front their target INR. Subsequent pages then show their current INR and the dose of warfarin to be taken over a set period.

The traditional way of calculating the dose of warfarin required to produce a target INR is prediction, based on previous readings. If a certain INR deviates unexpectedly from the norm, an estimated dose of warfarin is suggested. The dose is either reduced or increased depending on the INR, usually done a few days after the change.

These days, INRs are fed into an automated machine that works out the dose of warfarin needed by complex algorithms.

Factors that cause unexpected INR deviations include binge drinking, taking certain medication, a change in diet or even infection, amongst other things.

All the above factors either increase or decrease the activity of a liver enzyme called Cytochrome P450, which metabolises warfarin among other things.

It is not uncommon to see patients who have become muddled eventually overdosing on warfarin. This is potentially dangerous and can cause anything from bleeding gums, nosebleeds, and coughing up blood to black, tarry stools or easy bruising and continuous bleeding from minor cuts.

If your GP suspects an overdose of warfarin, you will need a vitamin K injection administered in the hospital depending on the INR.

Warfarin therefore needs continuous monitoring and taken appropriately prevents complications.

Some patients are now opting for the new class of blood thinners called Novel Oral Anticoagulants (NOACs) that *thin* the blood without the *hassle* of regular INR monitoring. They are not appropriate for all, but most find them brilliant.

Novel Oral Anticoagulants (NOAC)

NOACs are a relatively new class of drug, useful in patients who have blood clotting diseases. They are a convenient option for people who would like to avoid the hassle of warfarin monitoring. All NOACS end in the suffix *aban* (Rivaroxaban, Apixaban etc.).

Many practices are swapping warfarin for NOACS for their patients, unless there are any contraindications.

Heparin

Heparin is a common anticoagulant used to prevent blood clots in the veins (DVT) and lungs (PE). It is administered as an injection, usually in the abdomen.

Antimuscarinics

This category of drugs is mainly used for treating urinary incontinence from spasm of the bladder muscle. As the name implies, they block action of muscarinic receptors found in the bladder wall muscle (detrusor). The end result is less contractions and reduced incontinence. Common examples include Oxybutynin, Solifenacin, Tolterodine, etc. They sometimes cause a dry mouth but the newer ones less so.

Alpha Blockers

Alpha blockers are a class of drug used to treat high blood pressure. They are also used to treat enlargement of the prostate gland, also called benign prostatic hyperplasia (BPH).

As the name implies, they work on the alpha receptors present on the blood vessels and bladder neck. This causes an increase in diameter of blood vessels and relaxation of the prostate and bladder neck muscles. The result is lower blood pressure and increased urinary flow.

Alpha blockers are thus the ideal choice for men with both high blood pressure and lower urinary tract symptoms from the prostate. Its effect on BPH is quite quick.

Finasteride

Finasteride belongs to the class of 5-alpha reductase inhibitors. It is a drug mainly used to treat an enlarged prostate (benign prostatic hyperplasia) or hair loss in men. Its effect in shrinking the prostate is slow and it's frequently used in combination with alpha blockers.

Metformin

Metformin is an old drug, developed as far back as 1922. It is a common drug used to lower blood sugar, prescribed for type II diabetics. Metformin is also occasionally prescribed for women who have polycystic ovary syndrome (PCOS).

Metformin works by increasing tissue sensitivity to insulin, therefore facilitating glucose transport into fat and muscle tissues.

The dose of Metformin varies from 500mg once a day up to 1g twice a day depending on the blood sugar control.

Metformin occasionally causes bloating, diarrhoea or other gastrointestinal symptoms. Swapping to Glucophage, the modified release form, resolves the problem in most cases.

Metformin can lower vitamin B12, causing pins and needles or numbness in the arms or lower legs, known as peripheral neuropathy. If this happens, please ask your doctor to check your vitamin B12 levels, but be careful what range is considered *normal.*

In some cases, taking a good quality B12 supplement resolves the issue, although discontinuing the drug altogether might be a solution. However, it is important to note that diabetes in itself can potentially cause nerve damage (peripheral neuropathy) as the high glucose levels damage nerves.

Sulphonylureas, eg Gliclazide.

Their mechanism of action is by stimulating the beta cells of the pancreas to produce more insulin. They potentially cause a low blood sugar (hypoglycaemia).

You should ideally be prescribed a glucose meter and test strips for self-glucose monitoring.

Hypoglycaemia is by definition a blood sugar level of <4mmol/L and is a potentially dangerous condition.

Signs and symptoms of hypoglycaemia are numerous and vary from general malaise, drowsiness, confusion, and irritability to shaking, fits (seizures) and even unconsciousness.

If you are a driver who takes Gliclazide, or any antidiabetic tablets that potentially cause hypoglycaemia for that matter, you must inform the Driver and Vehicle and Licensing Agency (DVLA).

Glitazones, e.g. Pioglitazone

They reduce insulin resistance and therefore increase glucose transport into the cells.

Glitazones potentially worsen heart failure by causing fluid retention. They should therefore be avoided in these groups of patients.

Dipeptidyl Peptidase 4 (DPP-4 Inhibitors) eg Sitagliptin (Junuvia)

They are taken once a day and are tolerated by many patients.

Prandial regulators (Repaglinide)

They stimulate the beta cells of the pancreas to secrete insulin and are best taken before a meal.

Like Gliclazide, they can potentially cause hypoglycaemia.

Glucagon-Like Peptide-1 (GLP-1) agonists

Unlike the previously described agents, which are all oral formulations, the GLP-1 agonists are injections.

The GLP-1 agonists are thought to enhance insulin secretion by the beta cells of the pancreas.

Exenetide (Byetta) and Liraglutide (Victoza) are the two commonly prescribed ones and administered either as a 5mcg or 10mcg twice-a-day injection.

An interesting fact about Exenetide is its isolation from the saliva of the Gila (Hee-la) monster, a venomous lizard found in parts of America and Mexico.

Also available is a newer once-a-week formulation, marketed under the name of Bydureon.

Side effects tend to be mainly gastrointestinal in nature, including bloating, nausea and a generally unsettled stomach.

Canagliflozin

Canagliflozin works on special receptors in the kidney that help excrete sugar in the urine.

A relatively common side effect is frequent attacks of thrush and urine infections, due to accumulation of glucose in the urine.

Insulin:

If your HBA1C level remains relatively high despite the maximum dose of the acceptable drug combinations, the next step is insulin.

The topic of insulin is an extremely broad one, but I'll attempt to give you a broad overview.

In 1921, insulin was discovered in the pancreatic extract from dogs, by Canadian orthopaedic surgeon Dr Frederick Banting and a medical student, Charles Best.

A year later, injected purified insulin would save the life of a critically ill 14-year-old type I diabetic.

Since isolation of animal insulin from cows and pigs, advances have been made from genetically produced human insulin in the laboratory using recombinant DNA technology to synthesising insulin analogues, which have slightly different properties.

We therefore have four types of insulin based on their onset of action, namely rapid acting, short acting, intermediate acting and long acting.

Rapid-acting and short-acting insulins have a relatively quick onset of action, with effects lasting up to 12 hours or so.

The long acting insulins have a longer onset of action, potentially lasting up to 24 hours.

The intermediate insulins have an onset of action between the above three types.

Different insulin regimes are initiated in an attempt to mimic the way insulin is naturally produced by the pancreas.

Although the commonest way of administering insulins is via insulin pens, it can also be administered via insulin pumps, insulin jet injectors and insulin inhalers.

Some practices run in-house diabetic clinics, and most have *a diabetic nurse* who may seek advice from a GP, preferably one with a *special interest* in diabetes.

The first appointment is usually the longest and involves reiterating the basics of diabetes, various types of insulin and their action, symptoms of hypoglycaemia, and, most importantly, diet.

You will be prescribed the choice of insulin, lancets or a lancing device, and a glucose meter, complete with testing strips.

Repetitive injections on one site cause *lipodystrophy* (loss of fat tissue), hence the advice to rotate sites.

Frequent blood testing is mandatory while on insulin and is done by pricking the tip of the finger, usually via a lancet device, and slowly applying pressure to get a blood sample.

Last but not least, you need a glucose meter, which reads off the glucose level from a drop of blood from your fingertip.

Blood glucose readings are commonly called BMs, an abbreviation that somehow caught on from the testing strips produced by the pharmaceutical company Boehringer Mannheim, now known as Roche.

Essentially, a starting dose of insulin (denoted in units) is prescribed based on a rough calculation and monitored over time by frequent blood glucose readings.

Depending on your sugar readings over time, the dose of insulin is either increased or decreased.

After monitoring for a few months, your insulin regime might be changed altogether depending on the readings you get.

With time, you learn to understand your blood sugar fluctuations with respect to different foods, drink, exercise and other variables.

It can potentially be a difficult task initially, but in a few months, most patients are confident with their self-management.

Those who find it hard to control their diabetes and difficult cases are referred to hospital consultants for further management.

Lastly, it is worth noting that insulin potentially causes weight gain, a situation that ironically requires administration of even higher insulin doses.

For a type I diabetics, insulin is mandatory. However, if you are a type II or other related types, a strict dietary and lifestyle change can potentially spare you insulin, and all of the above tablets for that matter. There is more detail on this in Part 4 of this book.

Orlistat

Orlistat works by blocking the action of a group of enzymes called lipases, which break down fat in the stomach and pancreas. As a result, fat absorption is reduced and passed in the faeces. It is prescribed for patients to help with weight loss. Common side effects include gas, oily discharge and increased stool frequency.

Taking orlistat or any drug of this type for prolonged periods can potentially lead to vitamin depletion as the fat-soluble vitamins (ADEK) are blocked alongside the fat.

However, sustainable weight loss is only achieved with lifestyle modification and diet. I talk a bit more on this in Part 4 of this book.

The Combined Oral Contraceptive Pill (COCP)

The COCP is also commonly known as *The Pill* and contains the hormones oestrogen and progesterone. The difference between various COCPs lies in the proportion of oestrogen and progesterone in them, with some being more oestrogen or progesterone dominant.

Each pill packet contains 28 pills in total. Twenty-one of the 28 pills, also called active pills, contain both hormones. The remaining seven pills in the pack contain no hormones, hence the name dummy pill, and are in the pack just for orientation purposes.

Despite the COCP being a good method of contraception, it does pose a small risk of blood clots, also known as venous thromboembolisms (VTEs).

VTEs are bloods clots that occur in any part of the venous system of the body like pulmonary embolisms (PE) or deep venous thrombosis (DVT). The risk of VTEs is due to the oestrogen in the COCP, which increases the blood's ability to clot. This risk is significantly higher being a smoker over age 35, having a history of hypertension or migraines, a personal or family history of a DVT or PE, and a body mass index (BMI) of >39kg/m2 if less than 35 years old or >30kg/m2 if more than 35 years of age.

The Progesterone Only Pill (POP)/Mini Pill

As the name suggests, the POP contains the hormone progesterone only, in contrast to the combined oral contraceptive (COCP), which contains both progesterone and oestrogen.

Each pill packet contains 28 pills in total, and all contain the active hormone with no dummy pills present like the COCP.

So how is the mini pill taken and how does it work?

A pill is taken at about the same time every day continuously with no break between successive packs. Most POPs have a *three-hour window* within which it can be taken without being considered a missed pill. An exception to the rule is Cerazette, which has a 12-hour window.

The mini pill is an excellent choice of contraception for women who have contraindications to the COCP. This is because they don't contain oestrogen, which, as we know, increases blood clotting.

Depo Provera

Depo Provera, commonly known as *Depo*, is a progesterone-only injectable form of contraception. It is a good option for women who are inclined to forget the pill.

It is administered every three months, usually in the gluteus maximus (bottom).

Common side effects are mood changes, spotting (especially in the first few months) and overeating, leading to weight gain.

Implanon and Nexplanon

Implanon, commonly known as the *implant*, is also a progesterone-only form of contraception. It is a slender, short, flexible rod, which releases a progesterone hormone. It is usually sited in the inner part of the woman's upper arm and lasts up to three years.

Side effects include absence of bleeding (hence why some women choose Implanon) or spotting.

Mirena Coil

The Mirena coil is a small plastic T-shaped device with strings, coated with a progesterone hormone. It is inserted via an applicator in the vagina, preferably during menses, where the hormone is released locally. It is a great contraceptive option for women who have had children or who suffer from heavy bleeding. It is effective for up to five years.

Nuvaring

The Nuvaring is a flexible rubber ring measuring about 5cm, coated with oestrogen and progesterone. It is inserted into the vagina via an applicator for three weeks where it is kept in place by the vaginal muscles. It is then taken out for one week, similar to what one would do with the combined oral contraceptive (COCP) and another reinserted as before. It has all the contraindications of the COCP

Contraceptive Patch

The contraceptive patch is a sticky plaster-like square fabric laced with oestrogen and progesterone hormones. A single patch is applied to the skin of the upper shoulder, abdomen and thigh for one week, after which it is removed. Another patch is applied during the second and third week but none in the fourth week—similar to the combined oral contraceptive (COCP). Its contraindications are similar to the COCP.

---

1) Lewis SJ, Franco S, Young G, O'Keefe SJ. "Altered Bowel Function and Duodenal Bacterial Overgrowth in Patients Treated with Omeprazole." *Aliment Pharmacol Ther.* 1996 Aug;10(4):557-61

2) Hawrelak JA, Myers SP. "The causes of intestinal dysbiosis: A review." *Alternative Medicine Review.* 2004 Jun;9 (2): 180-97

3) Okuyama H et al., "Statins stimulate atherosclerosis and heart failure: pharmacological mechanisms." *Expert Rev Clin Pharmacol.* 2015 Mar;8(2):189-99. doi: 10.1586/17512433.2015.1011125. Epub 2015 Feb 6.

PART 4

AN ALTERNATIVE APPROACH TO HEALTH AND DISEASE

CHAPTER 45

WHY YOUR GP MIGHT NOT HAVE THE ANSWER TO YOUR HEALTHCARE ISSUES

Market participants don't know whether to buy on the rumour and sell on the news, do the opposite, do both or do neither depending on which way the wind is blowing.

Original quote by *State Street Global* financial magazine and used by John Bird on an episode of the *Bird & Fortune* sketch show on the subprime mortgage crisis.

The top three grumbles I get to hear as a GP are lack of appointments, the GP's predilection for paracetamol even for severe pain, and, lastly, the fact their GPs are never able to get to the bottom of their ailments. Instead of finding the root cause of their problems, they just throw more and more tablets at them with every visit—to quote a nice man I met, "Let's try this, let's try that..."

If you have ever wondered why your GP, who is supposedly an expert on your health, hasn't got the answers, please read on.

Disease Model

The disease model taught in medical school puts heavy emphasis on disease and less so on maintaining optimal health (homeostasis). While anatomy, biochemistry and physiology are taught in medical school, the relationship between the body systems and how they are maintained is not emphasised.

This is why your GP might advise you to take paracetamol for a viral infection and painkillers for a migraine or gallbladder pain but struggle to advise you on how to boost your immune system to prevent infections or advise you on what foods to eat to prevent any of the above conditions.

Doctors are taught extremely well on how to recognise and treat diseases based on symptoms. While this model is extremely useful with regards to acute disease when symptom control is appropriate, it falls short with regards to chronic illness where subtle imbalances have to be addressed and corrected.

In other words, successful chronic disease management lies in addressing the root cause of disease and not focusing entirely on symptom control.

There is now a growing number of GPs and hospital doctors all around the world who are embracing this holistic *systems-based* method of thinking, and I believe the future of medicine lies in the science of health and well-being.

With new advancements in how food, environment and lifestyle influence the expression of our genes (epigenetics), we are in for exciting developments.

Perspective on Disease

If you were to ask your GP if you could heal from any of your diseases without taking medication, I can almost guarantee you would be told it was impossible.

This response is not generally based on some hidden incentive on the doctors' part to benefit the pharmaceutical industry. The simple reason is doctors are not taught in medical school that any pathologies can be *reversed.*

Chronic diseases especially are viewed as progressively worsening conditions, and thus *reversibility* is almost an alien concept that most doctors would find bizarre. This fundamental outlook on disease from the outset translates to pessimism, with any ray of hope dashed—you are a victim, unable to change your course, thus the only logical advice is to *continue taking your tablets.*

I remember a patient at a diabetic meeting:
Despite successfully reducing his HBA1C level from 56mg/dL (diabetic range) to 37(non-diabetic range), one of the GPs suggested he was still diabetic! "Once a diabetic always a diabetic," were her words. None of the other GPs found this ridiculous. I envisioned the poor man who had most likely worked extremely hard to better his condition only to be essentially told nothing had changed.

No Time

As you are aware, your appointment is typically 10 minutes long. In those 10 minutes, your GP takes a history, examines, formulates a diagnosis and treats.

While this might be long enough for certain conditions, it simply isn't enough for complex cases, which require time and painstaking detail.

Here is a quick example:
In 10 minutes you could be diagnosed with knee arthritis and prescribed an anti-inflammatory. However, looking closely at your records, your doctor might realise you have been diagnosed with psoriasis a few times in the past. If your doctor were to *dig deeper*, they might notice you have been constipated for years. We are now in the digestive system, which needs to be explored even more—10 minutes isn't enough.

Division into Specialties

Specialists do a phenomenal job due to their expertise, but the drawback of specialism is further disease compartmentalisation. In other words, a cardiologist relates a particular set of symptoms to the heart and a neurologist also relates a particular group of symptoms with the nervous system, and so on.

The higher up the rung a specialist is, the less likely they are to know about anything just slightly out of their field—the big picture is lost. The moment your symptoms don't fit this paradigm, you have no specialist left to address your symptoms, and the answer is always *See your GP.* In fact, it isn't uncommon for GPs to have rows with hospital doctors about which specialist a patient should go to and who should prescribe a particular drug.

Diet and Lifestyle are Overlooked

Diet and lifestyle intervention are almost an afterthought, despite being in the National Institute of Clinical Excellence (NICE) guidelines and others.

Interestingly, doctors have little or no training on diet and equally have no knowledge of lifestyle modification. Incidentally, mastering these two factors is the only way to prevent the rise in chronic disease we are experiencing today. [1]

In the 1950s, '60s and '70s, the medical community refused the idea that plaques that caused heart disease could be prevented. The popular opinion at the time was that plaque formation had a genetic basis.

Ancient healing systems like the Ayurvedic system from India of more than 3000 years old, and traditional Chinese medicine (TCM) over 2000 years old, have long taught about the power of food in healing.

Presently, conventional medicine has made a few connections between diet and a few pathologies. A few examples include cardiovascular disease and saturated fats, gout and purine-rich foods, gallbladder disease and fatty foods, spicy foods and indigestion and so on. However, almost every pathology you can think of can be improved with food of some sort.

Mind-Body Split

The conventional medical model makes a clear distinction between the mind and the body. Diseases of the mind and body are therefore separate entities, with little emphasis if any on the interrelationships between them.

Many ancient modalities see the mind and body as one—the organism. This basic assumption leads to treating the patient from a more holistic point of view.

Appreciation of the interrelationship between mind and body, interpersonal and social relationships among other influencers of disease are explored. This further leads to various therapeutic techniques like mindfulness and meditation among others as powerful tools of healing.

Disregarding Supplements (Vitamins, Minerals, Herbs and Natural Substances)

Supplements, including vitamins, minerals and herbs, are great healing modalities when used correctly, but many doctors think anything to do with this is quackery.

Many herbal remedies form part of standard treatment in different countries like Germany and Switzerland, to name a few, and are prescribed by doctors.

Herbalism has a long history dating back to the Sumerians and ancient Egyptians. Traditional herbalism, ancient healing traditions like Ayurvedic medicine and traditional Chinese medicine (TCM), to name a few, have used herbs for thousands of years to treat almost every condition you could think of.

In he 1700s, many sailors died of scurvy at sea until 1747 when James Lind, a Scottish physician, found that the disease could be prevented and cured. He essentially conducted a clinical trial, feeding sailors citrus fruits packed with vitamin C.

In conventional medicine today, there are few instances of vitamin use: Folic acid, a B vitamin, is given to pregnant women as well as patients who take the immunosuppressant methotrexate.

Vitamin B12 (Cobalamin) is routinely prescribed for those with low B12, which can cause lethargy and nerve type pain.

Alcoholics are prescribed vitamin B1 (Thiamine), while vitamin D is prescribed for low levels.

Vitamin K is prescribed to reverse the effects of warfarin.

With regards to minerals, iron is prescribed in cases of iron deficiency anaemia, magnesium used to stop abnormal heart rhythms usually in the emergency department, magnesium sulphate for asthma attacks, lithium for bipolar disorder and so on.

In reality, many modern pharmaceuticals are *synthesised isolates* from naturally occurring substances. In other words, a particular substance or more, thought to be the active ingredient in a particular herb, is isolated and produced chemically in a lab.

The bark of the willow tree, for example, is a source of salicylates, used in the synthesis of the drug Aspirin, and Quinine, the anti-malarial, comes from the cinchona tree bark, for example.

Sadly, many dismiss herbs with the phrase *no evidence,* despite multiple papers and trials on herbs.

Curcumin from turmeric, which has been used for thousands of years, is now getting lots of attention and is probably the most studied herb, with over 5000 papers alone published.

Other commonly known herbs are Echinacea, which has powerful chemicals possibly beneficial for preventing colds [(2)], peppermint for IBS [(3)] and oregano oil for its antiparasitic properties [(4)].

You might think supplements don't work after trying something you bought in a local health shop. Firstly, this is to be expected to a degree as most people buy supplements based on erroneous self-diagnosis. In other words, the supplement they are taking might not be indicated for the ailment at hand.

Secondly, we have the extremely important issue of quality. Not all supplements are created equally—in fact, there is huge variation in the quality of supplements. This is a huge problem in the supplement industry, which is not generally as regulated as the pharmaceutical industry. Poor-quality supplements are one of the reasons people discard them with the fallacious conclusion that *complementary medicine* does not work.

That said, there are some supplement companies that manufacture supplements to the highest standards possible. These companies pride themselves on their quality and screen their products for heavy metals, pesticides and other contaminants. A high-quality supplement costs a bit more, but you get what you pay for.

I once attended a *College of Medicine* conference that focused on herbs and natural healing. Here, the world-renowned herbalist Professor Kerry Bones mentioned the herb Boswellia as a brilliant natural anti-inflammatory. He joked about using paracetamol as a placebo alongside it for pain control in his clinical trials on arthritis. [(5)] (P.S. Paracetamol is a lifesaver in our home!)

You might be surprised to learn that penicillin, many other antibiotics, statins and some anti-cancer drugs are derived from fungi (mushrooms).

Despite the barriers outlined above, complementary/alternative medicine is gaining popularity all over the world, with Harvard Medical School offering courses in *integrative medicine.*

The Whipp's Cross Hospital in London runs a dermatology clinic alongside the experienced and brilliant herbalist Alex Laird.

Here, patients are offered two choices to manage their condition: the traditional approach or complementary approach. Many now chose herbs to manage their conditions, and with great success I must add.

I have started seeing letters from some pain clinic consultants recommending turmeric (curcumin), magnesium and even cannabidiol (CBD oil) for chronic pain sufferers.

Finally, it is important to note that herbs have potential interactions with some medications. This is particularly relevant especially if they are *extracts,* which can be quite potent due to the way they are made. It is therefore best to get some guidance from someone who is knowledgeable or a qualified herbalist.

Over Reliance on Guidelines:

Sometimes as doctors we occasionally forget we are treating patients and instead cling to the rungs of rigid protocols and guidelines, despite the patient not getting better or even getting worse.

Patient individuality is overlooked, and we carry on like robots. Part of this has to do with defensive medicine, a concept we described in an earlier section.

Relentlessly aiming for a target sugar level despite side effects or persistently increasing the dose of a beta blocker while the patient can't move due to breathlessness or weakness are just some examples of this rigidity in thinking.

A GP friend of mine once joked the letters GP are more fitting for the term Google Practitioners!

Medical Sciences to Practice of Medicine Lag

Have you ever mentioned something you read about in the papers, journal or internet that your GP hadn't a clue about? I bet you must have thought it a bit odd a doctor didn't know. The answer to this seeming paradox is twofold.

First, a lot of the information reported is mostly in the experimental stage but good fodder for the media.

Second, and more importantly, there is a huge lag between the rapidly evolving field of medical sciences and the practice of medicine.

It is reported that it takes 17 years for medical science to reach doctors and ultimately clinical practice. [6] In other words, if you happen to have read the research on an innovative approach to a particular condition, you are 17 years ahead of your doctor. While it is true doctors attend educational courses, the content, which is geared towards clinicians, also mirrors this lag.

---

1) The world health report 2002: reducing risks, promoting healthy life. Geneva, World Health Organization, 2002.

2) Karg Ca et al., "Re-opening the stage for Echinacea research - Characterization of phylloxanthobilins as a novel anti-oxidative compound class in Echinacea purpurea." *Phytomedicine* 2019 May 22:152969. doi: 10.1016/j.phymed.2019.152969

3) Shen YH et al, "Complementary and alternative medicine for the treatment of irritable bowel syndrome." *Can Fam Physician.* 2009 Feb; 55(2):143-8

4) Force M et al., "Inhibition of enteric parasites by emulsified oil of oregano in vivo." *Phytotherapy Research.* 2000 May; 14(3): 2013-4

5) Kimmatkar N et al. "Efficacy and tolerability of Boswellia serrata extract in treatment of osteoarthritis of knee - a randomized double-blind placebo-controlled trial." *Phytomedicine,* 2003;10(1):3-7

6) Z.S. Morris et al., "The answer is 17 years, what is the question: Understanding Time Lags in Translational Research." *Journal of the Royal Society of Medicine* 104, no.12 (Dec 2011): 510-20

CHAPTER 46

LESSONS IN CHANGING PRACTICE

Is this the same man that two weeks ago told the Daily Telegraph 'I am and always have been a Conservative to the core of my being?' One week ago, he's the heir to New Labour and today he is a liberal conservative. No wonder he's against ID cards.

Tony Blair vs. David Cameron in the House of Commons.

About 15 years ago, I suddenly developed bloating and ill-defined gastrointestinal symptoms. I consulted with my GP at the time and was told it sounded like irritable bowel syndrome (IBS). The tablets prescribed didn't work, and I just learnt to live with the symptoms.

However, as things got worse, I was referred to a gastroenterologist who performed an endoscopy and a sigmoidoscopy. I was told there was *a bit of inflammation* in my bowel, but nothing more was found.

Fast forward many years later as a GP, I started noting patients who had similar symptoms like mine. Like me, they had tried the usual IBS tablets and proton pump inhibitors and seen various specialists, but their symptoms persisted.

After a few years of practice, I started noting it wasn't only patients with gastrointestinal symptoms who weren't getting better but a huge category of patients with a vast array of symptoms.

Migraines that just didn't go despite cocktails of medication from a neurologist; aches and pains despite multiple visits to the pain clinic; joint pain, stiffness and being tired all the time despite normal blood test results; resistant back pain despite having seen the orthopaedic team and spinal surgeon who could not find anything wrong; unexplained anxiety or depression with no triggers whatsoever were just some of these examples.

Occasionally, I would get a question from a patient asking why they had developed a particular symptom. In some cases, I replied with the word *inflammation*, but when asked why they had developed inflammation in the first place, my answer was, "It just happens." If they went even further to ask how they could prevent it, I was stumped.

It suddenly dawned on me how basic and fundamental these questions were, and I couldn't understand how as a doctor I wasn't able to answer them.

I attended numerous conferences in rheumatology, gastroenterology and neurology for answers but found many of the specialists didn't have a clue either. More worryingly, the majority of the specialists didn't seem to acknowledge there was a category of patients who weren't getting better. The few who did identify a category just thought they were neurotic—"It's all in your head."

I remember a rheumatologist at an educational event mentioning how obsessed his wife was with supplements. He thought they belonged in the bin as they didn't work. The audience seemed to share his point of view as they warmed up in laughter.

Towards the end of a diabetic educational event I attended, the speaker presented a case of poorly *managed type* II diabetes. The task for the audience was to suggest the next step in the *management plan,* in other words what medication was to be added at each stage depending on the patient's sugar level. I remember driving home after the event thinking all I had done was participate in a *medication addition exercise.* How was the patient in question actually going to get better by simply adding more and more medications to their already long list?

At this point I realised I had to find answers for myself. The best tools I had as a doctor were not working for me, or for my patients, and the experts didn't seem to have the answers either.

It was time to explore a new model, as the one I and many colleagues were using wasn't working for a cohort of patients who mainly had chronic diseases.

Jeff Bezos, the founder of Amazon, summarised it best: He said smart people were always *reconsidering* problems. I would soon realize I had to use a different approach, one that ironically didn't look at disease as a thing—this will make sense to you later.

I started voraciously reading books, scientific literature and attending conferences on health and nutrition. In addition, I also started experimenting with multiple supplements with some very good results.

We live in a modern industrial world, which impacts our health in many ways:

Lead toxicity [(1)], electromagnetic fields (EMF) from Wi-Fi and mobile phones [(2)], phthalates like BPA in plastics [(3)], pesticides [(4)], mercury [(5)] and so on.

These all change our bodies in subtle ways and cause symptoms previously never seen before. New pathologies are therefore emerging, and to treat them we have to first recognise them.

This might all seem nonsense to some, including some doctors who dismiss these factors on a whim without doing any research on the area themselves.

You have probably been mentioning your symptoms to your doctor for years, but because they don't recognise them, they can't help you.

Some doctors are quick to dismiss anything not taught to them at medical school. This is a rather curious situation because we ignore first-hand information from a patient in preference for something we have read in a book. Although as doctors we feel we are listening to you, what we are doing in effect sometimes is cross checking what you are saying with what we know. This is different from keeping an open mind and actually listening to what you have to say.

To really listen, doctors would need to adopt a model many companies are using today—that is actively taking on board feedback via social media and direct communication. This feedback in turn shapes the products these companies release, and in some cases entire product lines are designed by customers who submit ideas to them. This is called open innovation and is an area I actively take part in, but I digress.

If you read the first part of this book, then you are already familiar with the disease model GPs use. This is the model doctors are taught in medical school, and it does have a place to a degree, especially in acute disease.

Here is how it works:

You are labelled as having a particular disease based on a group of symptoms that occur in a given organ of your body. Following this, treatment of the organ involved eradicates your symptoms and you get better.

So, if you complain of dry, itchy skin all over, the problem is the skin; you get diagnosed with eczema and get a steroid cream to treat the skin.

You complain of a raging headache, with dots in your visual field; the problem is your head and you get diagnosed with a migraine. To relieve the symptoms, you get an anti-migraine tablet.

You complain of bloating, diarrhoea and constipation, these are stomach symptoms and you have irritable bowel syndrome (IBS). Treat the stomach with an *antispasmodic* and your IBS resolves.

You complain of a low mood; the problem is the neurotransmitters in your brain. You are diagnosed with depression, prescribed an antidepressant and you get better.

So, what are the problems with this model?

The first obvious problem with the conventional disease model is *compartmentalisation* of symptoms to a huge degree based on the organs or organ systems involved. According to the conventional disease model, your diabetes, eczema, migraines, joint pain, high blood pressure and more are all separate entities and generally not related.

This is erroneous as most organs or organ systems don't work in isolation but influence each other, leading to symptoms that might not fit a known diagnosis.

The second problem with the conventional disease model is the lack of appreciation for the *causes* of symptoms, instead the focus is on labelling what the cluster of symptoms are—a disease. The corollary to this is all symptoms, and thus diseases are treated the same.

A good analogy to explain this concept is to think of diseases like an arrival point or destination.

While we might all be present at a particular destination, how we got there can be different for each of us-everyone' story is different

Should your symptoms not fit a particular known cluster of symptoms called a disease, you might be classed as having *medically unexplained symptoms*, labelled as depressed or subtlety accused of making things up. I came across a saying—"I am not faking being sick, I am faking being well," *which* sums up the frustration of some patients.

Now, wouldn't it be exciting if you could find out what caused your symptoms in the first place, in other words the root causes? What if the symptoms in a given organ were due to a problem elsewhere and not necessarily in the affected organ itself? What if the multiple symptoms you were getting in different organs were all from a single cause? Would finding the root cause and eradicating it not be the optimal approach?

This *systems-based approach* concept is, however, not an abstract one and it is present to a degree in conventional medicine.

William Osler, known as *the father of modern medicine,* said as far back as the 18th century, "The good physician treats the disease; the great physician treats the patient who has the disease."

A clear example of treating the root cause can be demonstrated with regards to infectious diseases. Supposing you presented to your doctor complaining of a fever, coughing up blood, weight loss and fatigue, and a sputum culture showed tuberculosis (TB). What would the appropriate course of action be? Treat the TB with antibiotics or prescribe medication to suppress your coughing and reduce your temperature?

Another example where the systems-based approach is used to a degree in conventional medicine is thyroid disease. Thyroid disease can cause dry or oily skin, weight gain or weight loss, depression or hyperactivity, and so on, depending if underactive or overactive. Although the problem is the thyroid per se, its effects go beyond it. Applied fully, the *systems-based model* then goes beyond this and tries to find out what caused the thyroid dysfunction in the first place.

Take another example, Crohn's or ulcerative colitis, which is well recognised in conventional medicine as causing gastrointestinal symptoms as well as problems with the eyes, joints and skin. As you can see, what happens in one part of the body is not necessarily limited to it. Asking the question of what causes the inflammation that leads to Crohn's or ulcerative colitis is what the systems model tries to figure out.

The systems model looks *further upstream* if you like, with a strong focus on health, homeostasis(balance) and prevention, not just on disease.

The systems approach model recognizes different causes and individuality, aiming to treat the root cause of the problem and not just the symptom. It doesn't matter if your symptoms don't fit a label, category or disease. In fact, using this health model, diseases don't exist! It is all about creating balance by either removing the culprit or adding what is lacking. Once this is achieved, the body heals itself—in essence, disease is *reversed.*

So, if you have ever wondered why you are getting a particular symptom or disease, the reasons are infection, toxins, allergens, poor diet/nutrition and stress.

Without addressing these, you are essentially just managing symptoms.

---

1) R. C. Gracia et al, "Lead toxicity and chelation therapy." *American Journal of Health-System Pharmacy 64,* no.1 (2007): 45-53

2) De-Kun Li et at., "Exposure to Magnetic Field Non-Ionizing Radiation and the Risk of Miscarriage: A Prospective Cohort Study." *Scientific Reports* volume 7, Article number: 17541 (2017)

3) J. L. Carwile et al, "Canned soup consumption and urinary bisphenol A": A randomized crossover trial." *Journal of the American Medical Association* 306, no.20 (2011):2218-20

4) C. L. Curl et al, "Organophosphorus pesticide exposure of urban and suburban preschool children with organic and conventional diets." *Environmental Health Perspectives* 111 (2003): 377-82

5) L. Palkovicova et al, "Maternal amalgam dental fillings as the source of mercury in developing foetus and newborn." *Journal of Exposure Science and Environmental Epidemiology* 18, no. 3 (2008): 326-31

CHAPTER 47

THE MICROBIOME AND ITS FUNCTION

The universe is under no obligation to make sense to you.
-Neil deGrasse Tyson

I already mentioned the importance of the digestive system in Part 2 of this book. If there is one thing you could do to take care of your health and prevent disease, I would suggest you take care of your digestive system. The digestive system could be likened to a control centre of all the body systems.

Over 2000 years ago, the father of modern medicine, Hippocrates, is attributed to have said, *All disease begins in the gut.* Thinking about it, he probably came to this conclusion with the power of experience and observation.

Exploration of the gut concept then resurfaced in another form, started by the discovery of lactic acid bacteria in the mid-1800s by Louis Pasteur while he studied the fermentation of wine.

In 1905, Stamen Grigorov discovered the lactic acid bacterium that fermented milk into yogurt—he named it *Bacillus bulgaricus.*

A few years later, Elie Metchinkov, a researcher at the Pasteur Institute and winner of the 1908 Nobel Prize in physiology, caught wind of Stamen's discovery and soon adopted the idea that consuming milk with lactic acid bacteria was beneficial to health. His interest lay in health and the aging process, and, as such, he enthusiastically spread the word on the benefits of drinking sour milk, something he did himself on a daily basis. As proof of this theory, he cited the longevity of Bulgarian peasants, which he credited to their daily yogurt consumption.

More than 100 years later, we are exploring Metchnikov's ideas in even more detail with the concept of the microbiome/microbiota. So, what is the microbiome, also called the microbiota?

The gut microbiome is the name given to the community or group of microbes that live in and outside the body at any given time. These microbes live on the skin, in the mouth and in the gut and include bacteria, fungi and protozoa.

As we pass through the vaginal canal during birth, we acquire our first microbiome. More healthy bacteria follows via breastmilk and continuously develops. By age two or three, the microbiome has been generally well established [(1)].

There are various species of bacteria present at this stage of life, but mostly the Bifido and Lactobacillus types. As you can see, babies born via C-section thus have different gut bacteria, and this might explain the difference in incidence of some chronic inflammatory conditions like coeliac disease, ulcerative colitis, juvenile arthritis and asthma. [(2)] In addition, formula-fed babies have an increased risk of being overweight in the first year of life due to the difference in gut microbiome [(3)].

It used to be thought that the number of bacteria in the gut outnumbered the number of cells in the body by a factor of 10. However, as more research is being undertaken, it appears this number might not be accurate. However, whatever the number, it is undeniable that the bacteria in your gut are present in significant amounts. We thus all share bacterial and other microbial DNA to a large extent.

We all have a unique microbiome, which has a pivotal role in health. Ongoing research in this area is revealing more and more impressive developments.

Mapping it out completely and understanding its role is the basis of the *human microbiome project.*

Just because you have a gene does not mean you contract the disease. You can change certain factors like diet and stress and thereby change the gene's expression. This is the basis of the field of epigenetics, genomics, nutrigenomics and personalised medicine.

Our microbiome is influenced by the food we eat, stress levels, antibiotics and other medications among other factors. [4]

Once the balance of the microbiome is altered, harmful species of bacteria and fungi like Candida Albicans proliferate, leading to what is termed dysbiosis.

Dysbiosis can lead to multiple issues from food cravings [5] and obesity [6] to autoimmune conditions like inflammatory bowel diseases [7] and diabetes [8] as well as anxiety and depression. [9]

So, what are the functions of the microbiome?

Nutrition and Digestion

Your microbiome produces enzymes that help digest the healthy plant fibre, turning them into so-called short chain fatty acids. (SCFS) SCFS are the main source of fuel for the colon cells.

Secretion

The microbiota also secretes enzymes that synthesise nutrients, vitamin K and B vitamins.

Brain Health

You might be surprised to learn that about 70% of the immune system is present in the gut. Your gut is also supplied by the vagus nerve and a network of neurons called the enteric nervous system, sometimes called the second brain.

Your microbiome therefore provides the link between the gut and the brain—the so-called *gut-brain connection.* [10]

More specifically, the microbiome secretes neurotransmitters like dopamine and serotonin, hormones and brain chemicals called neuropeptides, which control mood. These in turn continuously communicate with your gut immune system, which also communicates with your hormones. As you can see, there is thus a two-way communication system between your microbiome and your body. As already mentioned, the microbiome synthesises B vitamins, which are in turn needed for producing brain neurotransmitters.

In summary, your gut microbiome has a pivotal role in health. Anything that puts it out of balance leads to dysbiosis, immune dysfunction and gut inflammation. Gut inflammation potentially leads to intestinal permeability, also known as leaky gut, [11] as well as brain inflammation. [12]

So, as you can start to imagine, once the equilibrium of the microbiome is altered, there is potential for the body to develop a myriad of symptoms. In the next section, we will use a step-by-step method to restore the microbiome and hence gut function.

---

1) Akihito Endo et al., "Long term monitoring of the Human Intestinal Microbiota from the 2nd week to 13 years of age." *Anaerobe* 28 (August 1, 2014): 149-56, doi:10.1016/) ANAEROBE. 2014.06.006

2) Kim Kristensen and Lonny Henriksen, "Caesarean Section and Disease Associated with immune Function." *Journal of Allergy and Clinical Immunology* 137, no 2 (February 1,2016):587-90, doi: 10.1016/j.jaci.2015.07.040

3) Forbes JD et al., "Association of Exposure to Formula in the Hospital and Subsequent Infant Feeding Practices With Gut Microbiota and Risk of Overweight in the First Year of Life." JAMA Pediatr. 2018 Jul 2;172(7):e181161. doi: 10.1001/jamapediatrics.2018.1161. Epub 2018 Jul 2.

4) Hawrelak JA, Myers SP. "The causes of intestinal dysbiosis: A review." *Alternative Medicine Review.* 2004 Jun;9 (2): 180-97

5) Joe Alcock et al., "Is eating behavior manipulated by the gastrointestinal microbiota? Evolutionary pressures and potential mechanisms." *Bioessays.* 2014 Oct; 36(10): 940–949. doi: 10.1002/bies.201400071

6) Ravinder Nagpal et al., "Obesity-Linked Gut Microbiome Dysbiosis Associated with Derangements in Gut Permeability and Intestinal Cellular Homeostasis Independent of Diet." *J Diabetes Res.* 2018; 2018: 3462092. Published online 2018 Sep 3. doi: 10.1155/2018/3462092

7) Andrea Brusaferro et al.," Gut dysbiosis and paediatric Crohn's disease." *Journal of Infec* January 2019Volume 78, Issue 1, Pages 1–7 https://doi.org/10.1016/j.jinf.2018.10.005

8) Sircana A et al., "Altered Gut Microbiota in Type 2 Diabetes: Just a Coincidence?" *Curr Diab Rep.* 2018 Sep 13;18(10):98. doi: 10.1007/s11892-018-1057-6.

9) G. De Palma et al. "Microbiota and host determinants of behavioural phenotype in maternally separated mice." *Nature Communications* 6. (2015): 7735

10) Emeran A. Mayer et al, "Gut Microbes and the Brain: Paradigm Shift in Neuroscience." *Journal of Neuroscience* 2014 Nov 12; 34(46): 15490–15496. doi: 10.1523/JNEUROSCI.3299-14.2014

(11) Arrietta MC, Bistritz L, Meddings JB. "Alterations in intestinal permeability." *Gut.* 2006 Oct;55 (10): 1512-20

12) Perry VH. "The influence of systemic inflammation on inflammation in the brain: Implications for chronic neurodegenerative disease." *Brain Behav Immun.* 2004 Sept; 18(5): 407-13

CHAPTER 48

MASTERING THE BASIC HEALING APPROACH TO THE DIGESTIVE SYSTEM

I didn't fight my way to the top of the food chain to become a vegetarian.

-Unknown

Here is a common scenario: You book an appointment with your GP complaining of bloating, gas, intermittent abdominal pain, diarrhoea alternating with constipation and low mood. You will most likely receive two diagnosis; irritable bowel syndrome (IBS) and depression. Naturally, you will be prescribed a tablet for your IBS as well as an antidepressant for your *depression.*

Supposing the tablets didn't work for either your IBS or your depression, but you persevered for a year or so and presented again as your quality of life was getting worse.

This time you might be referred to a psychiatrist and a gastroenterologist who will most likely request some blood tests and perform a camera test (endoscopy or sigmoidoscopy) to *rule out* any sinister causes.

Now, your blood tests came back normal and your sigmoidoscopy results shows mild inflammation only. The gastroenterologist suggests you double the dose of the proton pump inhibitor you were already taking.

Two years later, your symptoms are exactly the same, despite the third type of proton pump inhibitor and the maximum dose of the third antidepressant you have tried...

Here is another common scenario. You book an appointment with your GP with a rash and occasional low mood. You have phases where you are absolutely fine, but on others you experience a profound low mood for no reason whatsoever.

This time you are diagnosed with psoriasis and depression and leave the room with a cream for your psoriasis and a course of antidepressants. Your GP thinks stress at work might be a contributing factor here, but that's about it—maybe seeing a counsellor might help.

Three months later, your rash has improved dramatically, but you now seem to have bloating and excessive gas. The mood problems remain despite taking the antidepressant daily, and, in addition, you are now also getting headaches and fleeting joint pain.

You don't feel like increasing the dose of antidepressants as they just didn't suit you, and deep down you are questioning the diagnosis of depression. To make matters worse, your friends and family have also started noticing weight gain.

You really have to get to the bottom of things, and you present again this time and see a locum GP who requests some blood tests and suggests swapping antidepressants.

The good news is you haven't got rheumatoid arthritis, but your results show you are *borderline diabetic.* The locum doctor advises you to *eat a healthy diet and exercise,* with no further details. You are advised to take some anti-inflammatories, which seem to work, but they upset your stomach.

The above examples are all common examples I see on a daily basis. To resolve all of the above issues, you will need to *dig deep,* and a good place to start is *optimising* the gut microbiome.

A simple and effective method to use is the 5R protocol,:

R-Remove
R-Replace
R-Re-inoculate
R-Repair
R-Rebalance

Remove

The first step in the *gut restoration protocol* is *Remove.* The aim here is to remove anything that could potentially have consequences on your gut and consequently your health in general.

Food sensitivity testing can be complicated and expensive, so a simple place to start is to go on an *elimination diet* for a month or so. An elimination diet aims to remove any offending foods that might cause intolerances, sensitivities or allergies. An elimination diet should be attempted with care as there is a potential to be dogmatic about it by removing multiple classes of foods.

While each individual's food sensitivities and intolerances are particular to them, the commonest offenders are generally gluten [(1)], dairy [(2)] and soy.

Gluten is found in wheat, rye and barley, and thus you will have to cut out all breakfast cereals, bread and pasta. Needless to say, you will also have to cut out cakes and biscuits. Gluten is also hidden in other food types, but removing the main ones is a start. Some surprising foods that contain gluten are salad dressings and ketchup.

Wheat has been consumed for centuries by different populations, but, for various reasons, the incidence of intolerances has increased dramatically over the last 50 years or so. There are various theories to explain this rise, including the reduced diversity of the gut bacteria, the *glyphosate* present in the herbicides used to spray the wheat [(3)], the methods of preparation, or a change in the type of wheat consumed.

In the 1970s, Norman Borlaug won the Nobel Prize for hybridising a new form of *dwarf wheat,* which was more resistant to disease. The hybridisation process resulted in a change of the newly formed gluten's genetic structure in comparison to *ancestral wheat.*

Another consequence of the hybridisation was the resulting high glycaemic index, which causes sugar spikes leading to deposition of fat in the body. The glycaemic index (GI) is a scale that tells us how fast sugar levels rise in the blood. It is based on a scale of 1 to 100, with a GI of 100 assigned to glucose, used as a reference. The high glycaemic index causes rapid sugar and consequently insulin spikes, resulting in deposition of fat in the body. (See section on weight loss secrets.)

Gluten has been shown to increase intestinal permeability, a condition commonly known as leaky gut. [(4)] For years, leaky gut was laughed at by mainstream medicine as a farce, but things were set to change with the discovery of a protein called Zonulin.

Zonulin was discovered in the year 2000 by a group of researchers headed by world-renowned Italian paediatric gastroenterologist Alessio Fasano. Interestingly, it was discovered by accident while trying to develop a potential cholera vaccine.

Zonulin has been shown to control the spacings between intestinal cells called tight junctions, with high levels leading to increased intestinal permeability. [(5)]

In situations of increased intestinal permeability, the single layer of cells lining of the gut is breached. This allows pathogens, toxins and incompletely digested food material to pass directly from the gut into the blood. This does not only lead to gut disorders but a vast array of chronic inflammatory disorders as well as autoimmune conditions. [(6)]

Sensitivity to gluten is a complicated matter, determined probably by genetics, environment and other unknown factors. While not everyone would benefit from eliminating gluten, we have no way of identifying the subcategory of people who would.

In my experience, elimination of gluten can result in dramatic improvements in symptoms in some people after a few days only, while in others a few weeks.

The simple answer is to try to see for a few weeks or so. You have nothing to lose!

In addition to gluten, the flour used to bake breads, cakes and biscuits is mixed with calcium propionate, also known as E282, and acts as a preservative by inhibiting moulds. It is, however, toxic and has been shown to cause hyperactive/autistic type tendencies in animal experiments. [7] E282 is also founds in processed meats and some dairy products.

With regards to dairy, cut out milk, yogurt and soft cheeses. Hard cheeses like Parmesan tend to be less problematic.

Other potential food offenders include corn, peanuts, shellfish and eggs.

The next thing to do is consider going on a low FODMAP diet. FODMAP stands for **F**ermentable **O**ligosaccharides **D**isaccharides **M**onosaccharides and **P**olyols.

FODMAP foods are relatively difficult to digest carbohydrates, easily fermented by the gut bacteria, resulting in gas and bloating.

FODMAP foods comprise a vast category, including many fruits, artificial sweeteners, vegetables, dairy, legumes, and wheat.

The elimination diet we discussed above already takes care of some of the FODMAP foods, like wheat (Oligosaccharides) and dairy (Disaccharides).

The essence of a low FODMAP diet is to withhold the source of food otherwise used by the gut bacteria, in other words, starve them. This is particularly important if you have a condition known as small intestinal bacterial overgrowth (SIBO).

Small intestinal bacterial overgrowth is a relatively common condition that occurs when bacteria that normally reside in the large intestine (colon) grow in the small intestine. The symptoms of SIBO include flatulence, bloating, constipation and much more, [8] and your GP might have diagnosed you with irritable bowel syndrome (IBS).

Even though a low FODMAP diet has shown to reduce gastrointestinal symptoms, [9] it can be potentially quite restricting due to the multiple classes of otherwise *healthy food* you will need to avoid. This is one of the reasons I have saved it till last. A low FODMAP diet should therefore be implemented wisely to obtain benefit.

At this point, you might be asking yourself, "Why not just test for any offending foods? Surely this will tell us with precision where the problem lies."

The answer is not really. Many allergy tests are not 100% reliable and can occasionally reveal mixed confusing pictures, sometimes contrary to what a patient might say. For instance, you might know that eating asparagus causes diarrhoea, while your test does not show this. The best way is therefore to eliminate suspect foods and then gradually reintroduce them to gauge results.

In some cases, you might need a stool sample to check for parasites, using advanced DNA techniques for example. These advanced testing kits also map out your microbiome with the various proportions of bacteria present. You will need to see a private practitioner for this, however, as these tests are not available on the National Health Service (NHS).

Replace

The second step in the gut optimisation process is *Replace.* In this stage, we are trying to replace anything missing that might be beneficial to your gut. This includes nutrients, stomach acid, or even digestive enzymes.

We need enough hydrochloric acid (HCL) for the stomach's *intrinsic factor* to absorb vitamin B12. Chronic stress and acid blockers (proton-pump inhibitors) potentially reduce stomach acid, leading to mineral and vitamin deficiencies like B12 and magnesium. This situation leads to dysbiosis and potentially small intestinal bacterial overgrowth (SIBO). [10]

Small intestinal bacterial overgrowth is a relatively common condition that occurs when bacteria that normally reside in the large intestine (colon) grow in the small intestine.

The symptoms of SIBO include flatulence, bloating, constipation and much more, and your GP might have diagnosed you with irritable bowel syndrome (IBS). [11]

If you have ulcers, stay away from stomach acid, which could significantly worsen your situation. A simple effective stomach acid supplement is Betaine HCL, preferably in combination with Pepsin, taken alongside a protein meal.

Repopulate

The third phase of the protocol is *Repopulate*. This is the stage where we reintroduce foods loved by your *friendly* bacteria (prebiotic foods).

Raw foods, vegetables and fermented foods are a good start. Green leafy vegetables like spinach and kale are my favourite due to their versatility.

Simply spicing your food with onions, garlic and ginger is a great way to introduce prebiotic foods.

Some fermented foods include sauerkraut, miso, kimchi, tempeh, kombucha and kefir, which can be found in specialist shops or online.

Fermented foods contain probiotic bacteria, as well as fibre, enzymes and other useful natural products from fermentation. Kimchi, salted fermentable vegetables from Korea, for example, has been demonstrated to positively impact our gut bacteria when consumed. [(12)]

Fermented foods also optimize the PH of the bowel, aiding the microbiome to flourish and produce vitamin B12.

I tend to shy away from kefir as the lactose intolerant patients suffer.

The *Repopulate* phase is also the time to introduce a good quality probiotic supplement. Probiotics are beneficial organisms, usually bacteria, which are ingested for their health benefiting properties. [(13)] The non-pathogenic strain of yeast *Saccharomyces Boulardi* is also a probiotic.

There are probably thousands of probiotics on the market, but choosing a high-quality one makes all the difference. While the number of billions of bacteria is important, a good quality probiotic should contain a diversity of bacterial strains, be stable at room temperature and resistant to stomach acid and bile.

Repair

The fourth stage is *Repair*. Here we want to repair the cells, tissues and mucosal lining of the gut wall damaged by inflammation.

There are various herbs and supplements to do this, but vitamin C, which helps repair collagen, is a good starting point. The amino acid L-Glutamine is also a simple supplement to use as it is used by the gut cells for mucosal repair and preservation of the space between cells called *tight junctions.* [14]

Rebalance

This is the stage to examine all aspects of your life that might impact your gut and health. In other words, managing stress at work and at home, improving interpersonal relationships, implementing an exercise regime and optimising sleep.

This a generally overlooked area in conventional medicine but an extremely important part of your health.

The term stress was coined by Hungarian-Canadian endocrinologist as far back as 1936. He defined it as *the non-specific response of the body to any demand for change.* Since then, lots of work in the area of stress has been done, and a lot more is still unknown. However, the basic premise remains that the body's physiology changes irrespective of the type of stress it is subjected to. In other words, your body doesn't differentiate between the type of stress it encounters from nutrition, physical or emotional trauma.

In essence, stress increases the hormone cortisol, which is made from cholesterol. Cholesterol is also the raw ingredient for all hormones in your body, and, as such, when we are stressed, much of the cortisol is diverted disproportionately to produce cortisol. The result is your other hormones, especially the sex hormones like oestrogen and testosterone, suffer. This phenomenon is known as the *cortisol steal* and explains a lot of the female hormonal problems and erectile dysfunction in men due to stress.

In addition, in a highly stressed state your body reverts into a state of *sympathetic dominance.* What does this mean?

Your gut is supplied by the enteric nervous system and the vagus nerve, part of the parasympathetic nervous system.

In states of stress, the effects of the parasympathetic system are reduced, favouring the effects of the sympathetic nervous system. The result of this is poor digestion as blood is diverted away from the gut to the muscle organs ready for the fight-or-flight response. This is one of the reasons why watching TV or playing with your smartphone while eating or eating on the go is to be discouraged.

Stress at work is an extremely common presentation in general practice. You might feel stuck in a job with no options available to you in some cases.

Developing coping strategies is an initial step to help build your resilience.

The first step I find useful in tackling stress at work or at home is developing a positive outlook. Your boss might say things to do in the way of constructive criticism, but we might take them the wrong way; having said that, some people are simply toxic and project their insecurities on to you. Avoid such people like the plague.

A practice worth trying is meditation. Many immediately think of monks in a Tibetan mountain temple when they hear the word meditation, but it is far from that. A meditation practice could be as simple as getting completely immersed in your favourite song, playing your favourite instrument or taking a walk in a quiet park. However, put your smartphone away, unless you are listening to your songs or even a meditative voice through it.

Look into practices like Qi Gong and Tai Chi, which have a meditative element.

Daily walks after work in a park are extremely therapeutic. Walking barefoot in your garden if you have one is also a simple effective strategy.

When exercising, a combination of resistance training and high-intensity training produces optimal results.

Reduce *screen time,* on smartphones, tablets and TV.

Last but not least, sleep—an undervalued aspect of health in conventional medicine.

When was the last time your GP asked about your sleep unless you brought it up? Sleep deprivation has been shown to reduce levels of a hormone called melatonin. This leads to increased gut permeability (leaky gut), [15] obesity and insulin resistance. [16]

I hope you have found the five steps above simple and easy to follow. Some health issues are simple, while some are more complex, and the above steps are an introductory approach. If you have no joy, see a private practitioner in your local area, a nutritional therapist, or get in touch at www.guthealthmedic.co.uk and I'll try my best to help you.

Consultations with private *practitioners* are far from a 10-minute affair. A typical consultation will last at least an hour, with some lasting three hours or more.

During this time, every aspect of your health is explored and, ultimately, interrelationships between symptoms and systems are made. A treatment plan is formulated to help regain your health.

---

1) Antonio Di Sabatino et al., "Small amounts of Gluten in Subjects with Suspected Noncoeliac Gluten Sensitivity: A randomized Double-Blind, Placebo-Controlled, Crossover Trial." *Clinical Gastroenterology and Hepatology* 13, no.9 (2015): 1604-12,doi:10.1016/j.cgh.2015.01.029

2) Campbell AK et al., "Bacterial metabolic Toxins: A new mechanism for Lactose and Food Intolerance, and Irritable Bowel Syndrome." *Toxicology*. 2010 Dec 30; 278(3):268 -76

3) R. Mesnage et al., "Cytotoxicity on Human Cells of Cry1Ab and Cry1Ac Bt Insecticidal Toxins Alone or with a Glycphosate-Based Herbicide." *Journal of Applied Toxicology* 33, no.7 (Jul2013):695-99

4) Arrietta MC, Bistritz L, Meddings JB. "Alterations in intestinal permeability." *Gut*. 2006 Oct;55 (10): 1512-20

5) Fasano et al., "Zonulin, a newly discovered modulator of intestinal permeability, and its expression in coeliac disease." *Lancet*. 2000 Apr 29;355(9214):1518-9

6) Alessio Fasano. "Intestinal Permeability and its Regulation by Zonulin: Diagnostic and Therapeutic Implications." *Clin Gastroenterol Hepatol*. 2012 Oct; 10(10): 1096-1100

7) Raymond H. Thomas et al., "Altered brain phospholipid and acylcarnitine profiles in propionic acid infused rodents: further development of a potential model of autism spectrum disorders." *Journal of Neurochemistry* Volume 113, Issue 2

8) Ghoshal UC et al., "The Gut Microbiota and Irritable Bowel Syndrome: Friend or Foe?" *In J Inflam*. 2012;2012: 151085

9) Altobelli et al., "Low-FODMAP Diet Improves Irritable Bowel Syndrome Symptoms: A Meta-Analysis." *Nutrients*. 2017 Aug 26;9(9). pii: E940. doi: 10.3390/nu9090940.

10) Lewis SJ, Franco S, Young G, O'Keefe SJ. "Altered Bowel Function and Duodenal Bacterial Overgrowth in Patients Treated with Omeprazole." *Aliment Pharmacol Ther.* 1996 Aug;10(4):557-61

11) Amit H, Sachdev, Mark Pimental, "Gastrointestinal Bacterial Overgrowth: Pathogenesis and Clinical Significance." *Ther Adv Chronic Dis* 2013 Sep; 4(5): 223–231. doi: 10.1177/2040622313496126

12) Han K et al., "Contrasting Effects of Fresh and Fermented Kimchi Consumption on Gut Microbiota Composition and Gene Expression Related to metabolic Syndrome in Obese Korean Women." *Mol Nutr Food Res.* 2015 May; 59(5): 1004-8

13) Probiotic benefit Choi CH, Chang SK. "Alteration of Gut Microbiota and Efficacy of Probiotics in Functional Constipation." *J Neurogastroenterol Motil.* 2015 Jan 31; 21(1):4-7

14) Radha Rao, Geetha Samak. "Role of Glutamine in Protection of Intestinal Epithelial Tight Junctions." *J Epithel Biol Pharmacol.* 2012 Jan; 5(Suppl 1-M7):47-54 doi: 10.2174/1875044301205010047

15) Garth R. Swanson et al., "Decreased Melatonin Secretion is Associated with Increased Intestinal Permeability and Marker of Endotoxaemia in Alcoholics." *American Journal of Physiology-Gastrointestinal and Liver Physiology* 308, no.12 (2015):G1004-11,doi:10.1152/ajpgi.00002.2015.

16) Bo Xi et al., "Short Sleep Duration Predicts Risk of Metabolic Syndrome: A systematic Review and Meta-Analysis." *Sleep Medicine Reviews* 18, no.4 (2014): 293-97,doi:10.1016/j.smrv.2013.06.001.

CHAPTER 49

THE BASICS OF NUTRITION AND WEIGHT LOSS

Chronic disease is a food-borne illness—we ate our way into this mess, and we must eat our way out.

-Mark Hyman

A healthy diet forms the cornerstone of optimal health. Understanding this basic premise lays the foundation for success with regards to health and vitality.

So, what is a healthy diet?

In one sentence, a healthy diet is one relatively low in calories and high in nutrients, complete with minerals, vitamins, phytonutrients and antioxidants.

When we eat, carbohydrates, fats and proteins, called macronutrients, are broken down by enzymes into smaller simple sugars, fatty acids and amino acids respectively, which we absorb. In the process, energy is produced in the form of adenosine trinucleotide phosphate (ATP).

Almost everyone who complains to their GP of weight gain has blood tests done. These invariably include blood sugar (HBA1C), thyroid function test (TFT), B12, vitamin D and others. In almost all cases these tests *come back normal,* and you are then advised to *eat healthy and exercise.*

If you listen to the news or read articles on the internet, knowing what to eat is a daunting task due to conflicting information we get on a daily basis. Don't worry, it is not only you.

Many years ago, I came across the *cabbage soup diet.* It seemed extremely attractive and easy at first glance. At the time, I knew nothing about nutrition; I hadn't a clue about macro and micronutrients, vitamins beyond vitamin C, minerals, phytonutrients and more.

All I had to do was chop some cabbages, add carrots, tomatoes and onions and any other spices, and I was ready to go. After reading the book, I dashed to the local supermarket and bought everything I needed. I watched with excitement as my cabbages boiled and couldn't wait. I persevered for a few days, trying to get past the smell and despite being constantly tired and hungry. On the third day, I poured the soup down the drain.

If you have ever embarked on a diet similar to what I did, then you know diets don't work. Most diets seem attractive at first glance, with all the promises and testimonials that come with them.

When you see a diet advertised, you should ask yourself one question. Can you continuously eat the way this diet has been advertised? In other words, is it sustainable? If the answer is no, then there is no need to bother.

Weight loss is not just about aesthetics but, more importantly, about the health benefits you could potentially gain. Obesity affects almost every system of the body, from musculoskeletal (Knee, back and other joint pain) to cardiovascular (strain on the heart), respiratory (breathlessness), endocrine (insulin resistance) and more.

Accumulation of fat cells causes inflammation, [1] a process that underlies many chronic conditions like insulin resistance and type II diabetes, [2] high blood pressure, [3] obstructive sleep apnoea (breathing stopping while asleep), [4] and depression [5] amongst others.

Interestingly, some studies have identified that a bacterial substance called lipopolysacharide (LPS) plays a vital part in obesity, insulin resistance and diabetes. [6]

Obesity is a complex topic that involves the interplay of food, emotions, microbiome, environment, exercise and hormones. The main hormones involved in obesity are the thyroid hormone, growth hormone (GH), insulin-like growth factor (IGF), glucagon, adrenaline and testosterone to name a few.

In the next section, I will try to tackle this extremely complex topic with some simple effective tools that might potentially help you.

---

1) Sanshiro Tateya et al., "Recent advances in obesity-induced inflammation and insulin resistance." *Front. Endocrinol.,* 08 August 2013 https://doi.org/10.3389/fendo.2013.00093

2) Jianping Ye., "Mechanisms of insulin resistance in obesity." *Front Med.* 2013 Mar; 7(1): 14–24. doi: 10.1007/s11684-013-0262-6

3) Hall JE et al., "Obesity-induced hypertension: interaction of neurohumoral and renal mechanisms." *Circ Res.* 2015 Mar 13;116(6):991-1006. doi: 10.1161/CIRCRESAHA.116.305697.

4) Alan R Schwartz et al., "Obesity and Obstructive Sleep Apnea Pathogenic Mechanisms and Therapeutic Approaches." *Proc Am Thorac Soc. 2008 Feb 15; 5(2): 185–192. doi: 10.1513/pats.200708-137MG*

5) Floriana S.Luppino et al., "Overweight, Obesity, and Depression-A Systematic Review and Meta-analysis of Longitudinal Studies."
Arch Gen Psychiatry. 2010;67(3):220-229. doi:10.1001/archgenpsychiatry.2010.2

6) Cani PD et al., "Metabolic endotoxemia initiates obesity and insulin resistance." *Diabetes.* 2007 Jul;56(7):1761-72. Epub 2007 Apr 24.

CHAPTER 50

WEIGHT LOSS MISTAKES AND SECRETS

Know the rules like a pro, so you can break them like an artist.
-Picasso

As mentioned in the last section, obesity is a complex topic that involves the interplay of food, emotions, microbiome, environment, exercise and hormones.

These factors all play a part to varying degrees depending on the individual.

I have tried to come up with some general rules that apply to most, and for convenience and structure, I will discuss these points in the order of breakfast, lunch, snacks and supper. As you can see, these are loose definitions only.

Please note this might conflict with the *official advice* you have read or received. While in some cases there is scientific evidence to back what I say, in some cases it is backed by anecdotal evidence from my clinical practice. That said, you know your body best. Do not adhere blindly to what I say. There is no harm in experimenting and seeing what works best for you. If what you are doing is working, there is no need to change. However, if you find yourself gaining weight despite doing all that you have been advised, then it might be worth trying something new. Last but not least, remember no one diet fits all.

With this out of the way, let's start with the secrets.

BREAKFAST

Counting Calories

Although calories apply to all meals, let's get it out of the way here. The concept of counting calories is a long-standing one accepted as a truism. It is based on the premise that to lose weight the number of *calories in* must be less than the number of *calories out.* In other words, your body must burn more calories than you consume, thereby producing a calorie deficit. Although this makes sense, it is only half the picture, as *a calorie is not a calorie.*

The concept of calories in versus calories out is based on laws of physics and assumes a calorie is chemically inactive or inert. However, this is not the case in the human body as calories in different foods generate different chemical reactions in the body with varying results.

If I were to eat 1000 calories of a burger, fries and fizzy drink at my local fast food restaurant, while you ate 1000 calories of a mixed vegetable salad and a fillet of mackerel, I would be more likely to gain weight while you stayed thin.

Instead of obsessing on calories, focus on nutrient-dense foods, which are mainly vegetables, especially the green leafy variety.

Not Drinking Enough Water

This might sound like an obvious and trivial point, but some people don't like water—a friend of mine says he does not like the taste. Water helps in the detoxification of organs, especially the kidneys, getting rid of toxins and waste products from the body, without which you wouldn't be able to lose weight.

Drinking water has been shown to increase the body's resting energy expenditure (how much energy the body uses at rest). (1)

It is therefore a good idea to drink water just before meals, which may help reduce your caloric intake.

How much water should you drink? The answer varies from person to person.

The point here is to drink water if thirsty and not juice, teas, coffee and other beverages, which ironically might dehydrate you.

Investing in a good quality water filter is worth considering.

If you really can't stand the taste of water, try infusing your water with a slice of lemon, lime or orange to taste. There are many infusion type flasks on the market made for this purpose.

Drink Green Tea

Green tea contains many health-benefiting compounds, including L-theanine, as well as powerful antioxidants called catechins. These powerful chemicals have been shown to promote weight loss. [2]

Drinking Too Much Coffee

Tolerance to coffee (caffeine) differs from one person to the next and might even have a genetic basis. I know friends who drink up to five coffees or more a day and carry on with no problems whatsoever.

Coffee is packed with polyphenols and antioxidants, which have numerous benefits for the body. There is no need to stop drinking coffee if you enjoy its benefits.

However, for some people coffee can potentially overburden the adrenal glands, triggering chronic excess cortisol. This is particularly true of people who for one reason or another start gaining weight or start feeling sluggish. Chronically raised cortisol potentially leads to insulin resistance and fat accumulation, mainly in the mid-section.

It is worth noting that green teas, discussed above, also do contain caffeine, although in reduced amounts compared to coffee. A variety of green tea called *matcha*, for example, made from crushed green tea leaves, is particularly high in caffeine.

Eat Only When Hungry

Do you really need breakfast? You must have probably heard the saying breakfast is the most important meal of the day, but is this true? The answer is not really. Listen to your body and eat only when hungry.

When you eat a meal, the carbohydrate, protein and fat trigger your pancreas to varying degrees to release the hormone insulin. Insulin eases glucose (sugar) transport from the blood into the cells, which the body naturally uses for energy. Glucose is also stored in the liver as glycogen, and any excess is stored in the body as fat. When you go without a meal, your body starts using the glycogen stores for energy. (Provided you don't snack.) Once your body has used up all the glycogen stores, it starts to break down fat, aided by hormone sensitive lipase, into ketones, which it uses for energy. This is called ketosis and is the basis of intermittent fasting, a powerful weight loss strategy. [(3)]

Going without breakfast therefore increases the fasting time, thus accelerating ketosis/fat burning.

If you aren't hungry, it therefore pays not to eat anything and let the body go into ketosis. If you are hungry, however, the worst thing to do would be to skip breakfast only to then snack on unhealthy food once you get to work.

Eating Breakfast Cereals

The numerous adverts of our favourite breakfast cereal with smiling kids and happy families around the table are probably etched into our minds. However, these cereals are essentially nothing but processed carbohydrates.

All forms of processed carbohydrates have a high glycaemic index. This means they cause a huge increase in glucose levels in the blood over a short period of time. High glucose levels equally cause a rapid insulin spike from the pancreas, which helps transport the glucose from the blood into the cells. The excess glucose is stored as fat, mainly around the middle section of the body. In addition, high insulin levels also prevent fat burning by blocking the action of *hormone-sensitive lipase*—a hormone that would otherwise break down fat into ketones.

Toast for Breakfast

Bread for breakfast is an almost natural thing to do for most. However, if weight loss is your goal, then I am afraid bread has got to go.

We will talk a bit more on bread in the lunch section; however, the focus here will be on bread's glycaemic index.

The glycaemic index (GI) was a concept discovered in 1981 by Dr Thomas Wolever and Dr David Jenkins at the university of Toronto. They described the GI as a measure of how quickly a 25 or 50g of carbohydrate raised blood glucose levels. It is based on a scale of 1 to 100, with a reference GI of glucose set at 100.

The brilliant Dr David Unwin, a fellow GP, further put things into perspective by equating various foods with teaspoons of sugar.

To give an example, two slices of wholemeal bread are equivalent to about six teaspoons of sugar.

High glycaemic index foods cause rapid sugar and consequently insulin spikes, resulting in storage of fat in the body.

So, if in your quest to reduce the amount of sugar you consume you drink tea without sugar while eating a sandwich, you haven't scratched the surface yet.

Every little helps though...

Using Margarine Instead of Butter

Margarine is formed when vegetable oils are modified in a process called *hydrogenation*. Margarine was initially discovered as an alternative to butter and is composed of a kind of fat called *trans fats*. *Trans fats* have the potential to influence your metabolism, leading to insulin resistance, obesity, raised LDL, lower HDL and more. [4]

So why is butter better for you? Butter contains a fatty acid called butyric acid, also known as butyrate. Butyrate provides the cells that line the gut with energy. It also reduces the pH of the gut environment, thus inhibiting the growth of harmful gut bacteria and pathogens. In addition, it has numerous anti-inflammatory effects in the gut and beyond.

It is worth noting, however, that Butyrate is mostly formed when your good or healthy gut bacteria digests fibre. This is one of the important effects of consuming fibre.

Drinking Fruit Juices

Similar to cereal, fruit juice is commonly associated with breakfast. However, fruit juice is not the drink of choice if you are planning on losing weight—yes, even 100% juice!

Did you know a glass of orange juice contains an almost equivalent amount of sugar compared to a glass of cola? A can of cola contains about 40g (10 teaspoons) of sugar while a glass or orange juice about 39! Grape juice comes quite a lot higher, at about 60g. The only advantage the juice has is the vitamins in them.

Fruit juices cause high sugar and insulin levels in the bloodstream, leading to fat accumulation in the body. Whole fruit, however, contains fibre, which slows the absorption of sugar, causing a more gradual sugar spike. Consequently, the insulin spike is also more gradual and thus there's less potential for fat deposition.

Blending lots of whole fruit in the morning as a *healthy smoothie* is essentially also drinking fruit juices with similar potential problems discussed above.

Drinking Milk

In the previous section, I mentioned eliminating dairy products, which have the potential to cause inflammation leading to chronic gastrointestinal symptoms. [5]

Milk is composed of the sugar lactose and a protein. There is a percentage of people who are unable to break down lactose, a condition known as lactose intolerance. While this is genetic in some African and Indian populations, anyone can develop a degree of intolerance sometimes after a bout of gastroenteritis. This generally results after damage of the finger-like projections in the intestines (villi) that normally produce the enzyme lactase, responsible for breaking down lactose.

In addition, the protein casein, found in milk, can be difficult to digest. If your aim of drinking milk is calcium, then consider vegetables like broccoli or kale, which have relatively higher amounts comparatively.

Eating the Wrong Types of Yogurt

Many commercially available yogurts are laden with sugar. I recommend *Greek yogurt*, which has most of the lactose (sugar) filtered off in the processing. Add your favourite berries to taste.

If you are struggling to shed the pounds, or have ongoing bowel issues, then I recommend cutting out all dairy completely.

So, what should you eat for breakfast? I mostly eat leftovers from the night before. A patient of mine once exclaimed when I told her what I had had for breakfast.
"Salad for breakfast?, she said

Try to eat as many vegetables as you can, which you can either eat raw (salad), cooked (stir fry), or mixed in an omelette, or you can drink them (juicing and smoothies).

Salads don't have to be boring, and there is so much room for variations.

Olives, avocados and sardines are my favourite three foods always present.

Given salads are essentially predominantly raw foods, they contain a high percentage of natural enzymes and are a great source of food for your microbiome (prebiotic foods).

Add varying amounts of low glycaemic fruits like berries to vegetable juices or smoothies, which are not the tastiest of drinks.

The glycaemic index (GI) is a scale which tells us how fast sugar levels rise in the blood. It is based on a scale of 1 to 100, with a GI of 100 of glucose used as a reference.

A secret weapon I have especially for children is roasting. Add some balsamic vinegar, sea salt and olive oil to kale, broccoli, Brussels sprouts or a vegetable of your choice. Pop them in the oven and roast for a few minutes until crunchy.

LUNCH

Consuming Too Many Packaged Foods

There are no two ways about this, but you will need to learn how to cook your own food if you want to succeed at weight loss. If you have a chef, then you are technically cooking your own food.

When you cook your own food, you are in full control of what you put in.

Premade meals are simply not cooked in the same manner as home food is.

Most premade meals have lots of *added extras* in the way of hidden sugars, excess salts, colouring, preservatives and artificial flavourings just to name a few.

Aim for *whole foods* and opt for organic if you can afford it. The term *whole foods* is used here to mean foods found in nature.

The three main food groups called macronutrients are carbohydrates, proteins and fat. The proportion of each type to be consumed in my experience varies from one individual to the other.

If you must buy any packaged food, be extremely selective and vigilant as some might seem healthy on first impressions. Many years ago, I went through a phase of eating sushi for lunch. It looked healthy, and I thought I was making the best food choices at the time. One day I happened to read the label on the side of the pack and to my horror found sugar as an ingredient. Needless to say, I never bought it again.

I occasionally see some brands of smoked salmon laden with sugar. Watch out for some canned foods, which contain high fructose corn syrup. (HFCS) HFCS is an artificial sweetener obtained from corn starch syrup. It has a high fructose content, which among other things can overburden and damage the liver. [(6)]

Elimination Diet

The first strategy I use for anyone hoping to lose weight is implementing an elimination diet. I suggest a gluten-free and dairy-free diet. Note, this does not equate to eating processed food labelled as gluten-free.

Gluten has been shown to increase intestinal permeability—a condition commonly known as leaky gut, previously laughed at by mainstream medicine as a farce.

It all changed in the year 2000 when a group of researchers, headed by world-renowned Italian paediatric gastroenterologist Alessio Fasano, discovered a protein called Zonulin. Interestingly, zonulin was discovered by accident while trying to develop a potential cholera vaccine. Zonulin has been shown to control the spacings between intestinal cells called tight junctions, leading to increased intestinal permeability. The effects of increased permeability are widespread inflammation, leading to an array of chronic diseases.

While not everyone benefits from eliminating gluten, we have no way of identifying those who would. The simple answer is to try it and see if you feel better.

With regards to dairy, cut out milk, yogurt and cheese.

Eating Gluten-Free

A whole industry has blossomed around gluten-free products. Unfortunately, while gluten is mostly not present in some gluten-free foods, it is the extra stuff that is added which is the problem. These are usually high glycaemic flours and mixes, trans fats and more. Moreover, the fact that a food does not contain gluten does not automatically make it better.

Quinoa, a nutritious plant food from Peru, is usually a favourite alternative to pasta. However, some varieties have been hybridised in America with wheat and so contain gluten!

Eating the Wrong Types of Carbohydrates

Broadly speaking, the carbohydrates you consume can either be processed or unprocessed.

Examples of processed carbohydrates are breads, cereals, grains and pasta to name a few. Processed carbohydrates are definitely bad for you (see breakfast and snack section).

Unprocessed carbohydrates come mainly from fruit and vegetables. We have already discussed fruit, and we will focus here on vegetables, which can be divided into non-starchy and starchy vegetables.

Examples of non-starchy vegetables include asparagus, zucchinis, peppers, mushrooms, cucumber, broccoli, celery and more, and are generally fine.

Starchy vegetables include potatoes, beans, lentils, sweet potatoes, yams and more.

The trick here is to go for starchy vegetables with a low glycaemic index, which cause a lower sugar surge in blood sugar.

White potatoes, for example, have a high glycaemic index compared to sweet potatoes, which, although sweeter, are actually better for you.

"What about rice?" You might ask. Afterall, it has been consumed for centuries by millions of people around the world. Each population has a natural or innate *tolerance* to rice and possibly carbohydrates, based on genetics. My theory is some factor, possibly environmental, triggers a change in the microbiome, thus reducing this carbohydrate tolerance.

If you are struggling with weight, my advice is to consume as little rice as possible or cut it out completely. 1 bowl of rice equates to about10 teaspoons of sugar using the glycaemic index scale.

If you can't live without rice, I would recommend the long grain version of rice, which contains a form of starch called amylose. Amylose releases sugar slowly over time and thus has a low glycaemic index in comparison to the amylopectin found in *sticky rice*, which releases sugar fast and thus has a high glycaemic index.

Secondly, opt for brown rice when possible. White rice is essentially brown rice with the brown husk polished off. In the process, it loses its B vitamins, this renders it less nutritious if you like. This polishing process is thought to have started in Japan around the 18th century. Polished rice (*Hakumai*) was reserved for the Japanese upper class at the time as it looked more appealing, while brown rice (*Genmai*) was left for the peasants.

The overall winner is wild rice, which has the lowest glycaemic index of all varieties, complete with vitamins.

Lots of white rice and processed carbs can lead to a vitamin B1 deficiency.

Allow Your Carbohydrates to Cool

When you cook and then cool certain types of carbohydrate, they form what is known as *resistant starch*.

Resistant starches are unaffected by the digestive system, meaning, they are not broken down into simple sugars, which would otherwise cause blood sugar imbalances. Despite being resistant to digestion, they provide fuel for the gut microbiome. Resistant starches are essentially prebiotics and include legumes, potatoes, rice, plantains and more. Apart from its benefits to the microbiome, resistant starch has been shown to increase satiety. [7]

Interestingly, some studies [8] have shown that resistant starch persists after reheating previously boiled food.

Not Eating Enough Raw Foods

Ideally, a percentage of your foods should be raw. Raw foods contain vitamins and natural enzymes, which get denatured at high heat. Salads and vegetables contain fibre, which serves as prebiotics to feed your good bacteria.

Avocados are an extremely healthy food perfect for salads and have gained enormous popularity over the years. Avocados contain healthy oils called phytosterols, which help lower cholesterol. [9] They are also high in omega 3 fats, B vitamins and potassium.

It is worth mentioning that the elderly might have some difficulty tolerating high amounts of raw foods. In addition, consuming a high quantity of so-called cruciferous vegetables might be problematic for those with thyroid issues.

Cruciferous vegetables are a varied group of vegetables that include cabbages, broccoli, Brussels sprouts, cauliflower, kale and more. They are packed with phytonutrients called glucosinolates and other compounds that are considered as goitrogens. These goitrogens interfere with normal functioning of the thyroid gland.

It is worth mentioning that cooking some of these cruciferous vegetables reduces the amount of goitrogens present.

Not Eating Enough Vegetables

Strive to eat *a rainbow of vegetables*, which contain various phytonutrients, minerals, vitamins and antioxidants. In addition, vegetables provide fibre, which your healthy or good bacteria feed on and digest to produce butyrate.

Butyrate provides the cells that line the gut with energy and also reduces the pH of the gut environment, thus inhibiting the growth of harmful gut bacteria and pathogens. In addition, it has numerous anti-inflammatory effects in the gut and beyond.

Consuming vegetables is thus the smart way to eat to ensure you are feeding your gut bacteria (microbiome) first. This will eventually keep you full for longer and reduce cravings.

When you slip and binge on junk food, it isn't really an issue of willpower but the fact that you are fighting a losing battle; it's an uneven playing field as your microbiome has already got the better of you—but how?

The answer lies in the gut-brain axis we already mentioned in previous sections.

Here is how it works:

We know our microbiome is composed of different species of bacteria, fungi and protozoa. Now, each species of bacteria has a special affinity or liking if you like of a particular food type. For example, the Prevotella species prefer carbohydrates, the Bacteroides fats, and the Bifidobacteria prefer fibre, to name a few. When these bacteria require certain food types, they increase our food cravings by production of neurotransmitters like dopamine and serotonin, alteration of receptor types in the brain, and influencing our taste buds. These are the reasons why you have to feed your bacteria first and foremost!

Eating too Much Meat

This is an area I find has significantly variable results. While some people lose weight by eating lots of meat, some people don't. The quality of the meat and types of meat also make a difference.

In a recent study [10] it has been found that the activity of the gut microbiome produces a by-product called trimethylamine-*N*-oxide (TMAO) in subjects who consume high amounts of meat. High levels of TMAO have been linked to obesity and cardiovascular risk, to name a few.

I personally don't do well with beef and pork but find all other meats fine. I suggest limiting meat to about three times a week.

Irrespective of the above, you should aim to consume grass-fed beef in preference to grain-fed (corn, soy) ones. Grass-fed beef is generally more nutritious and contains more omega-3 fatty acids in comparison.

Omega-3 fatty acids are classed as good fats, which reduce inflammation as well as abdominal fat. [11][12] Higher levels of omega 6 fatty acids in grain-fed beef are pro-inflammatory and thus far from beneficial.

Eating the Wrong Types of Fish

Although fish is generally known to be a highly nutritious food, there are differences. All types of fish are a good protein source, but the most beneficial types for consumption are the *fatty fish.* Fatty fish contain beneficial omega 3 fatty acids, which reduce inflammation and the risk of heart disease. [11][12]

Before we go any further, it is extremely important to first of all make a distinction between *farmed fish* and *wild fish.*

Farmed fish involves raising mass concentrations of fish in controlled environments, like tanks or ponds for commercial purposes. These fish are mainly fed grains, soy and grounded fish to accelerate growth. To prevent infections due to overcrowding, they are constantly pumped with antibiotics.

Farmed fish therefore have some drawbacks, which include a smaller proportion of healthy omega-3 fatty acids and more inflammatory omega-6 fatty acids, a high concentration of antibiotics and harmful polychlorinated bisphenyls (PCBs).

PCBs are now banned chemicals manufactured in the early 1920s, now classed as *endocrine disruptors.* Their effects are not only limited to the endocrine system but the immune and nervous systems as well. Some studies have showed a link between PCBs and obesity. [13]

Based on the above, you might automatically think wild fish is the answer. The only problem with wild fish is mercury contamination. This is especially true with regards to large *predator fish* like sharks, king mackerel, tuna, swordfish and salmon among others, which feed on the smaller fish.

With regards to wild fish, I recommend the smaller oily fish like sardines, herring and anchovies for example.

Overall, one has to be practical about these things, and I think eating some farmed fish from time to time is reasonable.

Eating Low-Fat Foods

Avoid premade *low-fat foods* like the plague. Low-fat foods have their fat content taken out, which renders them generally less tasty. To compensate, extra sugar and additives are added to give taste, texture and colour.

Needless to say, a lot of these additives are detrimental to your health, while the excess sugar is what ultimately gets deposited in your body as fat.

Portion Control

Establishing potion size is not a straightforward exercise in my experience.

Most people think they are eating the right portion while, in actual fact, they aren't. The best way to establish portion size is to stop eating just before you feel full.

Eating Too Fast

Eating your food too fast reduces chewing time and has been shown to increase overall calorie consumption, and consequently weight gain. Eating your food slowly not only reduces calorie consumption but also improves digestion and thus absorption of nutrients.

Eating on the Go

Your gut is supplied by the enteric nervous system as well as the sympathetic and parasympathetic branches (vagus nerve) of the autonomic nervous system.

In states of stress, the effects of the parasympathetic system are reduced, favouring the effects of the sympathetic nervous system. *(Sympathetic dominance.)* The result of this is poor digestion as blood is diverted away from the gut to the muscle organs ready for the fight-or-flight response. This is one of the reasons why watching TV, browsing on your smartphone, driving or taking part in other activities while eating or drinking is to be discouraged. Take note, truck drivers J

SNACKS

Cakes and Biscuits

If you must snack due to feeling hungry, avoid processed foods like cakes and biscuits, which contain lots of sugar.

It was in the 1970s that Norman Borlaug won the Nobel Prize for hybridising a new form of *dwarf wheat,* which was more resistant to disease. In comparison to *ancestral wheat*, it had lower protein content and a higher carbohydrate one.

The result is an extremely high glycaemic index, which causes sugar spikes.

Insulin is released from the pancreas to help shuttle the sugar into the cells.

The excess sugar is then converted to fat, which accumulates in the body.

Processed flour in cakes and biscuits is devoid of nutrients, which have been stripped away when wheat is bleached. To make matters worse, when you consume them, your body uses its own stores of trace minerals and nutrients in order to digest these processed foods (empty calories). In the process, your body is robbed even more of its own nutrient stores.

In addition, breads, cakes, biscuits and pastries are preserved with calcium propionate, also known as E282, which inhibits mould. E282 has been shown in some studies to be toxic and can cause hyperactive/autistic type tendencies in animal experiments. [14] E282 is also found in processed meats and some dairy products.

Finally, products from refined grains are devoid of fibre. Fibre is essentially a plant-based nutrient that cannot be digested by the body.

Another name for fibre is roughage, which provides bulk to the stool and stimulates the bowel to continuously contract in a process called peristalsis.

In other words, dietary fibre *makes you regular.* A poor fibre diet, as in refined grains, inevitably leads to a sluggish bowel and constipation. This increases the potential for retaining toxins.

Eating Roasted Nuts

When most people think healthy snacks, they think nuts. Nuts are indeed a healthy food and in their raw state are a powerful source of good fats, proteins, fibre, vitamins and minerals. However, once nuts are roasted, the good fats potentially get oxidised, thus reducing their health benefits. In addition, most of these roasted nuts have low quality salt or even sugar added.

Some people get an uncomfortable feeling in their stomach or feel gassy when they consume raw nuts. This is due to phytic acid found in them, also present in some legumes and grains. Phytic acid can bind with minerals in the digestive tract, forming a mineral complex that cannot be absorbed, potentially leading to mineral deficiencies.

To combat this problem, a great tip is to soak the nuts overnight with added sea salt or Celtic salt – note, NOT table salt – to activate the enzymes in them. This is called *sprouting* and can be applied to beans and seeds as well.

The salt water helps break down the phytic acid, thus aiding digestion. In the morning, dry the nuts thoroughly and keep them safe for consumption.

Eat Healthy Snacks

Healthy snack options include carrots, hummus, cucumber, celery sticks, sardines, eggs, seeds, olives, raspberries, blueberries and pear.

Fermented foods like sauerkraut, miso, kimchi, tempeh, kombucha and kefir are other great snack options to consider.

Believe it or not, *dark* chocolate is another great snack. It is packed with magnesium, flavonoids (antioxidants) and the amino acid arginine.

Dark chocolate has been shown to improve blood flow to the brain, improving brain health, cardiovascular health as well as increasing HDL cholesterol. [15]

Please note I am not talking about milk chocolate here, and ideally the cocoa content should be 70% or more to qualify.

Underestimating Alcohol Intake

Discussing official alcohol limits in my opinion is somewhat of a pointless exercise. First, alcohol can be likened to liquid calories, so any amount would be an issue to a degree.

There is huge variability when it comes it alcohol tolerance, something that might have to do with our liver cells, P450 enzyme activity and even our microbiome. If alcohol makes you feel unwell or ill, this might be an advantage as you can immediately tell it is not good for you.

However, if you have got into the habit of drinking a glass or more of wine every night with no obvious issues, then you might develop a fatty liver without knowing it. The good news is a fatty liver is reversible. The bad news is a fatty liver changes your lipid profile, increasing LDL (bad cholesterol and triglycerides) while reducing HDL (good cholesterol). A fatty liver also sets off inflammation and insulin resistance (prediabetes).

Excessive alcohol consumption can also lead to cirrhosis, a condition that is irreversible. As a general guide, I would suggest at least four nights per week with no alcohol whatsoever.

DINNER

Avoid Eating Late

The effects of eating late probably differ from one person to another. The Spanish are notorious for eating particularly late at night, while in Britain we eat a lot earlier. There is lots of debate about whether the time of eating causes weight gain, with various trials coming to different conclusions. I say try it—aim to eat latest 8:00 p.m. and see what happens.

Avoid Fried Foods

When oils (usually vegetable oils) are heated at high temperatures, they undergo a process called *hydrogenation*. In the process, the unsaturated fats in the oils become trans fats. Fried foods therefore contain trans fats, which are unhealthy and promote weight gain. [4]

Consuming the Wrong Types of Oil

This can be a confusing area as the advice and literature seems to constantly change.

To start with, vegetable oils are fats that are liquid at room temperature.

In essence, the vegetable oils we are familiar with, like sunflower oil, corn oil, canola oil and so on, are highly refined polyunsaturated oils, rich in omega 6 fats. Omega 6 fats are thought to be inflammatory fats, thus potentially causing weight gain.

Now, coconut oil and butter contain different types of saturated fats that help reduce inflammation. [11][12]

Coconut and palm oil contain medium chain triglycerides, which help weight loss [16] and are a great source of brain fuel. In addition, they have antibacterial and antifungal properties.

Olive oil and olives contain a healthy monounsaturated fat, oleic acid, which helps reduce cholesterol [17] and blood pressure. [18] Olive oil easily oxidises, so make sure you buy those in dark bottles when you go out shopping.

Exercise (And don't tell me you haven't got the time!)

The benefits of exercise are huge, from joint health right up to the brain. With regards to weight loss, exercise does not burn fat per se but helps activate hormones necessary for fat burning. Exercise also increases the body's basal metabolic rate by increasing the number of mitochondria in the cells.

People immediately think of the gym with the mention of exercise, but it does not necessarily have to be so. You could exercise using your chair at work, stairs, sofa, outside on the lawn and so on—being inventive is the key.

A combination of aerobic and high-intensity exercise (high-intensity interval training) seems to provide the overall benefit.

If you really can't exercise due to health issues, try walking if you can. I recommend at least 30 minutes of walking per day at least four times per week.

Not Sleeping Enough

Although sleep is a vital part of human existence, it is hardly ever asked about during a traditional history taking.

With regards to sleep, both the quantity and quality of sleep are important. Lack of sleep alters gut microbiota, leading to systemic inflammation and insulin resistance. (19)

Lack of sleep also affects two hormones in the body that regulate hunger, namely ghrelin and leptin. Ghrelin and leptin have opposite effects; Ghrelin stimulates appetite while leptin suppresses it. If you are sleep-deprived, your level of ghrelin increases while your level of leptin reduces. The overall result is an increase in hunger and consequently weight gain. (20)

Just to reiterate how important sleep is, a working group assembled by the International Agency for Research on Cancer [IARC] concluded in June 2019 that *night shift work* potentially causes cancer in humans (a Group 2A carcinogen). Although this conclusion was based on animal studies, it is worth mentioning due to the clear mechanisms of action studied.

Medications

Some medications potentially cause weight gain as a side effect. Common examples include tricyclic antidepressants like amitriptyline, specific serotonin reuptake inhibitors like fluoxetine and citalopram, mirtazapine, contraceptives (hormones) and so on.

Finally, it is worth remembering these are guidelines only, which could potentially help provide some sort of structure in your quest for weight loss. If you suffer from a particular ailment, you will need to resolve this first for weight loss to be successful.

We are all constitutionally different, and what works for one person might not work for another. It is thus imperative to start some sort of food diary, which will help you monitor the effect of different food types on your metabolism and ultimately your weight.

Weighing yourself every week is a good idea in my opinion as this provides quick feedback on your journey. If you gain weight from eating a particular food type, simply stop eating it and try another. This approach is best reserved only for people who see a setback as an opportunity to get better.

---

1) Water-Dennis EA et al., "Water consumption increases weight loss during a hypocaloric diet intervention in middle-aged and older adults." *Obesity* 2010 Feb;18(2):300-7. doi: 10.1038/oby.2009.235. Epub 2009 Aug 6.

2) Zheng G et al., "Anti-obesity effects of three major components of green tea, catechins, caffeine and theanine, in mice." *In Vivo.* 2004 Jan-Feb;18(1):55-62.

3) Varady KA et al.," Short-term modified alternate-day fasting: a novel dietary strategy for weight loss and cardioprotection in obese adults." *Am J Clin Nutr.* 2009 Nov;90(5):1138-43. doi: 10.3945/ajcn.2009.28380. Epub 2009 Sep 30.

4) Kavanagh K et al., "Trans-fat diet induces abdominal obesity and changes in insulin sensitivity in monkeys." *Obesity.* 2007 Jul;15(7):1675-84.

5) Campbell AK et al., "Bacterial metabolic Toxins: A new mechanism for Lactose and Food Intolerance, and Irritable Bowel Syndrome." *Toxicology.* 2010 Dec 30; 278(3):268-76

6) Manal F. Abdelmalek et al., "Increased fructose consumption is associated with fibrosis severity in patients with nonalcoholic fatty liver disease." *Hepatology*, 2010; NA DOI: 10.1002/hep.23535

7) Gentile CL et al., "Resistant starch and protein intake enhances fat oxidation and feelings of fullness in lean and overweight/obese women." *Nutr J.* 2015 Oct 29;14:113. doi: 10.1186/s12937-015-0104-2.

8) Recooked white rice-Sonia S et al., "Effect of cooling of cooked white rice on resistant starch content and glycemic response." *Asia Pac J Clin Nutr.* 2015;24(4):620-5. doi: 10.6133/apjcn.2015.24.4.13.

9) Mahmassani HA1 et al., "Avocado consumption and risk factors for heart disease: a systematic review and meta-analysis." *Am J Clin Nutr.* 2018 Apr 1;107(4):523-536. doi: 10.1093/ajcn/nqx078.

10) Rebecca C.Schugar et al., "The TMAO-Producing Enzyme Flavin-Containing Monooxygenase 3 Regulates Obesity and the Beiging of White Adipose Tissue." *Cell Reports.* Volume 19, Issue 12, 20 June 2017, Pages 2451-2461

11) Calder PC., "n-3 polyunsaturated fatty acids, inflammation, and inflammatory diseases." *Am J Clin Nutr.* 2006 Jun;83(6 Suppl):1505S-1519S. doi: 10.1093/ajcn/83.6.1505S.

12) Metabolic syndrome Robinson LE., "N-3 polyunsaturated fatty acids: relationship to inflammation in healthy adults and adults exhibiting features of metabolic syndrome." *Lipids.* 2013 Apr;48(4):319-32. doi: 10.1007/s11745-013-3774-6. Epub 2013 Mar 1.

13) Jeanett L Tang-Péronard et al., "Association between prenatal polychlorinated biphenyl exposure and obesity development at ages 5 and 7 y: a prospective cohort study of 656 children from the Faroe Islands." *The American Journal of Clinical Nutrition*, Volume 99, Issue 1, January 2014, Pages 5–13, https://doi.org/10.3945/ajcn.113.066720

14) Raymond H. Thomas et al., "Altered brain phospholipid and acylcarnitine profiles in propionic acid infused rodents: further development of a potential model of autism spectrum disorders." *Journal of Neurochemistry* Volume 113, Issue 2

15) Baba s et al., "Plasma LDL and HDL cholesterol and oxidized LDL concentrations are altered in normo- and hypercholesterolemic humans after intake of different levels of cocoa powder."
J Nutr. 2007 Jun;137(6):1436-41.

16) St-Onge MP, Jones PJ., "Greater rise in fat oxidation with medium-chain triglyceride consumption relative to long-chain triglyceride is associated with lower initial body weight and greater loss of subcutaneous adipose tissue." *Int J Obes Relat Metab Disord.* 2003 Dec;27(12):1565-71.

17) Guglielmo Beccuti, Silvana Pannain., "Sleep and obesity."
Curr Opin Clin Nutr Metab Care. 2011 Jul; 14(4): 402–412.
doi: 10.1097/MCO.0b013e3283479109

18) Haban P et al., "Dietary supplementation with olive oil leads to improved lipoprotein spectrum and lower n-6 PUFAs in elderly subjects." *Med Sci Monit.* 2004 Apr;10(4): PI49-54.

19) Perona JS et al., "Virgin olive oil reduces blood pressure in hypertensive elderly subjects." *Clin Nutr.* 2004 Oct;23(5):1113-21.

20) Taheri et al., "Short sleep duration is associated with reduced leptin, elevated ghrelin, and increased body mass index." *PLOS Medicine.* 2004 Dec;1(3):e62. Epub 2004 Dec 7.

CHAPTER 51

STAYING ON THE RIGHT TRACK

It takes considerable knowledge just to realize the extent of your own ignorance.

-Thomas Sowell

As you can now appreciate, the human body might be complex, but you have the tools to influence it. There are a few good habits worth developing that keep you on the path of health.

Diet

We have already discussed diet in Chapter 43. In summary, aim for a diet rich in green leafy vegetables, healthy fats and good quality proteins. Eat vegetables of varying colours high in polyphenols and other beneficial nutrients. Eat high-quality meats or fish three times a week.

Supplement

I am a passionate believer in supplementing. As already mentioned, the soil is becoming nutritionally deficient due to modern agricultural practices and over-farming, and as such it makes sense to supplement with a high-quality multivitamin and mineral supplement as a baseline. There are other supplements that can be added to this, depending on your needs. These include a quality probiotic to help replenish your *good bacteria,* omega 3 fish oils, B vitamins and many more tailored to your needs.

Yearly Blood Pressure and Pulse

Set a yearly smartphone reminder for blood pressure and pulse.

If your BP is high each time at surgery but low at home, you may have *White Coat Hypertension.*

Some smart phone *apps* plot BP for you; alternatively use a simple spread sheet.

If the majority are normal, you do not need BP medication.

You actually don't need the hassle of trying to get in with a GP or practice nurse for this as you can buy a BP monitor and saturations (sats) meter cheaply.

Yearly Blood Tests

Although yearly blood tests are common in Europe and other parts of the world, the NHS only do a *health check* every five years from the ages of 40 to 74 only.

The aim of a health check is to pick up any abnormalities that might be present in the absence of symptoms.

If you were to ask for one outside the above range, you would likely get some resistance depending on who you see.

Does this mean abnormalities do not occur before age 40 or between a five-year period for that matter?

The answer is obviously no, but, as with any publicly funded system, limits are inevitably implemented.

If you can afford it, consider getting your yearly tests done at an accredited private laboratory and save yourself the hassle.

Screening

Women aged 25–49, make sure you get a smear every three years and aged 50–64 every five years.

Women aged between 50 and 70 get three yearly mammograms.

Self-Examination

A breast self-exam is encouraged for all.

I encourage men to perform genital self-examinations looking for lumps.

For men over 40, I personally recommend a yearly prostate specific antigen (PSA) test, especially if black.

This is not official guidance, which recommends a PSA generally only if symptomatic.

Home Testing

As far as testing goes, urine dipsticks are cheaply available as well as blood glucose machines.

It is, however, better to get a blood glucose machine from your diabetic nurse and ensure you get the appropriate accompanying testing strips.

If you are a diabetic on insulin and the traditional way of testing is an inconvenience, it might be worth looking into the *Freestyle Libre continuous glucose monitoring system.*

The *Freestyle Libre system* comprises a blood glucose meter/reader and a small sensor the size of a two-pound coin only.

The sensor, which continuously monitors blood glucose readings, is attached to any part of the body but usually the upper outer arm.

To know your blood sugar levels, simply scan over the sensor with reader to get an instantaneous read.

The beauty of this system is you can download the app and use your smartphone as a reader!

Spiritual Health

Last but not least, maintain a healthy positive attitude and mind.

This might seem like fluff, but emotions affect your health.

Being angry all the time, staying in a toxic relationship/environment, and being around negative people and friends foster *negative energy.*

Develop an attitude of gratitude and mindfulness.

Learn to let go, learn to forgive.

Make the best of your social interactions and always show genuine friendship, integrity and honour.

Be generous with others and take care of the environment as much as you can.

Last but not least, meditate—it will benefit you in ways you never dreamt of.

CHAPTER 52

THE WINNING HEALTH MINDSET

Every minute you spend in planning saves 10 minutes in execution; this gives you a 1,000 percent Return on Energy!
-Brian Tracy

Thank you for getting this far.

I am aware there is a lot to take in, but my overall aim is to spur your imagination to the endless possibilities there are with regards to health.

By now you realise the food you eat is paramount to staying healthy.

This is the absolute foundation on which everything rests.

Unfortunately, modern agricultural practices and over farming have rendered the soil nutritionally deficient according to multiple studies over many years.

This is one of the reasons why, if possible, you should strive to eat organically grown food sourced from a local farmer.

Staying healthy requires consistency, and as you have probably realised by now, the bulk of the work rests on you.

Knowing this basic principle changes your mindset and puts you ahead of any public health initiatives or general advice your doctor might give you.

Yes, you will always need your doctor, but you will be using them more as a guide for a journey you have already started.

A change in lifestyle is addictive and infectious.

As you implement something new and see changes, you will be more motivated to do more.

With time, your motivation will become infectious, and friends and family will take notice, and before long you will be an expert, a go-to person for health advice.

Change in the healthcare system happens at a slow pace, and you might have a few obstacles in your health journey.

You might struggle to see why your doctor doesn't come on board with regards to some ideas that seem like common sense to you.

If you can, aim to point your GP towards any new research they might not be aware of.

Doing this in a tactful manner could help build a good relationship between you and your GP.

However, remember in the majority of cases you will essentially be trying to make a doctor change a thinking process learnt and embedded in practice for years.

If your doctor is unable to get to the bottom of your health issues, don't let this deter you as they haven't got all the answers.

Do as much research as you can, and you will uncover so much information that you can use to your advantage.

I remember thinking, *The future is bright,* after attending a *College of Medicine* conference in London with speakers including school children, teachers, farmers, academics, writers, nutritional therapists, medical students and doctors.

It was one of the best conferences I have ever attended, and every single speaker was brilliant.

The school children who came all the way from the north of England were introduced by their local GP and school teacher.

The children recited catchy vignettes related to food and a video later showed them chopping up healthy vegetables cheerfully alongside their hardworking teacher who had taught them healthy eating.

Two medical students, Ally and Iain, who founded *Nutritank,* talked about their campaign to increase nutrition and lifestyle medicine education in UK medical school curricula.

Campaigns like this potentially have the power to fundamentally change the mindsets of doctors in the future, and I envisage a revolution in the approach to chronic disease, which unfortunately is on the rise.

One of my favourite quotes is *always be a student.* I don't know it all and am keen to learn from you.

I am happy to hear any feedback you might have, and, if you don't mind,

please also leave a review as it helps tremendously in getting the word out.

Finally, if you suffer from gastrointestinal symptoms, I might be able to help you.

Please get in touch at: www.guthealthmedic.co.uk

Thank you and stay healthy always!

-Leke Asong